SOME OF THE LOSING GAMES
THAT MEN PLAY

—The Macho Warrior with The Earth Mother
   (until she brings him down with a thud)

—The Stiff Upper Lip When In Pain
   (the next step is rigor mortis)

—The One Who Never Fails
   (even at suicide)

—The Decision Maker for Both Him and Her
   (and the one who takes all the blame)

—The Stud
   (getting it up until you collapse)

—The Bringer Home of the Bacon
   (even when no one is hungry)

Now there is a groundbreaking new book that tells the endangered male sex how to save themselves from these and other destructive stereotypes—

THE NEW MALE
From Self-Destruction
to Self-Care

"Dr. Herb Goldberg's *The Hazards of Being Male* has become the bible of the men's movement . . . *The New Male* is a worthy successor!"—THE AMERICAN MAN Magazine

"Challenging and needed!"—HOUSTON CHRONICLE

SIGNET and MENTOR Books of Interest

THE
NEW MALE

From Self-Destruction to Self-Care

by
Herb Goldberg

A SIGNET BOOK
NEW AMERICAN LIBRARY
TIMES MIRROR

NAL BOOKS ARE AVAILABLE AT QUANTITY DISCOUNTS
WHEN USED TO PROMOTE PRODUCTS OR SERVICES. FOR
INFORMATION PLEASE WRITE TO PREMIUM MARKETING DIVISION,
THE NEW AMERICAN LIBRARY, INC., 1633 BROADWAY,
NEW YORK, NEW YORK 10019.

Grateful acknowledgment is made for permission to quote from the following:
"The Hill Wife," from *The Poetry of Robert Frost* edited by Edward Connery Lathem. Copyright 1916, © 1969 by Holt, Rinehart and Winston. Copyright 1944 by Robert Frost. Reprinted by permission of Holt, Rinehart and Winston, Publishers.
"About a Man" by Mark Strand. From *The Late Hour* (Atheneum). Reprinted by permission; © 1977 The New Yorker Magazine, Inc.

This is an authorized reprint of a hardcover edition published by William Morrow and Company, Inc.

SIGNET TRADEMARK REG. U.S. PAT. OFF. AND FOREIGN COUNTRIES
REGISTERED TRADEMARK—MARCA REGISTRADA
HECHO EN CHICAGO, U.S.A.

SIGNET, SIGNET CLASSICS, MENTOR, PLUME, MERIDIAN AND NAL BOOKS
are published by The New American Library, Inc.,
1633 Broadway, New York, New York 10019

First Signet Printing, August, 1980

5 6 7 8 9

PRINTED IN THE UNITED STATES OF AMERICA

For my mother, Ella,
My sisters, Paula Nelson and
Bernice Wiesel, and their families,
My dear buddies George Bach and Marx Ayres,
And to the women who have been in my life
and who have given me my highest, most
euphoric moments and my lowest, most despairing
ones—may we someday meet happily on the
middle ground.

Acknowledgments

The "magical" part of writing a book is the people who appear during its development and either directly or indirectly make an important contribution. Without them a project such as this one would be significantly diminished.

Foremost, I would like to acknowledge with warm appreciation Ms. Nicole Howell, whose careful and faithful assistance in compiling research material as well as attending to the references and footnoting of this book were a source of great help and comfort. In addition, my thanks go to Ms. Rita Elwell, Ms. Donna Anderson and Ms. Beverly Britt for providing case studies, Mr. Earl Goldman for his contribution in the area of statistics on childhood emotional disorders, and Ms. Renae Jones for her fine work in typing the manuscript.

Finally, my editors, James Landis and Maria Guarnaschelli, who bolstered my work with their sensitivity, skills and support, and Mr. Francis Greenburger for his excellent work in finding a suitable home for this book.

HERB GOLDBERG

May, 1979

Contents

Introduction

In recent years there has been a dramatic change in the perception and functioning of the male in our culture. It has become increasingly apparent that the gender orientation known as masculinity has serious and troubling limitations and, consequently, has put the male clearly in crisis. He is accused of being chauvinistic and oppressive. He is fearful of abandonment by his increasingly autonomous and powerful woman. He is burning himself out physically and emotionally in pursuit of a success trip and other goals whose fruits are all too often questionable and meager. He hears and reads endless discussions about his declining sexual performance and increasing "dysfunction" supposedly caused by women's new assertiveness. He is lacking a support system with other men to help him through these crises, and he possesses little insight into the causes of what is happening to him and has few inner resources to draw on for nourishment during the difficult periods. He is truly a cardboard goliath, unable to flow self-caringly with the changing social scene.

Every crisis, however, provides fruitful soil for growth in addition to potential for disaster. Positive change and growth are more possible now than ever before. The social revolutions of recent years can lessen the male's time-honored burdens, help him reclaim denied emotion, expand his sensual responsiveness, bring new dimensions of honesty and depth of his heterosexual relationships, as well as alert him to the self-destructive compulsions within him.

It was my purpose in writing this book to explore how things have traditionally been for the male, and between him and her; how they are in today's era of changing women's consciousness, and how they might someday become as he begins to examine, reshape and expand his own role behavior and self-awareness.

Exploring the roots and implications of gender conditioning is, for me, the most exciting frontier in the field of psychology today. Through this book, I hope to contribute to a new understanding and recasting of the postures of masculinity in the direction of self-care, totalness and a feeling process that would facilitate the kinds of transparency, fluidity and fulfillment that the traditional masculine harness has previously made it near impossible for him to achieve.

HERB GOLDBERG

May 1979

PART ONE

HE

1. The Cardboard Goliath

ABOUT A MAN

Would get up at night,
go to the mirror and ask:
Who's here?

Would turn, sink to his knees
and stare at snow falling blameless
in the night air.

Would cry:
Heaven, look down!
See? No one is here.

Would take off his clothes and say:
My flesh is a grave with nothing inside.

Would lean to the mirror:
You there, you, wake me,
tell me none of what I've said is true.
                            —Mark Strand[1]

Women bend and men break. The blueprint for masculinity is a blueprint for self-destruction. It is a process so
deeply embedded in the male consciousness, however, that
awareness of its course and its end has been lost. The masculine imperative, the pressure and compulsion to perform,
to prove himself, to dominate, to live up to the "masculine
ideal"—in short, to "be a man"—supersedes the instinct to
survive. His psychological fragility and volatility may even
cause him to destroy a lifetime of work and relationships
in a momentary impulse.

The diagnosis of chauvinism is superficial. More often it
is a gross and misleading distortion. Closer examination of

a man's behavior reveals a powerfully masochistic, self-hating and often pathetically self-destructive style.

The brittle male conducts his life by his *ideas* about masculinity. Living up to the *image* is the important thing. Though the moment-to-moment experience may be painful and generally unsatisfying for him, his mind is continually telling him *what he is supposed to be*. As long as he is able to be that way, he can fend off the inner demons that threaten him with accusations of not being "a man."

As his isolation and distrust, the hallmarks of "successful" masculinity, increase, so do his drive for power and control and his inner rage and frustration. He senses the human experience drifting beyond his reach forever. By trying to control the world, even "improve" it or change it, he may simply be trying to make it a place in which he can safely become human—more loving and less aggressive. But the plan fails. His great hunger to prove himself, plus his anger and distrust, drive the possibilities of intimacy away. As his life unfolds and he is well into living up to masculine expectations, his behavior and choices for emotional nourishment may very well become more desperate and bizarre.

Traditional masculinity is largely a psychologically defensive operation rather than an authentic and organic process. A man's psychological energy is used to defend *against*, rather than to express, what he really is. His efforts are directed at proving to himself and others what *he is not*: feminine, dependent, emotional, passive, afraid, helpless, a loser, a failure, impotent and so on. He burns himself out in this never-ending need to prove, because he can *never* sufficiently prove it. To his final day he is driven to project himself as "a man," whether on the battlefield, behind the desk, in lovemaking, on the hospital operating table, in a barroom or even on his deathbed. And when he fails, his self-hate and humiliation overwhelm him.

He would sooner die than acknowledge the things that threaten him most. And yet his deepest imprint is feminine, for it was a woman, not a man, who was his lifeline and his deepest source of identification when he was a baby and a young boy. The femininity is therefore naturally a part of his core. The stronger that identification is and the more it threatens, the more powerfully will he need to deny it. Prisons, as well as violent street gangs, are filled with men who have "Mother" tattooed on their arm, and "motherfucker" as the trigger insult that may well bring death or serious injury to the one who dares to utter it.

In the traditional contemporary American home, the feminine imprint is particularly deep because the father sees himself as an incompetent, bumbling parent whose only legitimate territory is the office or the factory. He defers to the innate "maternal wisdom" of his wife in the early child-rearing process. Or he is by necessity simply minimally present, consumed by economic pressures. He is a father in name rather than in behavior; his role is to keep the bills paid and provide for the necessities of life. In many cases, divorce has made him largely a stranger to his family.

The emotions are there, but the admonitions against expressing them have progressively caused them to be blocked out of consciousness. As a boy the message he received was clear: Feelings are taboo.

Recently I conducted a marathon therapy group for married couples in a small city in the Midwest, where most of the men still behave in gender-traditional ways. I began by asking each man to write about his feelings, about his life as it was for him, and about his marriage. Five of the eight men insisted that they had *no feelings* inside themselves at all. With assistance, they eventually began to get in touch with their emotions, and it was not hard to understand why they had been blocked. Feelings of frustration, resentment, conflict, loneliness and of not being cared for lay underneath. The men were afraid of these emotions and would not know how to deal with them if they acknowledged them. On the surface, in self-protection, all of these men were "macho"—detached, hyperrational and tough—in short, machinelike. Of course, all of them drank before coming home each day after work, and heavily on weekends. They were burning out rapidly in every way.

The feminist movement has brought the man's rigidity forth in maximal relief. If his fear of change weren't so powerful, he would embrace the movement for the life-giving and life-expanding possibilities it offers him: a release from age-old guilt and responsibility toward women and from many onerous burdens. And if he could redefine himself and perceive women differently, he could begin to achieve the rebirth in heterosexual relationships that would come from equal responsibility and comfortable self-expression. However, unable to change, he is afraid of women's changing, too. As a result of his rigidity, the transformation in women only spells danger in the form of abandonment and potential emotional starvation.

It is my interpretation that on the deepest archetypal level the feminist movement is partially fueled by an intuitive sensing of the decay and demise of the male. Women are rushing in to take men's places, as much for survival's sake as for any sociological or philosophical reasons. He has become a hyperactive, hyper-cerebral, hyper-mechanical, rigid, self-destructive machine out of control.

In 1910 there were 106.2 men for every 100 women in the population at large. By 1970, about the time when the feminist movement began to develop momentum, there were approximately 94.8 men for every 100 women.[2] In 1978, by age sixty-five, there were only 75 men left for every 100 women. Little boys fall prey to major illnesses, such as hyperkinesis, autism, stuttering and so on, at rates several hundred percent higher than little girls. The suicide rate for men is also several times higher than for women, to say nothing of the many indirect and less obvious ways in which men kill themselves. And the behavior of the up-and-coming generations of men suggests that the self-destructive trend may be accelerating.

In an article entitled "My Lost Generation," the author describes the men he grew up with in the 1960s in this way: "When I speak of my lost generation, I mean mainly the men. I am told by veteran editors that, by as early as 1965, more good women and fewer good men began passing through their offices, getting assignments and eventually becoming writers. . . . There has been a change, a shift. In the sixties, we used to sing a song that now seems a little too sentimental: 'Where have all the young men gone . . . ?' It is still a good question. Many of my friends have gone to graveyards, real and otherwise."[3]

The nature of masculinity is such that the male is unable even to recognize that he is in hazard. His life seems

He 9

to him to be totally within his control. Unaccustomed to self-examination, he blocks out awareness of the way he lives and the conditioning that created it. He stoically accepts his lot as a given, or at best a challenge that the "real man" will accept and cope with and only the "sissy" will not.

These attitudes were brought home to me when I was investigating the interpersonal lives of adult men. I asked them if they had any close male friends. Many seemed surprised by that question. "No. Why? Should I?" was the usual reply. They perceived their isolation, their lack of friendship with other men, as "normal." It was not something even to be questioned or examined.

The lack of close friendships between men may, in part, reflect the fact that they, too, experience the sterility, aridity and superficialty of intimate relationships with each other. How long can conversations about cars, politics, business and sports prove fulfilling and nourishing?

The repression of emotion, the denial and suppression of vulnerability, the compulsive competitiveness, the fear of losing, the anxiety over touching or any other form of sensual display, the controlled intellectualizing, and the general lack of spontaneity and unself-conscious playfulness serve to make the companionship of most men unsatisfying and highly limited. Men are at their best when a task has to be completed, a problem solved, or an enemy battled. Without such a structure, however, anxiety and self-consciousness accelerate too rapidly to allow for a sustained pleasurable experience.

This is also what makes feminist independence a threat. If a man cannot turn to other men in a crisis; if there is no support available to see him through periods of transition and change; if he can only bond comfortably with other men in pursuit of a tangible goal or to defeat a common enemy, he has no basis of intimacy for reaching out to them. It is particularly uncomfortable in moments of weakness, vulnerability, humiliation or pain.

His relationship with his woman is suffocated by the heavy weight of his dependency and draining demandingness, as he turns to her for everything. If she abandons him, his emotional lifeline will have been cut. At the same time, he never clearly defines what it is that he needs or wants from her. He detaches himself, with occasional moments of explosiveness, to control the torrent of unexpressed feelings. She will in turn either come to hate him for it or "suffer through it" masochistically.

Finally, there will be rapid physical decline, because health-giving things are mainly feminine. To take care is not masculine.

Before the age of liberation and feminism he could rationalize this self-destructiveness: He was doing it for his wife and family. That made it all valid and worthwhile. Today the enlightened and honest woman is owning up. "You're not doing it for me: you're doing it for yourself. And if you're doing it for me, please stop, because I'm not getting anything from it. It's boring. It's dead and I hate it."

But the sham is revealed. In spite of the fact that she no longer wants what he is giving her, he can't stop giving it. This is the man who is told by his female companion that she does not want him to intervene or "protect" her in an argument or when a man makes a provocative comment, yet he can't hear her and persists in spite of her wishes. What is clear is that he is doing it for his *own* needs. A former police chief of Los Angeles, noted for his "macho" attitude, a man who liked to call himself the "meanest man in town," revealed this in a recent interview: "Men have the responsibility to protect women in the classical sense—to open the door of the car for ladies." When the interviewer asked, "You still think so today?" he replied, "I still do it. *The heck with them if they don't want it.*"*[4]

As a cardboard Goliath, the male cannot easily shift direction. It was recently reported by Dr. Sandra Bem, based on her extensive research, that "while high masculinity in males has been related to better psychological adjustment during adolescence, it is often accompanied during adulthood by high anxiety, high neuroticism and low self-acceptance. . . . Boys who are strongly masculine and girls who are strongly feminine tend to have lower overall intelligence, lower spatial ability, and show lower creativity."[5]

If he continues to cling to the traditional masculine

---

* Italics not in original.

blueprint, he will be a victim of himself. He will end his life as a pathetic throwaway, abandoned and asleep. He needs, therefore, to recognize what was aptly described in the ages-old philosophy of Lao-tzu:

> All living growth is pliant
> Until death transfixes it.
> Thus men who have hardened
> Are "kin of death."
> And men who stay soft
> Are "kin of life."[6]

2. The Razor's Edge of Compulsive Masculinity

To be strong, the prisoner once wrote, a man "must be able to stand utterly alone, able to meet and deal with life relying solely upon his own inner resources." To show he was such a man, he once held his hand over a candle flame without flinching. This is G. Gordon Liddy, 46 . . .[1]

It happened on Highway 126 in Fillmore, California, on April 26, 1976. A car with four young men passed another containing three male occupants. The young men in these two cars had never seen each other before.

One of those in the passing car made an obscene gesture at the guys in the passed car. If one is even slightly familiar with the hair-trigger defensiveness of the masculine psyche and the stereotyped, predictable quality of its reactions, the next scene in this freeway drama could be easily predicted.

First, one can easily imagine what went on in the minds of the young men who received this obscene nonverbal communication. "We'll teach those assholes about flipped fingers! No one does that to us and gets away with it!"

Both cars stopped, and there was a fight. Afterward, as the three men drove away, a single shot was fired, and one fifteen-year-old in the passed car was shot in the head. He was dead on arrival at Santa Paula Hospital.[2]

I term this *macho-psychotic behavior*, because it results from what I believe are moments of temporary insanity, those apparently defensive, uncontrollable reflex acts arising from the compulsion to prove one's musculinity.

The incidence of fights and killings in bars and other places where men gather, between individuals whose only contact or communication was an obscene gesture, a slurring remark, a threatening look or some other kind of similar challenge, is high. So commonplace, in fact, that most incidents of this kind rarely find their way into the newspaper.

Supposedly, the drive to survive is the most powerful motivation in the human being. For many men, apparently, this is not so. Rather, the need to prove oneself, "the razor's edge of compulsive masculinity," suffocates the survival instinct and creates a temporary state of insanity when there is a challenge or threat to one's masculinity.

It is important to differentiate at the outset genuine heroics from compulsive proving behavior. Heroic behavior involves an actual danger, or a threatening enemy who intends to harm, and from whom there is no escape. This might be in the form of a fire endangering lives, the rescue of a person in trouble, or protection against someone with clearly destructive intent. However, in the case of the young men in the car, when nothing but the masculine ego was at stake and still life and limb were risked, it is safe to say the persons involved were in a possessed state, temporarily blinded to reason, out of control, out of their minds, and in a *macho-psychotic* condition.

The male driven to prove his masculinity is also in a state of addiction, not much different from the person who is hooked on alcohol or pills. His behavior cannot be affected or changed by logic and reasoning. For example, some therapists have used the tactic of taking alcoholics to the morgue to show them corpses of skid-row alcoholics with their livers eaten away by cirrhosis. The experience has no lasting effect in getting them to stop drinking. So, too, the driven male is beyond reality testing and cannot be affected by the kind of reasoning that tells him he is behaving self-destructively. *In that sense, masculinity can be seen as a psychological defense because it is beyond being affected by reason.*

Tragically, such behavior is only occasionally of an obviously and blatantly self-destructive kind. In most cases, the razor's edge of compulsive masculinity cuts much more subtly, and assumes the mask of hero behavior, and the person is applauded.

One of this country's contemporary economic success stories is a forty-nine-year-old self-made millionaire in CB radios. He had gone through a career in the military and small-time sales before taking a plunge in the business of citizens-band radios, where he went from scratch to a twenty-five-million-dollar business in three years.

A neighbor of his had had open-heart surgery, and one of his friends had a heart attack while driving and wrecked his car. This motivated him to have a physical examination.

His doctor informed him that he was 90 percent blocked. After inquiring about his chances of survival without surgery and being told he would have a maximum of fifteen months of life, he underwent a nine-and-a-half-hour operation.

On the eighth day his wife picked him up from the hospital and said, "You want to go home?" to which he replied, "No, I want to go to the office." Only eight days after major surgery!

In an interview he said, "And now I'm back on the merry-go-round, working harder, longer hours. Traveling more. More stress. More strain. This is just what I shouldn't be doing after my open-heart surgery. But it doesn't seem to be affecting me. I stop every once in a while and say, 'Why am I pushing myself so hard?' And I say, 'Why not? I feel great.' "[8]

On an underlying level, there is an equation between autonomy and masculinity, between overcoming obstacles and resistances and masculinity, between being fearless and all-powerful and masculinity and between not being passive and dependent and masculinity. The need to prove these things supersedes rational self-care and results in compulsive, self-destructive behavior.

The difference between men and women in these areas, between rigidity and fluidity, between compulsive defensiveness and a more reality-oriented response rests in women's greater ability to express strength *or* weakness, independence *or* dependency, activity *or* passivity, rationality *or* emotionality, courage *or* fear, hetero-sensual *or* homo-sensual feelings without threat to their self-image. The man, however, is hooked on his one-track, all-or-nothing response, which appears regardless of the dictates of external reality.

Nowhere does the razor's edge manifest itself in America as clearly, and in such socially approved form, as in the game of football.

The drive in football is enforced at an early age. The "pee-wee pill poppers" are young teen-age boys who go on crash diets of diuretics, laxatives and other pills with possible dangerous side effects in order to lose weight to meet the rigid age-weight classifications. They can then compete in the intermediate divisions, where they stand a better chance to be winners.

One league commissioner reported, "I recall one incident where a kid was so weak from dieting that his father carried him to the scale. I refused to weigh him. Last year I saw one kid slumped on the floor and another who walked around in circles from losing so much weight. They were in too bad shape to be weighed. In both cases the problem was parental. I know of another case where the kid was so weak he contracted pneumonia."[4]

Reinforcement of the compulsion to prove is graphically demonstrated by the appreciative roar of the crowd when a football player is injured or knocked unconscious and returns soon thereafter to the game. It is as if the crowd were saying in unison, "What a man!"

The long-range effects of such "heroics" are being brought out in public for the first time. Until recently, ex-athletes were like ex-soldiers who proudly displayed the wounds they received in battle. To complain or to blame would have cast doubt on their masculinity. Each took it in silence "like a man."

However, some ex-players with lifelong chronic problems received from college football injuries that were not properly treated or given time to heal because the player was needed back in the game are coming forward. Some are filing lawsuits against their coaches, team doctors, or universities.

One player for a leading southern university six years ago was on crutches until just before the game, when his ankle was heavily taped. It wouldn't function, so the team doctor injected it with Novocaine. He then had to have his ankle injected before and during each game for four weeks, because it never got a chance to heal. He now lives in chronic pain from his problems with it.

Another player reports teammates playing with tears

streaming down their faces from pain in damaged knees. But the coaches kept them out there, because the team needed the bodies.

Moses Easley, ex-Indiana football player, said, "You know, as a nineteen-year-old I had all those crazy macho ideas. But it all turned out to be nothing but sadomasochism, walking around all season in bandages. It was crazy. I wish I'd never played football at Indiana."

Andy Lowe, former defensive end for Texas Tech, dislocated his left knee in 1971 and had an operation. He was only supposed to play heavily taped, but his coach didn't like his lateral movements, so they removed the restricting tape. A teammate landed on his knee and Lowe, who is now suing, says, "My leg below the knee just hangs there like a hunk of meat." He may have to have the leg amputated.

Reports on college football players conducted by Dr. Kenneth Clarke at Penn State indicate that for high school and college football players there are 28 significant injuries among every 100 football players. A number of players have indicated that their coaches often instructed them not to tell the team doctors about their injuries, fearing the doctors would order the players sidelined.[5]

The support of early marriage may represent this culture's fear and hatred of unharnessed masculinity. When a very young man marries, to the delight of family and community, are they not breathing a sigh of relief and unwittingly saying, "Another potential animal is off the street"?

A thirty-four-year-old American serving as a mercenary was killed by the Angolan government. He had four children, ranging in age from nine to three and a half, and had been married eleven years. He did it for the money.

His wife commented, "In his own misguided way he was taking care of us. He was a family man." Before he left, he was attending college and working two jobs, maintaining cafeteria equipment and packing parachutes, in addition to serving one weekend a month with the National Guard. He had served in Vietnam.

Despite the fact that he had nailed himself prematurely to the cross of compulsive masculinity, doing all the things "real" and "responsible" men should do, he died in a condition of self-hate, as he described it just before the end.

He wrote his wife: "This will be my last letter to you, because I know I'm going to die. I'm just one of those people who never made good. It will be very hard on you all, and it is all my fault, as most everything that has gone wrong has been. All I can say is that I'm sorry, and I wish I could make it up to you. Please pray that God will let me into his house so that one day I can see you all again. All my love and goodbye."[6] *The priest at the funeral called his wife "an inspiration," but decided against any eulogy for the dead mercenary.*

The man who is obsessed with work, with meeting responsibilities, who drives himself to an early demise after procreating, making money, possibly becoming successful or powerful (most men *never* do!), has lived his life as a sleep-walker in harness. He has equated the compulsively driven need to live up to the masculine imperative with a "meaningful" life.

Even the notion of a man being satisfied because he has "done his work" and feels prepared, therefore, to die may, in an age of expanded consciousness, prove to be another defensive illusion and romantic variation on the theme of compulsive masculinity. The pioneering, creative psychologist Abraham Maslow, known as the father of humanistic psychology, died at the young age of sixty-two. In an interview shortly before his death he spoke introspectively about an earlier heart attack that had come right after he completed what he felt to be an important piece of work. "I had really spent myself. This was the best I could do, and here was not only a good time to die but I was even willing to die . . . it was what David M. Levy called the 'completion of the act.' It was like a good ending, a good close. . . . Partly this was entirely personal and internal and just a matter of feeling good about myself, feeling proud of myself, feeling pleased with myself, self-respecting, self-loving, self-admiring . . ."[7]

The value placed on work as being the ultimate raison d'être of a man's life, as articulated by even this highly respected and sophisticated psychologist, needs to be seriously questioned. Is it perhaps not just another subtle variation on the razor's edge of compulsive masculinity?

Finally the world of fraternity hazing, in which getting accepted by one's "brothers" often involves submitting oneself to humiliation and outright sadism, presents in microcosm the conflict between the external masculine imperative to "act like a man" and the internal craving for intimacy and belonging. It is also an apt metaphor for the dilemma of modern masculinity.

The destructive aspects have been frequently reported by the press. At the University of Wisconsin, a student named David Hoffman died from excessive alcohol consumed at a number of bars while on the "death march," an initiation ritual of his fraternal club. A nineteen-year-old junior at Queens College, going through the rites involved in becoming a member of the Pershing Rifles fraternity, was jabbed with a knife that accidentally plunged through his main artery and killed him. At Michigan State, one senior lost interest in joining a fraternity after he developed a burn on his nose as a result of being forced to rub it along a carpet as part of the initiation rites.[8]

Then there was the Sundowners, a social drinking club at the University of Nevada, Reno, where one man died and another just managed to survive after suffering a complete respiratory arrest subsequent to a bizarre and savage drinking rite that lasted several days and involved the consumption of quarts of tequilla, bourbon, wine, artichoke liquor, gin and so on.

Listen to the tragic explanation of a man who was an honorary pallbearer for the victim, who had played football with him and was tending the bar where the victim had drunk the night he died. He expressed poignantly the distorted manifestations of affectionate expression between men who are psychologically blocked from such direct affectionate display.

"I think the guys quote, unquote who absued him the most were the people who wanted to get to know him and wanted to leave an impression of themselves upon him, to show him that they had a feeling for the club, and they wanted him to possibly have that same feeling. What the witnesses saw was a front. They saw guys yelling and calling bad names, pushing them against the wall, trying to take their hats away. They didn't know the guys liked him. . . . The two who were the most active in John's initiation, I heard one say to the other when it was over, 'I just love the guy.' "[9]

3. Alive at Twenty, a Machine at Thirty, Burned Out by Forty

> I've always grown up late. I think a lot of men begin to die when they're in their 20's, when they make a commitment to a fixed life. I was never able to do that. I feel sometimes as though I've never grown up, and I like that. There are still possibilities.[1]
>
> —Sterling Hayden, actor and author of *Voyage*

There is a notion, or "fact," interpreted as a biological phenomenon but seeming to me to be more psychologically symbolic of the life-constriction process of men, that they reach their sexual peak in their late teens and then go into a decline. Women, however, are said to peak in their late twenties and early thirties.

It is, in fact, one of the tragedies of the rhythm of the male-female developmental process in our culture that men are in the process of shutting down in the same age period when women are unfolding, falling asleep while women are awakening. Consequently, feminine blossoming is met by masculine defensiveness and rigidity. This is manifested more obviously and powerfully today than ever before, as women increasingly give themselves permission to grow into total personhood beyond sex-role stereotypes.

Chris White had been a star athlete in high school and was appointed to a military academy, where he was in officer's training until age twenty-two, when he had to be dropped because of a shattered knee.

In high school and at the academy he was outgoing, had many friends and possessed an easygoing, fun-loving style. After leaving the academy, he married his beautiful high school sweetheart, Donna, who was now building a career in public relations. He took a job with one of the largest, most prestigious encyclopedia sales companies in America.

20

Though only twenty-three, Chris was already well along in the process of becoming a machine, and his call for help, which clearly took all the courage he could muster (he thought about it for two months before telephoning me), seemed motivated by some unconscious, self-preserving instinct that was pushing him into reexamining himself. He was in painful conflict over things that were going on at his job and in his marriage.

When he arrived for his appointment, he was wearing a gray suit with a vest and tie. His hair was short and perfectly in place, and his overall grooming was impeccable. His manner and speech were careful and conservative. It was hard to believe that he was only twenty-three.

Chris was approaching a stage in the life cycle described in a research article, "Natural History of Male Psychologic Health," co-authored by psychiatrists George E. Vaillant and Charles C. McArthur. According to their study of the male life cycle from age eighteen to fifty, men tended to hustle hard between twenty-five and thirty-five. "Poor at self-reflection, they were not unlike latency children—good at tasks, careful to follow the rules, anxious for promotion, and accepting many aspects of the 'system' and instead worked hard to become specialists."[2]

My patient came to see me, as most conformist males do, with great reluctance and trepidation and *only* because he thought his problems would yield rapidly to clear-cut and usable solutions. He told me that he did not want the bills sent to his home, because he didn't want his wife to know of the visits. He feared it would upset her. It was clear that in his mind one or two hours of talk would take care of everything.

He was in particularly painful conflict about his job, which he initially took because it afforded him the prospect of a lucrative future. His manager was prodding him to begin by selling encyclopedias to his friends, and he found it embarrassing and uncomfortable because, as a result of his sales approach, many of them were beginning to avoid him. His manager insisted, however, that this was the only way to get the ball rolling and become successful. He even urged him to lie and tell his friends that he needed the sales to win a contest.

Equally discomforting was the fact that his manager

had sent him back to his former academy to sell encyclopedias. The administration at the academy turned him down because of previous bad experiences with other alumni who had returned to campus to sell various products. His manager was threatening to file a lawsuit against the academy in order to gain access, claiming that the company's rights were being violated. Chris White felt manipulated, resentful, confused and fearful that he would alienate former friends and acquaintances and get a reputation as a troublemaker.

Then there were the problems in his marriage. He loved dogs and wanted to get a German shepherd, but his wife didn't want a dog, so he deferred to her. But inside he deeply resented it.

In addition, there were the times when he had felt particularly troubled and lonesome and wanted his wife to spend the day at home to talk with him and make love, because he had been working evenings and rarely saw her during the week. She refused, explaining that she was in the middle of important projects and was needed at the office. He felt hurt because her job seemed to be more important to her than he was.

Once a fine and enthusiastic athlete, he now spent his weekends at home papering and painting walls and gardening. Though his wife was only twenty-three, like himself, he saw her already developing into a henpecking, dominating person like his mother. Still, he felt too guilty to confront her and reluctant to forcefully assert his needs, because he perceived her as being fragile.

He would meet attractive women during the week who aroused him sexually, and he wanted some freedom, but again he hesitated to discuss this with his wife, because he thought it would "wipe her out." Periodically, he fantasized about getting a divorce but rejected the idea because he felt both their parents would be too deeply upset. Besides, everybody had said that they were the perfect couple—attractive, ambitious and bright.

He would come home at night occasionally wishing that his wife had been killed in an automobile accident so that his conflicts could be resolved without guilt. He hated himself for these thoughts. He was beginning to brim over with anger and frustration but could see no alternative except to use more self-control to overcome these feelings, which he wanted me to help him with quickly.

Like many other men in their early twenties, Chris had directed all of his energies toward "making it" while denying important feelings and needs. Deadening his inner experience and at the same time accommodating himself to externally imposed role expectations that were in opposition to his inner feelings led to machinelike behavior.

By age thirty, most men are well along on the journey of proving themselves and becoming dehumanized "things."

I was recently invited to the thirtieth birthday party of a rising star in the business world—the brother of a close woman friend of mine. The party was attended by members of his football alumni association and some business acquaintances and friends from his army days. The invitation said the gifts were to be funny. As the party was ending and he opened them in pained good humor, the forced "witty" comments of his friends and himself, as well as the gifts, all focused on whether or not he could still "get it up" or "keep it up." The general idea was that at thirty he was over the hill and on the way to becoming an old man.

The men at the party were active sportsmen, and outdoor games could be played in the handsomely decorated, spacious backyard. Instead, they sat around drinking beer and discussing real estate and business.

The powerful decline from age twenty to forty takes place on every level as the man goes from being:

1) Urgently sexual at twenty, to sexually mechanical at thirty, to sexually anxious, defensive and grateful just for being able to perform at forty.

2) Restless, passionate about his ideas, eager to push the limits and experience of his life at twenty, to conservative, "appropriate" and accepting of "reality" at thirty; to holding on tight and just trying to maintain his place at forty.

3) Physically active, energetic and finding pleasure in movement and play at twenty, to exercising purposefully in order to fight his waistline and stay in shape at thirty, to engaging in physical activity at forty, if at all, in a compulsive, serious and measured way, motivated by a fear of heart attacks and other physical ailments.

4) Playful, curious, adventurous and hungry for plea-

sure at twenty, to controlled, with his pleasure outlets limited to dinners out, movies, television, photography and shopping at thirty, to passive and reluctant to try new things or to forsake the sporting event on television at forty.

5) An optimist and laughing boisterously at twenty, to a pragmatist, realistic and with a more inhibited sense of humor, at thirty, to cynical, with a snicker if he laughs at all, at forty.

6) Buddyship oriented and close to male friends who are important to him at twenty, to being more guarded around other men and getting together socially usually only in the company of wives or girl friends at thirty, and at forty in a situation where friendships have evaporated because the men are either divorced, overburdened or living elsewhere and without time or motivation to participate in any close male relationships.

7) Blunt and honest often to the point of rudeness at twenty, to appropriately tactful, phony and manipulative by thirty, to not really knowing what he feels or believes in at forty, because everything has by now been discolored by his overriding motivations of expediency and proving himself.

The roots of this decline are clearly not mysterious, nor need one rationalize these changes as being "normal" passages. In fact, in a self-aware, self-responsible, humanly creative world, I believe that people would scoff at the notion that stages are predetermined and predictable. They would recognize these so-called stages as being nothing but comfortable rationalizations for conformity and loss of mastery over one's existence and developmental pace.

The decline is set in obvious motion in his early twenties *because* he is making critical and often permanent and irreversible life decisions at an age when he is figuratively asleep in terms of his self-awareness and understanding. In his late teens and early twenties he is driven by the external pressures of his culture to prove himself a man, long before he is aware of what it is that he really wants for himself, apart from what he has been told and therefore presumes that he should want. He gets prematurely locked into cages, cornered and trapped in life situations with few, if any, comfortable or apparent options.

It is, in fact, a humanly destructive culture that does not do everything in its power to prolong this early decision-making period. It should prevent the behavior that turns his adult years into something akin to military conscription, in which doing one's duty and paying dues in the form of seriousness, responsibility, adjustment and self-denial are paramount.

To add insult to injury, after he has prematurely locked up and thrown away his life, he may be labeled a chauvinist, an alcoholic, a wife abuser, a manic-depressive or a cold, uninterested family man. He is left defenseless because he hasn't the ability to examine the obvious roots of these expressions of rage and self-hate. He has also not had the supportive psychological climate which would make it possible for him to free himself from the destructive binds that triggered his twisted responses.

Much attention has been paid recently to the "male menopause," the newest rationalization for male deterioration, a process that supposedly occurs in a man's forties and fifties when his functioning starts to break down. This so-called climacteric strikes me as a sort of death rattle, a last glimmer of awareness and cry of protest and pain before the total demise of the self. I personally do not accept the rationalization that the "male menopause" is simply the result of panic over declining potency, biological changes, the fast pace of modern life or the breakdown of traditional values. To my mind it is the noise of the male organism shattering under the weight of oppressive, dehumanized conditioning.

This decline, caused by years of repression and emotional denial, makes him dangerous to others as well as to himself—particularly to his sons and other young men. Because he has placed himself on the cross and endured unending frustration, he has a strong vested belief in and commitment to the values for which he sacrificed himself. It would be threatening indeed for him to acknowledge that he has been a sleepwalker, self-destructively conformist and deluded. His defenses against this awareness will cause him to resent and block the more spontaneous, growth-oriented and meaningful life-style of younger men, which he interprets as irresponsible and adolescent. He will try to thwart it by withholding support so that it cannot be maintained for long without extraordinary effort and ego strength.

He will gladly invest in his son's professional training or back him for a start in business if the money is available, but he won't encourage what he considers an "unproductive" process of self-discovery and an expansive orientation toward life. He wants younger men to pay the same dues he paid, to travel the same road he walked. And the more he has committed himself to his own self-denying style, the more difficult will it be for him to break through the defenses that continuously reassure him about the rightfulness of his behavior.

While many modern women are at least willing to reexamine the time-honored, "sacred" roles of mother and wife that have been their chief source of identity, and also to acknowledge their stifling aspects, men continue to negate their feelings and pretend they are comfortable in their roles. Most probably they cannot perceive any alternatives, because these roles affirm their manliness. And that is *the* important thing. Any changes would threaten that status and arouse intense anxiety.

Some men do escape this process constriction and live a more expressive existence. They are the late-bloomers, the "child men," the creative people—the ones who have never fit into the traditional mold. These men stun with their individuality and are either adored or scorned, considered lusty and free or crazy misfits, depending on whether they have been able to make their style functional and materialistically profitable.

These are men who have found it impossible to conform, because they have never lost touch with the person inside and are therefore not able to regiment themselves into a style that will require them to suppress their individual humanness. The pain and struggle they experience as young men for being deemed misfits or "different" are repaid in the long run, if they find their niche, because they remain more fluid, interesting, sensual, playful, passionate, ever-changing and even charismatic. While other men of their age are withering, they are blossoming and retain a youthful, timeless quality, because they have navigated by their own senses, perceptions and rhythm. They are the Zorbas, the Picassos, the Chaplins and many others who are not well known but who continue to be lusty and who can relate to young and old without an awareness of age difference or consciousness of barriers.

Others who sometimes escape the process of constriction are those who experience a shattering crisis early in life and are able to learn and benefit from it and reorganize their lives in a new and more authentic way. These are men who perhaps had some personal problems and also possessed the openness to reach out for professional help. They opted to stay with their own self-discovery long enough to break through and undo harmful attitudes and reaction patterns that would have otherwise suffocated them.

The point is that no man will escape the inevitable end points if he conforms to the traditional processes of rigid masculine conditioning. These processes and the patterns they generate are overpowering and their consequences inevitable. The conceit of most men is that they feel they *can* make the traditional journey and somehow magically avoid what they have seen occurring in others.

A culture interested in liberating men would slow the life decision-making pace down greatly. Jobs would be seen for what they are; tasks and role behaviors needed to keep the society functioning—not *the* reason for being alive. A young man would be discouraged from establishing permanent relationships early in life and certainly discouraged from fathering until his own identity was well under his conscious awareness and control. Ultimately, the best method of population control would be self-aware, self-caring men who simply would not reproduce early and abundantly, because the price that had to be paid for living under this kind of pressure would obviously be too great. Only fools would risk it.

By becoming self-aware, I believe, he would develop physical and emotional patterns that would greatly extend and expand his life and his youthfulness. There would be less urgency to assume heavy responsibilities early. The pressure of time that many contemporary men feel would be seen as an artifact of the destructive conditioning and early burning out which the masculine game plan produces. His stages or passages would also be revealed to be the penalties for his lack of consciousness.

Self or other abusive behavior, be it alcoholism, child or spouse abuse, indulgence in the purchase of prostitutes as a manifestation of the inability to have the kind of sex life he needs and desires, drugs, compulsive overwork or cynical detachment would be revealed to be symptoms of self-hating, self-destructive, frustrated, trapped male, rather than the chauvinistic "bad boy" behavior of the inherently "evil" man.

4. Sleeping Is Feminine

Ronald Blake was a thirty-nine-year-old radio talk show personality at the time he went into the hospital for a corneal transplant operation. He was known throughout the South as "The Tennessee Iron Man" for his all-night program, which he often conducted without any accompanying guests. It was just he and his call-in listeners. He was at the peak of his career at the time of the surgery. It bothered him that he would be laid up for at least a week after.

His beautiful new wife was at his bedside throughout. Theirs was a brand new marriage, the second for both. She was fourteen years his junior and an aspiring actress-singer.

"I really feel restless," he told her, while chain-smoking in his private room only one day before surgery. "I'm gonna go crazy just lying here. I'll try and talk them into letting me broadcast live from my bed."

The radio station manager loved the idea, because Blake was one of their superstars, and the publicity value of their "Iron Man" broadcasting live from the hospital would be enormous. Nevertheless, he gratuitously asked Blake if he was sure he could handle it and that it wouldn't slow his recovery.

With the adrenalin flowing and his beautiful wife sitting nearby, he boasted, "I feel fantastic. They'll be the greatest shows I've *ever* done. No problem here!"

Being persuasive and charming, he succeeded in getting his doctor and the hospital administration to go along with him, as long as he remained under their constant supervision. The staff thought it would be good public relations for the hospital, which they wanted to have recognized as being a progressive one. It would also help the morale of other patients, many of whom tended to be overly fearful of resuming normal activities after an operation, they rationalized.

Blake loved the idea, too. He would be a model for all of the sick people who wallow in self-pity, and that excited him. He was sure his audience would love him for his courage, and that his audience would grow. It would reinforce his "Iron Man" image and at the same time reassure his wife that she didn't have a middle-aged invalid on her hands.

She brought champagne to his room, and he recruited her to help him with the logistics of the broadcast. It would be good experience for her too because he knew she wanted to break into show business.

Warned that a cold or infection would severely impede and possibly even be disastrous for the healing process, he popped Vitamin C pills continually. When he felt feverish or headachy, he simply increased the dosage, without even discussing that with his physician. He saw himself as an expert on this vitamin, because he'd read a lot about it, so he figured he couldn't go wrong by self-prescribing these "harmless" pills.

Six days later he was discharged from the hospital, and by then he had become "fast friends" with most of the staff. He had proven to everybody that the "Iron Man" label was no hype by turning his recovery into a party without any complaining, self-pity or special attention.

Three months later he collapsed right after his nightly program and was taken to the hospital with double pneumonia. Two years later he died "unexpectedly" and suddenly of a heart attack.

Blame it on the Y chromosome, the supposedly weaker male form, which allegedly makes the male more vulnerable than the female to certain disorders. Or blame it on biological inferiority, or even on man's evolutionary history which has been credited with making the male less well adapted than the female to the contemporary stresses of civilization.

The facts remain that men are far more susceptible to degenerative diseases than women. By 1974, the rate for mortality from malignant neoplasms was 1.49 for men in comparison to women, an increase from 1.08 in 1950. For heart diseases, the mortality rate is more than twice as high. Cerebrovascular disease has risen from a sex mortality ratio of 1.07 in 1950 to a value of 1.21 in 1974.[1] By the next century, it is predicted, men will be living ten years less than women.[2]

It is indeed very much in the masculine psychological tradition to search only externally for the explanations and causes for his physical and emotional problems. The genetic, biological and historical focus turns the issue into an intellectual puzzle, a scientific problem to be solved. Little emphasis is placed on anything that would involve self-awareness, emotions, relationships or psychological introspection. Besides, most men are still pretty well convinced that psychology and the introspective, self-awareness orientation is mystical, tender-minded garbage.

Yet from a psychological perspective, it is both an obvious but subtle and difficult awareness to grasp that the basic processes, attitudes and behavior patterns that are life sustaining and health nurturing are commonly identified as feminine. At the same time, on a physical care level, traditional masculine values and attitudes can be seen as synonymous with physical self-destruction. For example, it is masculine (1) to be able to take as much pain as possible without giving in to it, (2) to hold liquor, (3) to recuperate from serious illness quickly, etc., etc. In fact, there is even something feminine just about being sick in the first place, perhaps because it involves acknowledgment of vulnerability and helplessness. Many men who are ill are embarrassed to acknowledge it and, in fact, will deny it as long as possible. *That's masculine!*

The factors which have resulted in the equation between self-care and femininity have also, I believe, created what I term a *body-psychotic* condition for many men. What that means is they have lost touch with their bodies. In effect, one could say they have *no body*, in the same way the psychotic personality has lost his sense of self, and has *no self*.

The masculine imperative, meaning the pressure to live up to the mandates of masculinity, has caused him to lose his body awareness. As a little boy, he was taught to tune out body signals and to perceive certain attitudes toward his body and his health as masculine, while others were considered sissyish or feminine. Consequently, it is not uncommon to find workaholic middle-aged men, alcoholic, hyperactive, overeaters who are chronically driven. These are the men who tell you they "feel great" one day, and then "suddenly" fall prey to a major illness or even drop dead the next.

This lack of awareness of their physical deterioration, while engaged in the most obviously self-destructive of habit patterns, is a manifestation of the *body-psychotic* condition. *Stress, self-poisoning, fatigue and emotional pain do not register.* Their early conditioning as men has numbed that awareness and made it anxiety provoking to give in to them even when they *do* experience it. These men are detached from the voice of their body. They do not experience the body's growing signals of distress and the accumulation of dis-ease, until they break down altogether.

It is pathetically ironic that the very characteristics that constitute the heart-attack-prone Type-A personality, the personality and response configuration of the man most likely to succumb, are the same characteristics that have been said to lead to success. They include being highly competitive, compulsive about deadlines and quotas, being highly achievement-oriented and pushing oneself constantly. He has been written about as follows: "The Type-A person works hard and fast to succeed, and in striving toward his goals he suppresses feelings such as fatigue that might interfere with his performance. Type-A's get angry if someone or something else gets in the way of their success . . . rises to master challenges out of a need to control the world."[3]

To embarrass such a man, telephone him in the afternoon, and say, "I hope I didn't wake you from a nap." "I wasn't sleeping!" will most probably be his quick and defensive reply in a guilty tone, or one which would suggest that you had impugned his manliness. Or even telephone him very early in the morning and apologize for having awakened him. "I've been up for quite a while," "I wasn't asleep," or "I was just about to get up" will probably be his reply. It will be most important for him to *deny* that he'd been asleep.

He reacts like a little boy who has been caught stealing. Guilty! He has been caught napping, "asleep at the wheel." He feels accused of nonmasculine behavior. Gently ask him on the freeway, after a long stretch of driving, if he'd like you to take over because he looks tired. "No, I'm fine! I'll let you know when I've had it." Then he will continue to deny and fight his fatigue as long as possible.

Sleeping is feminine because sleeping is a passive activity. Passivity equals femininity. During sex, for example, the man is traditionally supposed to be on top and active while the woman is supposed to be on the bottom, more reactive than active and in traditional feminine behavior, passive and submissive.

Because passivity equals femininity, passivity might also unconsciously equal homosexuality. On the deepest level, particularly for the most masculinely defensive of men the unconscious equation might be seen as follows: Sleeping equals passivity, passivity equals femininity, femininity in a man equals homosexuality; therefore sleeping, beyond a certain minimal point, would be equated with homosexuality. Consequently, it could be predicted that the more macho the male, the more uncomfortable he would be with long stretches of sleeping, taking of naps, inactivity or any forms of passivity or "doing nothing." A typically macho attorney, describing the difference in attitude between himself and his wife, said, "Sleeping is a necessity. She likes to lie in bed in the morning. I like to get up early." When he's in trial, he often gets up as early as 2:30 A.M. "I like to get ready to do battle. I'm never happier than when I'm in court," he said.

In fact, most men would proudly tell you how little sleep they need in order to function. The unspoken message is, "See how masculine I am!" The scientist who could develop a pill that would allow men to go without sleep altogether would undoubtedly become an instant billionaire.

Sleeping conjures up other, more consciously negative associations such as laziness. There is the inner voice of past authority warning him as a boy always to be doing something and, particularly, not to sleep his life away. "Do you want to spend a third or more of your life sleeping?" He does not see sleep as enriching and extending his life, in quality and quantity, but rather as being a waste of it.

The masculine psychological imperative does not allow him the psychological space to grasp what Shakespeare so aptly perceived, when he wrote in *Macbeth:* [4]

> ... Sleep that knits up the
> ravell'd sleave of care,
> The death of each day's life,
> sore labour's bath.
> Balm of hurt minds,
> great nature's second course,
> *Chief nourisher in life's feast.* *

His conditioning, his anxieties and his compulsions even prevent him from fully experiencing his need for sleep. He may become an organism without a passivity cycle, and in this way he is unlike any other organism. For years he blocks out the fatigue, kicks himself back into activity as he would a tired horse, and to accomplish this he uses pills, cigarettes, coffee, liquor, stimulating diets, vitamins and whatever else will allow him to deceive his body into suppressing its exhaustion.

The result is that he ages and burns out prematurely. But in the short run, being able to do with little sleep is a triumph and a habit that he feels will keep him one step ahead of the crowd, a winner! By age forty he is already a physical caricature of his younger self; paunchy, balding, wrinkled, with poor eyesight and general physical enervation manifested by various aches and pains. Rather than reveling in good body feelings, he is now physically defensive, obsessed with heart-attack prevention, weight reduction, reducing his drinking and maintaining his potency.

His resistance to passivity also ties in with his goal orientation. That is, he won't do something if it doesn't have a purpose because he can't afford to "waste his time." As one young man so aptly expressed this orientation, "I can't even take a walk without feeling I'm wasting my time. If I'm not going somewhere specific or for a reason, I feel

* Italics not in original.

uncomfortable. I have a constant gnawing feeling of anxiety and guilt."

When he exercises, it is also for a purpose: to keep in shape. When he touches a woman, it is for a purpose: to have sex. When he has a lunch date, that too has a purpose: business and making money. And when he plays or otherwise spends time with his child, it is for a purpose: to make sure the child is exposed to the right things, to ease his own guilt over not being an involved parent and to pay his dues and reassure himself he is fulfilling his responsibilities as a father.

Because passivity is feminine, everything, including his greatest pleasures, eventually becomes a job because he is always goal oriented. He plays to win, so playing becomes a form of stress. When he doesn't play as well as he "used to," he might stop playing altogether, because he didn't play for the fun of it originally so there is no point in playing if he will lose. When he makes love, as the dominant one, he must have an erection. Failing that, as he someday must, what was once pleasure will become a source of anxiety, a terror and a job.

Not only is sleeping feminine, but it is a part of the self-destructive nature of masculinity that the healing, recuperative, life- and health-sustaining attitudes and processes are essentially considered feminine, while body-destructive attitudes are considered masculine.

1) *Emotional expression is feminine.*

Women are emotional; men are supposed to control themselves. So men's emotions undergo repression, and they fall victim to stress-induced, psychosomatic illnesses.

2) *Giving in to pain is feminine.*

Boxers, though bleeding and half conscious, stay in the ring and fight until they're forced by the referee to quit. Even then they will protest the call if they have *anything* left at all. Or, as one football coach told his limping player as he urged him to continue, "I've never seen a guy die from a sprained ankle." To another, he remarked, "You play with the small hurts, boy!"[5]

The male learns to equate his masculinity with his ability to take pain. The equation he lives by is a simple one. "The more pain I can take without giving in, the more manly I am." Only after the cumulative symptoms have become so great that they throw him over, does he give in to them and only then because he has to. He can disown personal responsibility and blame the illness. "*It* knocked me flat."

3) *Asking for help is feminine.*

He drives around the neighborhood for a half hour rather than pulling over to ask for help with the directions. When he's hurting, often nobody knows. "I don't want to impose on or bother anybody," he says. The feelings of discomfort he experiences when asking for help outweighs the benefits he believes he'll receive. On a deeper level, he may be asking himself the painful question: "Am I lovable when I'm not strong and healthy?"

A recent research study showed that although 65 percent of psychiatrists asked said that they saw more women professionally, 77 percent added that they didn't see more women who actually required psychiatric treatment. According to the researchers, that seemed to indicate that men don't make their first appointment until their symptoms become really severe. Women feel culturally freer to seek help because for a woman it is not viewed as an admission of weakness.[6]

4) *Paying too much attention to diet, especially when you're not sick, is feminine.*

He has been taught, and he believes, that because he's a man he needs to eat more heavily, even if, in fact, his work is less physically exerting than the woman's. Therefore, although he sits behind a desk all day in his office, he eats like a warrior embarking on a two-week hunt.

Eating meat is masculine. Perhaps it is the association of meat with blood. He has been told that the great warriors of old drank blood. Facts do not deter his magical belief in the idea of meat proteins making him strong, even though recent research indicates that "the only thing produced by excess intake of protein is high performance urine," and that protein is not a good source of energy because it has to go through many complex biochemical changes before becoming available as an energy source. Nor does additional protein enhance physiological work performance.[7]

Not only is it a myth that extra protein gives strength,

but a diet high in meat and dairy products, along with re-
fined flour and sugar, has been tied to six of the ten leading causes of death in the United States, including heart
diseases and certain kinds of cancer.[8] Recently, when the
U.S. government put two hundred obese rats on strict protein diets similar to those blamed for the deaths of sixteen
women, 95 percent died within a month.[9]

5) *Alcohol abstinence is feminine.*

In many small towns across America, the fear of reflecting negatively on one's masculinity by not drinking in the
company of one's male friends, almost every evening after
work, is far greater than any concern about what the alcohol is doing to the body. Drinking, after all, is *the* primary
basis for men relating to each other socially and of proving their masculinity. Again the equation he learns is
simple and blatantly self-destructive. "The more liquor I
can hold, the more masculine I am."

Never mind that recent studies show that alcohol enhances the carcinogenic impact of other agents, so that alcoholics are more prone to mouth, throat and liver
cancers.[10] Or that cirrhosis, brain damage, vitamin defi-
ciencies, premature aging and a significantly shortened life
span are other results of regular alcohol consumption.

It is a reflection on the interpersonal anxieties and the
limited capacity of men to find satisfying sober pleasures
in their life, that they need the liquor *in spite* of what they
know it will do to them.

6) *Self-care is feminine.*

Pampering oneself, taking long, leisurely baths, exploring oneself in front of the mirror, going to health spas,
and taking "beauty rests" are all "feminine" activities.
Men have "more important" things to do, namely, working
and being otherwise productive. A man who is unduly involved with his physical well-being is suspect. He is labeled
narcissistic, effete, a hypochondriac or worse. Conversely,
the man who is the most reckless in attitude toward his
physical well-being is seen as being most masculine.

7) *Dependency is feminine.*

Getting sick often means having to let other people take
care of you. Letting other people take care of you, worse
still, expecting them to, is feminine. The man who can

stand alone, does not rely on others, expresses no dependency and is least needful is the most manly.

8) *Touching is feminine.*

The nourishing, healing and comforting roles of touching are well documented in psychological literature. But touching, especially when it is purposeless (meaning it is not a prelude to sex or a formal greeting), arouses the man's anxiety and makes most men uncomfortable.

He learns that lesson early. Asking to be cuddled, held, kissed, stroked, rocked is for girls. Boys shake hands and that's about all the physical contact they share unless they're celebrating a victory, and then a pat on the ass or an arm around the shoulder is acceptable. A barber interviewed in a film about men called *Men's Lives* commented, "For many men, the only time they get any touching is when they come in here."[11]

So his body is tense and he looks to inanimate outlets for relaxation, such as eating, drinking liquor, watching television, etc. The human touch is acceptable only when it is for a purpose, such as a massage to "loosen his muscles," or touching before intercourse, mainly to loosen *her* up and to make *her* feel good. Otherwise, he is a rare, pathetic species in this world, one who has learned through conditioning that being touched is taboo because touching is "feminine."

In summary, masculinity in the care of the body means:

1) The less sleep I need,
2) The more pain I can take,
3) The more alcohol I can hold,
4) The less I concern myself with what I eat,
5) The less I ask anybody for help or depend on them,
6) The more I control and repress my emotions,
7) The less attention I pay to myself physically, *the more masculine I am.*

It is basically futile to warn or preach to a man that he should rest more, eat or smoke less, express emotions, etc. Like the neurotic who needs his symptoms to preserve his psychological balance, the man makes an unconscious equation between self-care and femininity, and he will therefore resist and ultimately abandon and subvert the most sincere intentions and efforts to change.

A typical conscious masculine rationalization for avoiding a change in self-caring behavior patterns is, "Why should I stop? I might get killed crossing the street, or get hit by a falling rock. So I'll live a few years less. At least I'll be enjoying myself when I'm here." Or "I don't want to be a 'health nut.'"

The changes, if they are to come, must emerge from a reclamation of his total self, the consciousness of himself as a whole person. As long as passivity, emotions, dependency, self-care, etc. equal femininity in his conditioning, while self-destructive proving and the tuning out of and learning to deny and overcome body messages is masculine, warnings and beseechments will fail. He, himself, must realize this conditioning and refuse to self-destruct just to prove himself. The awareness of what he has allowed to happen to himself, however, must come first. Resistance to following a self-destructive course in order to live up to an image could then follow.

He who can risk change, and reclaim the right to self-care and experience the satisfaction and pleasure of physical self-awareness and health, will never again return to self-destructive patterns. The body's signals of protest and the bad feelings he would experience when he behaves self-destructively would act as a constant, haunting reminder. And the incredible pleasure of being in tune with rather than the victim of his body would replace the momentary validation of his masculinity afforded by his former physical self-destructiveness.

5. The "Secrets" of Success

"You have a friend at Chase Manhattan."
—Advertisement

Judging from the continual flow of books on the subject, there is an insatiable appetite for literature on the techniques and secrets of becoming successful. Many of these books allege to lay bare the eternal, hidden, unspoken truths of life and human motivation, the attitudes required for "making it," the stuff that others dare not speak or will not reveal and that will open the palace doors to gold and riches.

The philosophies expounded range from inspirational, positive thinking, "pep-talk" approaches to various jungle philosophies that spell out in endless variation the cynical themes: "It's a dog-eat-dog world." "Do unto others before they do unto you." "Altruism is naïveté." "Every person is only out for himself," or a la Machiavelli, "The nature of men is such that most forget more easily the death of their fathers than the loss of their property."

The real "secret" of writing and publishing these books is that there exists in most people a belief in the illusion of techniques, a seemingly eternal, unshakable fantasy of the existence of a "magic key," a perfect formula, a combination of moves and strategies that will unlock the doors to success. Due to this propensity, there can exist at the very same time, widely read, popular books which offer totally contradictory advice and philosophies. Each manages to find its own group of ardent, convinced supporters.

The "secrets of success" that cannot be taught are deeply ingrained personality traits. These qualities, when combined with a specific skill or outlet or direction, and

40

sound intelligence will almost assuredly produce success. These ingredients include:

1) *Basic Distrust*: These men keep their own counsel, increasingly so as they climb the success ladder. They reveal their inner life to no one. Perhaps they are unknown even to themselves. For them, trusting is naïveté and dangerous vulnerability. It is the kind of human interaction that they believe will only interfere with and possibly sabotage their upward mobility.

Their unspoken philosophy, the one behind their surface cordiality and attentive and polite facade, was perhaps best articulated by George Smiley, the fallen chief of British intelligence in *The Honourable Schoolboy*, a spy novel by John Le Carré:

> . . . I have learned to interpret the whole of life in terms of conspiracy. That is the sword I have lived by, and . . . the sword I shall die by as well. These people terrify me, but I am one of them. If they stab me in the back, then at least that is the judgment of my peers.[1]

2) *Need to Control*: A counterpart of *basic distrust* is the *need to control*. This need allows one to avoid vulnerability and spontaneity and is also intrinsic to the traditional masculine style.

The highly aggressive, success-driven man has it to an extreme. He will avoid situations and people he cannot control. Eventually, his relationships are reduced to business-related ones. "Best friends" are his accountant, lawyer, business manager, etc. His wife, who is probably in the background, is appropriately submissive in relation to him. In his personal relationships, he is more or less obviously a tyrant, and the unspoken, reigning rule is: "Do it my way or leave."

Relationships which are not readily controlled and which result in conflict or excessive demands on his personal time are systematically eliminated.

3) *Manipulation*: He treats people as objects for manipulation.

One part of this orientation was cogently expressed by Dorothy Schiff, one-time owner, publisher and sole stockholder of the *New York Post*, and for many years one of America's most powerful women. In a published interview she commented, "Most people to me are nothing but personnel problems."[2]

Discussing her personal life, she commented, "Unforeseen problems always arise in my marriages. Maybe very common problems, but they always take me by surprise." When the interviewer asked her what sort of problems she was referring to, she replied, "That the other person has needs . . ."[3]

Extremely goal oriented as part of his pursuit of success, the success-driven man operates in detached, rational fashion, without allowing feelings, his own or those of others, to interfere.

According to some researchers, this approach is even prerequisite for the successful empire-building style. Psychologists David C. McClelland and David H. Burnham, in an article titled, "Good Guys Make Bum Bosses," pointed out that a bad boss is "a man whose main drive is for affiliation—to be friendly with everyone, including the people who work for him. His desire to be liked leads him into wishy-washy decisions, and he cares more about the happiness of particular individuals than the well-being of the whole working group."[4]

Social-industrial psychologist Jay Hall expressed it this way: "Good managers challenge their people; poor ones comfort them."[5]

The qualities of men who create effective organizations which expand into empire bases are described in the psychological book *Power: The Inner Experience*.[6] They include:

1) a strong need for power
2) a weak need for affiliation
3) a strong need for control

Manipulation, turning off one's human side in order to get results and reach a goal, is very much a constant part of a young boy's conditioning in our culture. He is rewarded for *winning*, nor for *caring*. Caring, he is taught, is the province of women, the territory of the Red Cross nurse. He learns also that an excellent grade in school or a triumph in sports is applauded and remembered, while the process involved in getting it is not. In other words, it's not so much a case of "What did you learn?" but "What grade did you get?", not so much "How you won," but "Did you win?"

Translated into everyday behavior, *manipulation* means that when someone else has something to offer that is desired or needed, involvement with and interest in that person is strong. A person who is not needed, however, becomes invisible. Relationships are cultivated and maintained for their usefulness. People are extensions of objects, used for specific purposes and then discarded or set aside until the need for them arises again.

Like *basic distrust*, *manipulation* as a style of relating is a deeply rooted part of the personality. It emerges from early conditioning experiences which put the primary focus on achievement, goal orientation and winning. He learned that only total control spelled safety, and that "love" was contingent on being successful. Some have more of that dehumanized jungle ability to manipulate than others. It cannot really be taught because it is not a question of a handful of moves but is rather a constant, all-pervasive style that is always in operation.

4) *Repression of Human Needs*: Dr. Thomas Stockmann, the maverick of Henrik Ibsen's *An Enemy of the People*, expressed his style as follows: "I am one of the strongest men in the world . . . the strongest man in the world is he who stands most alone."[7]

Repression of human needs, coupled with intelligence and drive, would allow a man to become a fine achieving performer, a well-oiled machine. Without the intrusion of human needs for physical and emotional contact and interaction, a man can comfortably obsess himself and his work in his office, laboratory, shop or wherever his success drive is being nurtured, and work a fifteen-hour-a-day, seven-days-a-week schedule. Not only is intimate human contact not required, but nongoal-oriented activities and people involvement are seen as an intrusion, an irritant, an obstacle to bypass as quickly as possible.

His social life is an instrument for his success. His wife and children are a part of his career building. Dinner, social engagements and trips become increasingly more business connected and purposeful. Otherwise, vacations and weekends are a waste of time at best, dreaded at worst.

He navigates as a "winner" must; self-controlled, logical, detached and decisive. The success drive engulfs everything and his life-style becomes a triumph over intimacy.

He disconnects from those people in his life who don't facilitate his goal. A troubled child of his, or a wife with emotional problems puts him into a particularly difficult conflict. He cannot easily fire them or deny their existence. If it would work, and if he could, he would hire his own resident psychiatrist to attend to that uncontrollable part of his life.

In general, as personal contact becomes more intrusive and annoying at home, he would verbalize his feelings as follows, if he were being transparently honest:

1) Let the housekeeper take the kids to the zoo.

2) Use your vibrator for your damn orgasm if you're frustrated.

3) Talk to a shrink if you've got a problem.

4) Take a class in the evening if you need something to do.

5) Send the kids to boarding school if they won't shape up.

For himself, the words "I need" on an intimate level choke in his throat before they can be expressed. *Need* is not to be felt and certainly not to be exposed. He is locked into his posture and as he becomes increasingly invested in it, it becomes ever more threatening to examine and get in touch with deeper needs.

More success and more power become increasingly easier to pursue and acquire, because all other activities are less comfortable for him. To be a workaholic is his refuge. It protects him from an awareness of the dehumanized life he has created. Rather than enjoying the benefits of the success he has acquired as he originally imagined he would, all he really ends up feeling comfortable with is more work and more success.

Success-driven men are fiercely goal oriented. They are machines in acceleration and with no brakes. They are men who finally can stop only by crashing, physically or emotionally.

They pay the price with their humanness. By middle age, they have become isolated islands unto themselves. Their emotions have béen submerged and only surface occasionally, usually in erratic outbursts of anger or frustration. They become increasingly more rigid in their need to control others, and distrustful to the point that they expose themselves to no one. Relationships are segmentalized, meaning that people are related to in terms of the function they perform rather than as whole individuals.

The sudden mood swings and eruptions, alternating between rage and depression and so common in men who reach the loftier heights of success, can be interpreted as the inner life voice experiencing annihilation and screaming, out of control, to inform him that his humanness is being consumed.

If he can avoid a psychological encounter with his inner life and handle the turbulence with stabilizing drugs, he will. Success-driven physicians, equally as phobic about encountering themselves, will accommodate his need to avoid self-recognition. Many of them can understand and empathize with his style very well, because they share it.

In the end, the rewards of his success are revealed as masturbatory. There is really no one to share them with when he gets "there," no one close enough who really cares or knows him and whom he genuinely trusts and feels close to. The satisfactions of the success are, in the main, only symbolic. Control over others, money, renown are his, but they are all just a part of the preparation for living. Originally seeking out the success and power to make himself safe from a threatening world, he barricades himself to the point that not only is he protected from the "dangers" but he is shut out from the whole process of living itself.

Our society is full of success-driven men at the end points of their success voyage, living in a nightmarish world of not knowing whom to trust, unable to find satisfaction in intimate contact, unaware of what they want and feel, and rigidly resistant to opening up in order to find out.

While achievement and accomplishment are important

for a sense of self worth in most people, the success-driven man has substituted the acquisition of symbols for human intimacy and satisfaction. In a psychologically aware society, such a life-style would not be praised or respected but would be recognized for its dehumanized quality and its destructive impact on the person himself and those around him. It would be seen for what it is, a pathological, dangerous disorder.

6. Afraid to Fail, Even at Suicide

There is a statistic the meaning of which, once understood, illuminates one of the deepest and most powerful aspects and motivations of masculine behavior. The implications of it are at once far-reaching, pathetic and chilling.

Women attempt suicide at least four times as often as men. The disparity is probably larger, because women tend to attempt suicide with milder means than men, preferring pills, for example, to guns. Many of these attempts therefore are not recognized as such and are not officially recorded. Men, however, *succeed* at suicide close to three times more often than women. Put another way, nearly 90 percent of suicide *attempts* are by women, whereas over 70 percent of *completed* suicides are by men. Again, the difference is probably greater, because many male suicides are probably disguised as accidents—for example, automobile accidents.

This disparity in suicides increases considerably with age. While men at all ages commit suicide at rates approximately three times higher, by age sixty the rate for successful suicides is at least five times as high for men. Also, men of sixty or older kill themselves at rates approximately four times greater than men under twenty.

Clearly, for the male, age does not bring security, wisdom, serenity, mellowness and philosophical acceptance. The depiction of grandfather on the porch, contentedly rocking and smoking his pipe, is a romanticized distortion. Aging makes men psychologically *more* vulnerable, brittle and prone to self-destruction.

The suicide attempt has often been interpreted by those in the helping professions as an indirect "cry for help." *This interpretation, however, is generally true for women only.* The man who sets out to commit suicide means to

47

achieve it. A study of methods employed by male suicides showed that in over 50 percent of cases firearms were used, while approximately 20 percent were by hanging.[1] Suicide-prevention centers report that they get at least twice as many calls for help from women. One male registered nurse at a Los Angeles mental-health center, who works with the suicidal male and female over the hot line and directly in his ward, reported that many men will use guns or knives and tell him over the phone that they have these weapons at hand. Other popular masculine methods, according to him, are jumping off buildings or driving off a cliff. He therefore becomes more alarmed when a man calls up, because he will more than likely go through with the act.

The tragic element in masculine role conditioning is that crying for help is considered feminine behavior. When a man is confronted with overwhelming problems and pain, it is very difficult for him to admit his inadequacy. Asking for help is not an appropriate masculine approach, so when the situation becomes unbearable, only one solution is possible: death.

A study by Kate Frankenthal, M.D., pointed out this inter-sex difference in a recent report for the Sixth International Conference for Suicide Prevention. Women attempt suicide as a cry for help, and such demonstration of weakness is fitting. However, the man has been taught that masculinity requires that he face death fearlessly. So when he contemplates suicide, he is going to succeed and "die like a man."*[2] *In other words, even at the moment of self-destruction he is under the same pressure to succeed and not to fail.*

He is thus caught in an impossible bind. If he asks for help, he impugns his masculinity. If he goes it alone, he crumbles under the weight. The latter is apparently preferable for most men. So instead of reaching out, he quietly gets his life in order, pays the bills, checks on his insurance and tries to exit in a way that won't be an imposition on anybody. The fact that he prefers death to impugning his masculine self-image is the most telling comment about the nature and self-destructive power of his conditioning.

* Quotation marks not in original.

Once one grasps the insidious and deeply self-destructive nature and meaning of his conditioning, one can see how it would be a great humiliation for him if he happened to survive his suicide attempt. First, he would have to face what he would interpret as the scorn of those who knew him and would condemn him for having "copped out." Second, he might have to acknowledge and deal with the very feelings (fear, rage, vulnerability) that drove him to it. Confronting one's inner emotions is a dreadful threat. Third, and as frightening for him, he might only wound himself and survive as an invalid. In his mind, this would make him a dependent and hated burden, because all of his life he felt lovable for being the strong man and the caretaker whom others could depend on. Finally, he would jeopardize his future employability. Without a job, he believes, he would be better off dead.

One study showed that 15 percent of the people who committed suicide had received but not followed a recommendation for psychiatric hospitalization within a few weeks of their death. Men apparently resisted it because it would mean a loss of earnings. They feared that the psychiatric label would make them unemployable in the future.[3]

In a paper by Harry Levinson titled "On Executive Suicide," published in the *Harvard Business Review*, the author pointed out that when a highly successful man is at the end of his rope, he must not admit to having problems and must not under any circumstances give way or seek help. In fact, to seek help from a friend or the company doctor is considered a sign of weakness and failure to cope. Moreover, if he seeks help from a psychiatrist or a psychologist, he will fear being seen as either weak or crazy or both. "When a conscientious executive with tremendous self-demands recognizes that he is failing to cope effectively with a situation under circumstances in which he must control intense negative feelings, he may see limited alternatives. If he does not seek professional help, escape from an apparently hopeless situation can seem possible only by developing psychosomatic symptoms, by attacking himself in the form of accidents or, in the extreme, by committing suicide."[4]

It is traditional in our society, which depicts the male as

"top dog," to account for the devastating male statistics, namely, significantly shorter life span, significantly higher disease and death rates, and a preponderance of emotional problems in boys, with biological or genetic explanations. This has even been done in the case of suicide, where one psychological researcher-theoretician rationalized the higher suicide rate in men as reflecting a general biological law that the male clings to life less and is less resistant to stress than the female.[5]

One need not conjecture further about this kind of explanation once it is recognized how deeply embedded the fear of failure is in the male. As a young boy, he is repeatedly given the message that success and winning make him lovable and worthwhile. There is hardly a more devastating label than that of "loser." Some boys get the message in an extreme form through their father's rejection and his intensely negative reaction when they do poorly. Indirectly, the boy gets the message because he is adored when he triumphs. He also observes the powerfully positive reaction of his parents to other boys when *they* are successful winners or prove themselves to be the "best." These early evaluations contaminate his pleasure in many activities as he grows older. If he can't win or do very well at something, he won't do it at all. This progressively narrows his range of involvements until he winds up as primarily a spectator to most activities except those in which he can excel.

One study on the phenomenon of "skidding" and "occupational mobility" described the possible connection between suicide and failure at work. Most men identify themselves with their occupations. When achievement at work goes badly, so does their self-image. One hundred and five consecutive male suicides in a large southern city were studied by a Tulane University sociologist. He found that:

1) Among the suicides, considerable downward mobility ("skidding") was found and relatively little upward mobility.

2) Decreasing incomes characterized more than half the suicides, whereas men of the experimental control groups (non-suicides) were showing gains.

3) When the occupational level of the suicide and his

father were compared, considerable mobility, mostly down-ward, was discovered.

The researcher commented, "It is not difficult to form the impression that these men felt acute dissatisfaction with their performance and standing in their respective business and professional circles."[6]

The fear of failure infects and ultimately destroys every man who has not succeeded in wresting himself from its powerful grip. Most important, it prevents him from ever discovering what it is he really *wants*, because what he *doesn't* want is so much more powerful a force in his life. *He doesn't want to fail.*

Because of this phenomenon, he is unable to learn and benefit from his experiences of failure except to search for ways to avoid future failure. That is, when problems arise at work, in a relationship, sexually or even in competitive activities, he cannot read the potentially health-giving, growthful messages that may exist in the failure of his resistance. His organism may simply be shouting, "No!" or "Get me out of here!" However, he cannot read the "No!" All he hears is the encroaching, haunting chorus chanting the word "failure." So he hangs in when he should let go, tries to succeed when his resistance is overwhelming, while struggling at the same time to avoid self-loathing.

The deeply embedded fear of failure also makes every victory one that is short-lived and essentially hollow, be-cause each success, more than representing an accomplish-ment, is an avoidance of non-success or failure. Therefore, on a deeper level, *each important success makes important failure that much more imminent*, because each important success raises his standard of performance expectation that much higher. The level of yesterday's success becomes to-day's level of failure. Those who become extremely wealthy and successful, motivated by the need to prove themselves, to perform and conversely, therefore, by the fear of failure, become the most vulnerable. One highly successful motion-picture director expressed this suc-cinctly: "With each film it gets worse—and this is my tenth film. The waiting is awful. When I started directing I told myself it'd get easier with each film. It doesn't. In the beginning it was easier because I was just happy to be working."[7]

As far back as 1954 the late and noted psychiatrist Dr. Don Jackson reported in his paper on suicide for the *Scientific American*, "Professional people commit suicide more commonly than nonprofessionals, white collar workers than laborers, officers than enlisted men."[8]

It is commonly noted that many men who become rich and highly successful are not able to let go and enjoy the fruits of their work. If anything, as they become successful and wealthy they seem even more driven, more compulsive in their work routines than when they were poor.[9] The more open and aware among them often comment that, indeed, life tasted better and they enjoyed themselves more when they had less.

Of course! At their new pinnacle so much more energy is required just to maintain the new level of failure avoidance, because *anything* but *more* represents failure. So the pressure increases, their pace quickens, and if there is nothing to interrupt them, their road all too often ends in either interpersonal isolation, a heart attack, alcoholism, an emotional breakdown or the collapse of everything they put together.

Once this underlying motivational dynamic is recognized, the often defensive and enclosed behavior of the powerful, the successful and the wealthy person becomes easier to understand. It also becomes clearer why the rate of suicide among older men increases so dramatically and out of proportion to women of the same age and to younger men. At an age when, so mythology tells us, wisdom and comfortable detachment should be in operation, the experience of failure becomes that much more inevitable and pervasive. Previous successes, no matter how great, provide no cushion.

When the fear of failure is a stronger motivator than the desire to grow, a psychological time bomb becomes embedded within the masculine conditioning, a disease process that makes every traditionally brought up male a potential suicide in one way or another.

The self-caring man will not react in a terrorized way to failure of any kind. Instead, he will embrace it for its potentially important self-revealing messages. Failure in a relationship would be seen as a growth-yielding, freeing end. A resistant penis would be seen as a signal to explore and take responsibility for real feelings toward the person he makes love to. Failure in his job would show him how he might be misdirecting his energy. Even illness would be welcomed for its information about self-destructive habits that need to be corrected.

Once he is free to value himself for his capacity to live his life fully, rather than simply perform and avoid failure, others will relate to him accordingly. The fear of failure will no longer serve as a criterion for the way he evaluates himself. Its removal, however, will not be an easy process, because it has become so much a part of the way he acts. But, once liberated, he will cease to focus on how people react to his level of success.

7. The Impostor Fantasy

I felt like a fraud.
So I learned to fly an airplane.
At 50,000 feet I thought:
"A fraud is flying an airplane."
So I crossed the Atlantic in a rowboat.
I docked at Cherbourg and thought:
"A fraud has crossed the Atlantic in a rowboat."
So I took a space shot to the moon.
On the trip home I thought:
"A fraud has circled the moon."
So I took a full page ad in the newspaper and
    confessed to the world that I was a fraud!
I read the ad and I thought:
"A fraud is pretending to be honest."[1]

—Jules Feiffer

A thirty-three-year-old New York attorney is admired and
acclaimed for his activist-humanistic orientation, specifically, the pains and risks he takes helping migrant farm
workers and non-English-speaking prisoners with their le-
gal problems. For no financial compensation and on his
own time, he also writes and distributes a newsletter that
reports on police and judicial abuses in the treatment of
these aliens.

Speaking during one of his moments of self-loathing, he
confessed, "People think of me as a humanist, a guy who
cares. Basically, I think most of the men I work with and
help are a bunch of schmucks. They're assholes as far as
I'm concerned. I'm really doing this for *me*, not *them*. My
public image is of a 'together' white dude, not just another
phony liberal or closet racist. But half the time, when I'm

talking to myself, I'm thinking, 'That lazy nigger!' or 'That dumb Chicano!' "

However, it disturbed and haunted him to think that he might be a phony, because he had always been an idealist. But now he was beginning to feel like an impostor and was considering quitting his job, even though his work was still admired and he was considered one of the very best at what he did. "I don't know if I can go on living with myself this way," he said.

A thirty-eight-year-old psychologist committed suicide. For a number of months before he killed himself, he had become increasingly depressed about his work. His wife reported that he would ruminate out loud in a self-hating, depressed tone. "I'm *not* the wise old man with answers. I'm *not* what people see in me. I'm sitting in my office listening to people and they'll be crying, and I can't get into their pain no matter how hard I work at it. All I can think is, 'That's tough shit! I'm sorry you're feeling bad, but so does the whole world. Everybody's anxious or depressed. That's just the way it is.' "

He was obsessed with the idea that he had no right to continue being a therapist. In fact, it began to feel impossible to him even to pretend, and his self-hate increased until it became unbearable.

Similarly, a child and family counselor, well known for his fine theoretical publications on the dynamics of family life and childhood problems, found himself with a failing marriage, a drinking problem, and a twenty-year-old son who was into hard drugs. The thought, "How come my family and personal life is so messed up when I'm supposed to have all the answers?" tortured him. "What if the families I worked with knew all this?" he thought. "I'd probably have no practice."

A motorcycle policeman was arrested for masturbating near his motorcycle while "peeping" into the bedroom window of an attractive stewardess. He talked about himself to the psychiatrist he was sent to see by his attorney. "For years I've been making drug arrests and hiding the fact that I was heavily into marijuana. I'd go to parties not knowing whether to smoke a joint, and I know even my friends wondered if I was going to bust them. When I was twenty-two I had a sixteen-year-old girl friend who I went to bed with. Now, that's statutory rape, right? I'd do crackdowns on porno places, but I've enjoyed my share of porno films. It's been driving me crazy—being two people—a cop and the real me. Maybe I had to blow it this way, and do something crazy to save my sanity."

A forty-seven-year-old orthopedic surgeon, with an additional graduate degree in biochemistry, was the director of his own clinic and the administrator of a small hospital. In spite of his extensive education and training, he was obsessed with the fear that he would someday be revealed as an ignorant poseur. "During a case conference I'll be sitting there terrified that someone's going to ask me some questions and discover that I don't know *anything*."

His fear of being "revealed" intensified when he made the decision not to devote as much time to his work and instead to spend more time studying classical guitar and being with his three young children. Rather than enjoying this, he became increasingly frightened that he'd soon be professionally obsolete and make a fool of himself and be forced out of his medical group.

He was particularly intimidated by an older colleague who arrived at work every morning at six-thirty and spent an hour and a half reading medical journals. He felt certain that this colleague would eventually see through him and find out that he wasn't keeping up. While he had rarely received anything but very favorable feedback about his work, he continued to be haunted by his feeling of being an impostor, to the point that he tried to befriend everyone in his clinic, from other doctors to the nurses and aides. He reasoned that he would be safer if everybody liked him and would be on his side when he was finally exposed.

A thirty-seven-year-old political-science instructor remarked, "I don't really know whether I care about the things I say or not. I've been told I lecture and write with a lot of passion, but actually I don't even know what I really believe in. I do know it's publish or perish, so I put on paper what I know will get published. As far as I'm concerned, most of it is just shit, but I'm playing the game. I might as well be selling shoes, though, when it comes right down to it."

A television newscaster in a large eastern city was earn-ing ninety thousand dollars a year as an anchorman. His drinking problem, however, was getting worse, and he decided to quit and take a job in a smaller West Coast city for considerably less money. "All the while . . . I kept thinking, 'Someday they're going to find out that there's a thousand guys out there who can do the job better, and how do I keep them from finding out?' It was a constant strain."

And the young owner of a health-food store expressed a feeling that I've heard from many men: "There are two voices inside of me," he said. "One voice says I'm brilliant, sensitive and the greatest. The other voice says that I'm a total con, a bullshit artist and everybody can see through me. Once upon a time I really believed in health foods—fresh fruits, wholesome breads, nuts. Now all I want to do is sell the vitamins, because that's where the money is, even though I know most vitamins do nothing but feed on people's suggestibility and wishful thinking."

On a self-assessment questionnaire about masculinity that I distribute to men who come to my lectures, there is one statement they are asked to answer as to whether it is true of them. The statement reads, "I often secretly feel like a phony or an impostor at work, like I'm faking it, and that sooner or later I'll be found out."

A large number of men from a wide variety of professions—engineers, planners, safety specialists, firemen, naval flight officers, physicians, computer scientists and so on—answer yes to this question. The impostor fantasy, the feeling that one is faking one's job, that one is the opposite of the image one projects, and the fear of being exposed that results, is a common experience.

These impostor fantasies take various forms. The "intellectual impostor fantasy" involves feelings of having fooled people into believing one knows far more than one really knows, and fearing that one will someday be revealed as ignorant.

The "role impostor fantasy" involves feelings that one is faking one's commitment to one's job: "I'm not really dedicated like they think I am. I act enthusiastic, but I don't really believe in the product I'm selling. I'm not committed to the welfare of this company."

The "personality impostor fantasy" is expressed in

feelings such as: "I'm not really the nice guy I come on as. I'm not the stable, mature, together and happily married man they think I am, and I'm not the sensitive, concerned, self-sacrificing person I present myself as." Behind this feeling is often another one which says, "Basically I'm just out for myself and they don't know it."

The "emotional impostor fantasy" involves the sense that one is projecting feelings to specific individuals that one really does not feel. "The people I work with think I like them, but really I see them as boring and stupid. I wouldn't spend a minute with any of them if I didn't have to." A doctor said, for example, "I don't really care about my patients like I seem to." Likewise, a salesman confessed, "My customers are just accounts to me—they're not even people, even though they think I'm their best friend."

Finally, there is the "role-conflict impostor fantasy," illustrated by one teacher's feeling that he expounds and is supposed to symbolize values, beliefs and commitments to his students that are not at all what he really believes or how he really sees things. One counselor commented, "I teach people to be open to communication and honest with their feelings, but I don't do it myself. I don't even know if I believe it is a good thing."

In all of these instances, the men were haunted by the fantasy that their *real* feelings, the *real* person underneath, would one day be exposed. *These men were not conscious or evil manipulators. Rather, they were individuals caught in a conflict between what they were and what their image said they were supposed to be.*

The impostor fantasy is rooted partly in the belief that to assume certain roles one must acquire certain kinds of feelings. The person playing the role himself believes this to be true and tries to match his identity to the role requirement. For example, good doctors are "supposed to" feel dedicated, caring and self-sacrificing; clergymen are "not supposed to" have carnal appetites, materialistic motivations, hateful feelings and so on. They are "supposed to" have loving, spiritual feelings.

These role images are also reinforced by associating the role with a certain specific mode of dress, speech, grooming and manners. Imagine for a minute the reaction of the public to a president who was giving a speech while un-shaven and standing in his jockey shorts, or a gynecologist who smiled and made jokes while he examined a patient. The job might be performed at a high level of competence, but the "inappropriate" accompanying aspects would be totally disorienting.

A psychologically aware society might applaud a political candidate who openly acknowledged his pleasure and appetite for power, money and glory, and who frankly communicated his personal prejudices regarding certain races and religions. He would thus be acknowledging his humanness and he could then be evaulated on the basis of his ability to do the job rather than on his ability to project the required image. Instead, there remains a childlike craving to believe there are superhuman men, that politicians, for example, have no prejudices and are motivated by their concern and love for the people, and we are repeatedly disillusioned because, rather than being beyond "base" human motivations, they are, in fact, heavily mired in them.

The belief in the "good," "selfless," "pure" person who has transcended human emotion and frailty is one that not only dehumanizes relationships but creates endless problems and a highly destructive potential, and at the same time blocks psychological growth. It is much like the woman who never gives up her belief in the existence of the "perfect man," her Prince Charming, and is therefore repeatedly attracted either to men who *seem* to her to be that way but inevitably fall short, or to manipulators who know how to give her what she wants for a short time, to their advantage, and who then abandon her, leaving her with deep hurt, increasing cynicism and a sense of futility about *all* relationships.

Her continued pursuit of this "perfect man" prevents her from ever learning to deal with the problems inherent in relating to real men. In addition, it ultimately dooms her to isolation and prevents her from growing into reality. Likewise, society's belief in the "bigger than life" personality in any role makes it constantly vulnerable either to ruthless manipulation or repeated disillusionment. Either way, cynicism and a sense of hopelessness intensify, while growth is aborted and psychological reality is avoided.

The height of role-expectation insanity was reached during President Carter's election campaign. His election potential was significantly jeopardized when he acknowledged having "lust in his heart." That this statement was even considered a disturbing admission in a society that has made the movie *Deep Throat* one of the largest box-office successes in history and that constantly uses sexual symbolism to advertise and sell many of its products is astounding. But we want our political heroes to fit our role fantasies and to *pretend* rather than to be.

Role-impostor problems are complicated by the fact that men in our society are psychologically isolated from each other, secretive and ready to use another man's self-exposure and vulnerabilities to their advantage. This isolation produces in a man the feeling that he is the only one who has a certain problem, or that he is different or "sicker" than others because of experiencing emotions and thoughts that he believes other men don't have. Liberated, caring and humanized men would applaud and vigorously support the man who exposed his real feelings, fantasies, experiences and conflicts, *no matter what they were*, and would reject those who used such self-exposure to their advantage. The act of opening oneself up would be seen as an act of faith and trust that provides a basis and a beginning for humane bonding among men.

I have heard professionals from a wide variety of fields comment that they do not like to socialize with men in their own profession because the experience is boring and unpleasurable. When I was a fledgling psychologist, I remember my own self-consciousness at parties and professional gatherings as I worried about saying or doing something that would betray personal hang-ups. I felt that I was supposed to be free of them because I was a psychologist. I had the feeling that I would be analyzed, evaluated and criticized if I let my guard down. Apparently, many of my peers had similar feelings, because the atmosphere at social events tended to be cautious and stilted, and the conversation consisted of impersonal intellectualization and role posturing. Any professional gathering where people behave according to their prescribed roles inevitably becomes a constricted and unfulfilling experience.

Perhaps the most frightening possibility in all of this is

that some men have actually repressed their own identity and replaced it with their role image. These are men whose wives and children even refer to them as Doctor, Judge, General or Mister. Invariably, they are respected and perhaps beloved by those who relate to them professionally, while they drive their intimates "crazy" because their responses are always impersonally "correct," controlled and in keeping with their image. It shuts intimates out, and the emotionally unreal communications that result are laden with underlying, repressed emotions the role player is not aware of. My belief is that the more a person has assumed his role as a constant identity, the more emotionally troubled his intimates, wife and children will be.

There are some who consciously and healthfully realize that when it comes to their role, they must be in this world but not of it. They know what the acceptable role behavior is, play the game out of necessity but do not judge themselves for being "phony." Other men who experience impostor fantasies, however, torture themselves with self-loathing. The latter group are closer to humanness and self-awareness than the third group of men who wear their role mantle comfortably and without conflict and experience only what they are "supposed to" experience. Their role and personal identity have merged into one. In fact, it would seem that any man who still had a semblance of humanness and who had not been swallowed up by his role image would experience impostor feelings, because no person with an identity of his own could be what his role dictated he should be. After all, role expectations and demands are static, while human emotions are not.

In effect, those who do not experience a conflict between their inner experience and what their role dictates that inner experience should be have been consumed by the demands of their role. They are role robots, effective performers, perhaps, and therefore socially laudable, but destructive on a human level because of their machineline, out-of-touch behavior. Children of these role players have to struggle for sheer emotional survival in the face of counterfeit responses. They become confused and disturbed by a father who is socially highly respected but is unable to be real beyond his role, and who never realizes what his personal impact is until the children manifest emotional problems. These may take the form of drug addiction, sexual acting out, nervous breakdowns or suicide attempts. They are indications of a child's need to call himself to his father's attention, to reach him emotionally and to free himself from the annihilating interaction.

My physical appearance is a youthful one, and my dress is casual. I struggled for many years with the knowledge that prospective patients would be intimidated by this. I knew that many of them would want their psychotherapist to have a mature, conservative, "father figure" type of appearance, a person who "looked like" a doctor. I toyed with the idea of growing a beard, wearing a suit and tie, or even horn-rimmed glasses, though my eyes were perfect. I realized, however, that I would be committing a kind of psychological suicide, to say nothing of reinforcing an orientation that *causes* emotional problems, and that any success I gained on that basis would be at the cost of my humanness and the patient's potential for ever seeing beyond stereotypes, role images and authority poses. The need to see and believe in the professional as being in a certain mold and somehow larger than life, a father figure, is to my mind a major stumbling block to psychological growth and also prevents patients from trusting in and drawing on their own resources.

By insisting that professionals dress and behave in predictably role-appropriate ways, we reinforce and perpetuate an atmosphere that will ultimately reward either the most manipulative men (in other words, those who are most skillful at "seeming") or those who have actually repressed their own identity and humanness and replaced it with role-required image behavior.

The impostor fantasy seems to me to be the beginning of a role identity crisis that can lead to important human growth. Indeed, it has been my experience that those who suffer the most from impostor feelings are, in fact, potentially the most real. Those who are the most comfortable with themselves as role players have, in effect, become unreal people and have committed an identity suicide.

The impostor fantasy indicates that there is an experi-

enced gap, an awareness of a difference between externally
imposed role expectations (the "supposed to be") and the
internal experience of oneself. The feelings of being on the
verge of a breakdown that the impostor fantasy may generate—"My act is falling apart"; "I can't play the game
anymore"—may actually be a healthy resistance to remaining a "role thing." It may be a critical moment of potential growth, even though it is terrifying, because it
suggests the fear of losing the protection and security the
role and "uniform" provide.

To *feel* like your role, therefore, is a form of insanity: a
loss of self. It means that one has replaced one's own fluid
self with a stagnant, externally imposed set of behaviors
and reactions. This may be equally true when that role is a
nonprofessional one, such as "good husband," "good father," "good provider," "strong man" and so on.

Parents of disturbed children, for example, are rarely irresponsible, overtly hostile people. More often they are individuals rigidly working at playing out their role as "good
parents," while on a deeper level they contain a hurricane
of repressed resentment, resistance, anger and even murderous rage—all of the "not supposed to" feelings that are
being blocked out because they are threatening for the role
image of the "good parent" to acknowledge. Every communication of theirs, therefore, becomes a loaded, confusing one consisting of the "correct," "loving" response on
the surface and the angry, rejecting emotional one underneath which is transmitted in various forms through nonverbal communication and body-language. The child is
bombarded with a flood of "push-pull," "come here-go
away," "I love you—I hate you" messages. It is literally
a "love that destroys," and the child would ultimately be
emotionally far healthier if he received an overt message
such as, "I hate being your father and I wish you were
dead." The child might grow up angry and feeling rejected,
but would probably not grow up crazy. He would at least
know his reality, even though it was a painful one. So long
as intimates and society are punitive in response to a person who has feelings he is "not supposed to" have, emotional repression, hiding, hypocrisy and crazy-making communication will be perpetuated.

Men have been victims of image strangulation because

their social attractiveness and lovability have so commonly been linked with their roles and success. The role-oriented male must continue to successfully live up to his image in order to retain his attractiveness. The prospect of not being able to maintain this becomes terrifying. It spells the end of being lovable. Maintaining a role image, however, seals one into receiving a false, image love. It is one of the most excruciating impossible binds that men face.

Role behavior and the human experience, which seem to have become so powerfully merged, need to be separated. The liberated man would react just as negatively to his attractiveness being contingent on his role as an aware, liberated woman would to her attractiveness as a person being measured by her breast size or her figure. In a society interested in humanness and not in performing puppets, we would applaud the person who resists playing out role stereotypes and who is transparent and open with his changing feelings, hostilities, fantasies and prejudices. Otherwise, we are asking for, and will continue to get, a society run by successful manipulators, role poseurs or role robots, and we will experience all the shock, pain and insanity that are inevitably the price.

In a human society a person who became his role would be the object of pity and revulsion because of having become a human aberration, diseased at best, a dangerous monster at worst. There would be no "great men" with clay feet, because we would know that any man who had become "larger than life" was a human fraud, be he the great religious leader, healer, teacher, poet or whatever. It has traditionally been society's insanity that it believed people could really *be* their image and still be human.

Despair, anxiety, fears of a breakdown and suicidal impulses may occur when the gap between role requirements and personal feelings increases and creates the impostor fantasy. However, the existence of this fantasy must be accepted as an inevitable phenomenon and in a human society we would encourage and embrace this experience as the beginning of a process which would allow the person *esse quam videri,* to be, rather than to seem.

PART TWO

HE
AND SHE

8. The Actor and the Reactor; or Why She Can Label Him Exploiter, Oppressor and Chauvinist Pig

The traditionally socialized woman has had to deny and repress her aggression, her autonomy and her sexuality. The process of doing this begins at a very young age, so that her inability to experience, express and assume responsibility for these important parts of her humanness is largely beyond her conscious control. For example, it wasn't until recent years that most women could even acknowledge their *own* sexual drive—an inner-originated impulse, need or "horniness"—the way men traditionally have. Hers was typically a *reactive* sexuality. She "did it" *for him*, or *he* "turned her on."

This orientation was both the bane and the glory of married men in times past. While she was perhaps never quite the sexual partner he imagined for himself, he was assured that she would not walk around during the day getting turned on by other men. It made him feel safe to know she wasn't a sexual being in her own right. In his eyes, sex with her was a gift, a token of appreciation, a sacrifice, payment made for being protected and provided for or simply an expression of her love for him.

Traditionally she also did not experience or act out her aggression directly. Her identification was with fragility and weakness. She was the passive, peaceful one. In times of danger or challenge he aggressed for her. She was the cheerleader on the sidelines while her football-playing man fought it out on the football field, or she was the Red Cross nurse waiting with coffee, sandwiches, bandages and sympathy when he faltered, fell exhausted or staggered wounded from battle. Helplessness and dependency were her mode and were a part of being feminine.

The business of getting a "Mr. Right" meant marrying

the most ambitious, worldly, aggressive, successful and powerful man she could. He would then take control, make decisions and be the dominant figure. In return he received reinforcement from her, ranging from adoration to affirmation of his masculinity. He knew he had a "good woman" if she still reacted lovingly even when he failed. Her part of the contract was that she would not threaten him by competing with him or making him look bad in the eyes of other men.

In essence, she was trained to be the *reactor* in her relationship with him. That is, he would initiate or take responsibility and she would react to his ability to do so. He led, she followed. He dominated, she submitted. He made the sexual advances, she reacted to them. He owned his sexuality, his aggression and his autonomy. She disowned hers. *He was the actor. She was the reactor.*

This interaction, which traditionally continued throughout their lifetime in various forms, was launched and given momentum early in the courtship ritual. In it we can see the basis for the traditional male-female interaction. In spite of feminist consciousness, androgyny advocacy, ERA and the like, most of these time-honored *actor-reactor* transactions in the courtship phase are still alive and visible.

This is the way it goes. He sees her and is attracted to her. At a party, on the street, in an elevator, a classroom or wherever they chance to meet. Perhaps she notices him too and is also attracted. Nevertheless, it will be his responsibility to initiate the opening conversation. Then she signals her interest through her reactions. If she is very interested, she will be animated and enthusiastic. Less interested, she will be more guarded in her responses. Hardly or not interested at all, she will look through him as if he didn't exist or, worse still, through her reaction make him feel like an inappropriate intruder. He needs to be able to read these signals correctly, because it will again be his responsibility as the *actor* to say, "I'd like to see you. May I have your telephone number?" The rejection, if he has misjudged her degree of interest, is uncomfortable at best.

If he has not misread her and she gives him her telephone number, he breathes a deep sigh of relief and feels pleasure, particularly if he is very attracted and is imagining that she might be THE ONE, potentially his MAGIC LADY. The knot in his stomach loosens and a burst of adrenaline pours through his bloodstream, creating a euphoric anticipation. "I think she likes me," he says to himself.

If he's really turned on, however, this feeling of relaxation and joy will soon be mingled with anxiety and apprehension. He has only passed a perfunctory screening exam and there will be many more tests to come.

He has her phone number and is feeling that he'd like to call her immediately. However, that might make him seem too desperate, too lonely and hungry, which he believes would be a sure turn-off for her. He doesn't want to behave as if there was no one else in his life until he met her. To acknowledge such neediness is very "unmasculine."

He calculates that he'll wait at least two days before calling. Two days is enough time for him not to appear too eager and not so long that she is likely to have forgotten his name or met someone else important to her in the meantime. So he waits. Each hour seems long until the time he can finally call, pretending casualness and nonchalance when he does. After a few minutes of time-filling, time-killing conversation, he says, "I'd like to take you out." Particularly if he believes he's competing for a much sought after prize, he will suggest Friday or even Thursday evening, because it would be too great a risk if he asked her out for Saturday night, the night usually reserved for THE SPECIAL PERSON, if one exists. If she said no, he might not know how to interpret it. "Is she *really* busy on Saturday night, or does she *really* mean that she *really* doesn't want to see me?" he will wonder.

While he's asking her about Friday, perhaps trying to convince her by telling her about the places he'd like to take her, the tension in his stomach increases until she finally answers. The knot then becomes either a flash of despair or a jolt of further anticipatory excitement.

If she says yes and his fantasies of a magical experience have been ignited, he begins scouring the newspaper and his memory for "exciting" things to do, impressive places to eat, and he thinks about what clothes to wear that will make him most attractive. Sometime before the date he may even get his car washed and take a few workouts so that his body will have that extra little definition that makes him look more masculine and appealing.

Comes the evening—and as will be the case throughout the courtship except for special circumstances or under emergency conditions—he will get into his automobile and drive to pick her up. This is taken for granted, even though most women have cars and driver's licenses and driving is not a particularly hazardous activity requiring "masculine" skills. Nevertheless, probably because it is his mandate to be in control, a leader, it also translates into his being the driver. The man who says to his prospective date, "Would you pick me up?" risks his image and may be seen as imposing or insulting. ("He's taking me for granted. He doesn't even care enough to make the effort to pick me up.") Besides, his car is part of his image, an extension of his identity and often a part of the armament at his disposal to excite and seduce her with. The commanding way he drives demonstrates his way of being.

Occasionally this ritual of "picking her up" assumes ludicrous proportions, such as when she lives a good distance away and he has to drive to her house only to bring her back to the part of town he lives in for dinner, then drive her back home before returning to his. The driving part of the date has taken on the trappings of a part-time job.

He arrives at her place at the agreed-upon time, and the *actor-reactor* interaction, if we are looking at the traditional male-female pattern, begins to manifest itself in all of its unbalanced glory.

As a "democratic" *actor*, he says to her, "What would you like to eat?" If she is a genuine *reactor*, she will reply, "It doesn't really matter," or she will throw it back to him by saying, "What would *you* like to eat?" At this point he's in a double-bind dilemma. If he makes the decision unilaterally, he may appear too quick and selfish. If he continues the discussion, he risks appearing indecisive.

His compromise ploy is to use a fairly safe alternative. He may say something like, "How about Italian or Chinese?" However, if she is a heavily conditioned *reactor*, she might answer this one by saying, "They both sound good," or "Either one—I really have no preference," at which point he will recognize the necessity for taking matters in hand. He says, "Let's go to an Italian restaurant.

Do you have a favorite one?" to which a *reactor* might again reply. "It doesn't really matter that much," or "There's lots of places I like," or even more probably, "Not particularly, do you?" A motivated *actor* comes prepared. "I know a neat little intimate place I'm sure you'd like. It's run by an Italian family—just a hole in the wall, but the food's great. It's called Mamma Giovanni's and it's on River Street." She responds with enthusiasm, "That sounds great!" So they get into his car and drive off.

The loaded and ironic aspects of being the *actor* now become even clearer, because during the meal he will feel as ego-involved with the quality of the food as if he had cooked it. In other words, if she really likes it, he'll feel good about himself because *he* made the choice, and therefore sees it as reflecting on *him* favorably as a person. However, if the food is poor, the service slow or the decor unattractive and she reacts negatively, he will take it personally and might feel that much less attractive to her because of it.

After the meal, the check arrives. His date may well be an aware, independent and liberated woman whom he would not dare relate to in old-fashioned, chauvinistic ways. Nevertheless, he is unable to raise the issue of payment be it the first or fifth date, or to simply say, "The bill comes to thirteen dollars; that's six-fifty for you and six-fifty for me plus money for a tip." It would sound rude and make him look cheap, even if she is at about the same income level as he is.

Contemporary advice columns dealing with this often inform men that they should not feel offended or see it as a rejection if a woman insists on paying her share. The option, however, is still seen as hers. None of these writers point out how preposterous it is in this age of liberation for it to be taken for granted that payment is his responsibility. Nevertheless, even when he is with a woman he knows to be liberated, he would find it uncomfortable and generally out of the question to confront this issue head-on. To be seen as "cheap" is to be unsexy and unlovable. The waiter even colludes with this as he hands the man the check, face down, as if the whole business was dirty and the woman was not to be involved with such a low-level matter.

My objection to this is not regarding the act of a man's paying for a woman, particularly if his income significantly exceeds hers. Rather, I react to the presumption that payment is his responsibility and that this is taken for granted and only altered at her insistence.

Back to the date. The check is paid, and now he's faced with the second major dilemma of the evening: what to do after dinner. He says to her, "What would you like to do now?" to which, as a *reactor*, she is likely to reply, "I don't know," or "What do you suggest?"

Again he chooses and pays, and again, if the movie or the nightclub or any other activity is *his* choice, his principal concern will be, "Is she enjoying this? Did I make a good choice?" Again it is the phenomenon of his identifying with the choice and feeling responsible for its quality. A good movie means that he's sensitive and tasteful. A boring movie means that he's not. Good music means that he's cultured and aware. If she doesn't like the music, he feels that his judgment is faulty and she won't like him.

Added to all of this, throughout the evening he might also be straining to generate and maintain interesting conversation. He sees it as his responsibility to keep her entertained in every way, even in creating a stimulating conversational flow.

If he's still very excited about her at the end of the evening, experiencing her as special, he might be looking for a sign that she is also attracted to him, be it through a spontaneous holding of his hand, putting her head on his shoulder or kissing him. If he is like most single men in our society, he is starving for affection, touching, intimacy and feedback that tell him he's lovable. While these needs of his are repressed most of the time, they get unleashed when he is in the midst of the fantasy that he has found *the* woman for him.

During the drive home, he tries to interpret her behavior. Is she sitting near the door (that means she's not turned on), or is she moving close to him (that means she likes him)? Is she talking in animated fashion (that means she's interested and wants to connect), or is she yawning and seeming to be tired (that means she's not)? Is she telling him that she has to get up the following morning at 6:30 A.M. for a ten-mile Sierra Club hike (that means goodbye at the door), or is she expressing delight at the prospects of a leisurely, lounging day tomorrow (that means he'll be invited in)?

Sometimes the signals are mixed and confusing and require acuity to interpret them. That is, she may be sitting close to him but yawning at the same time, or she might be engaging in animated conversation while she sits tight up against the door.

His signal-reading ability had better be accurate, because he is particularly vulnerable in the sexual area. If he comes on to her and she responds with delight, then he'll be floating, suddenly transformed in his eyes into the most attractive man in the world. If she responds coldly, however, and with an attitude that seems to be saying, "What are you doing?" he will flood himself with self-hating messages and name-calling: "I really blew it with my impatience and aggressiveness." Echoes of past accusations may then reverberate inside him: "Horny! Insensitive! All you really want is sex!"

The *actor-reactor* model has been set in motion. Throughout, he has assumed the role of *actor* by initiating the date, making the choices, paying, asserting himself sexually and so on. With only occasional exception, unless she is a nontraditional woman, she has been reacting, positively if she is turned on and interested, negatively if she isn't.

The evening's interplay is crucial to an understanding of the bedrock of the male-female interaction. It exposes the roots and reveals the reasons why a woman today can righteously point accussingly at a man and in bottomless-well fashion assert that he is responsible for every heinous crime and exploitation while she paints herself as an innocent victim. That is, *Reactors are never guilty. Actors are responsible. Therefore, only actors can be portrayed as evil or exploitative.*

Actors are either heroes or bums, liberators or destroyers, winners or losers, and sooner or later every man falters, fails or falls, at which time he will stand accused while his latent self-hate, guilt and negative self-accusations will reinforce this sense of responsibility.

In its extreme form, the experience is comparable to that of an impressionable lay person in the company of a clergyman. The latter behaves as if he had no animal impulses, no animosities, no anger or hate, no selfishness or materialistic desires. This inevitably incites self-conscious feelings of being inferior, sinful, undeveloped, dirty and so on in the lay person. Likewise, the woman who, for example, does not acknowledge her own sexual hungers can generate feelings of being animalistic, horny, insensitive and boorish in the typical guilt-prone male who does express these desires.

It is this *actor-reactor* dynamic that has made it possible for feminist writers to accuse men of driving women crazy or exploiting and abusing them. Passive-submissive role players, be they male or female, always end up feeling used and "pushed around," until one day they scream out, "You're not going to do *this* to *me* anymore!"

Even enlightened, psychologically sophisticated and educated male writers and professionals fall into the trap of not recognizing the loaded quality of this dynamic and accuse themselves and other men. For example, according to Ashley Montagu, in his book *The Natural Superiority of Women*:

> 1) Woman is the creator and fosterer of life; man has been the mechanizer and destroyer of life.

> 2) Women love the human race; men behave as if they were, on the whole, hostile to it.

> 3) It is the function of women to teach men how to be human.

> 4) Because women have had to be unselfish, forbearing, self-sacrificing and maternal, they possess a deeper understanding than men of what it means to be human.

> 5) By comparison with the deep involvement of women in living, men appear to be only superficially engaged. Compare the love of a male for a female with the love of the female for the male. It is the difference between a rivulet and a great, deep ocean.[1]

Psychiatrist Dr. Lester Gelb wrote an essay entitled "Masculinity-Femininity: A Study in Imposed Inequality."

In it he wrote, "It took me many years to realize that when a woman described many of the men who wanted to take her out as 'no damn good,' she was likely to be right."[2]

The *actor-reactor* interaction causes the man to appear to be an exploiter and also generates feelings in him of being responsible for the woman's happiness or unhappiness. For example, the following excerpt from the book *Divorced in America*, by Joseph Epstein, illustrates a man's feelings toward his ex-wife:

> You had had a letter from their mother, now your ex-wife, two days ago. In it she explained having come up with some mysterious female problem. One sentence in the letter affected you particularly. "Whenever I am away from you for any length of time," she wrote, "I seem to become sick." You wired her two hundred dollars through Western Union yesterday morning, for this illness would keep her from working for a week or so. Wavering between guilt and anger, between fantasies of reconciliation and vengeance, your feelings toward your ex-wife seemed beyond sorting. For the most part, you felt awful about her. You ardently wished she would remarry soon and solidly, to a wealthy, intelligent, gentle, tolerant man—in part because you really wanted good things to happen to her, *but in even greater part so that you could at last stop worrying about what exact share you had in the unhappiness of her life.*"[*3]

The more powerful his need for control and dominance, the more vulnerable he is to being portrayed in this way as a bad guy. David G. Winter of Wesleyan University, Abigail J. Stewart of Boston University and David C. McClelland of Harvard University recently studied the relationship of power-motivated husbands and their submissive wives. They concluded: "The power-motivated man, it appears, not only tends to distrust and exploit women in fantasy and through adolescent sexual 'con-

---

* Italics not in original.

quests,' he also appears to suppress them (or their career aspirations) in real life."[4]

This is just another of the endless examples of what eminent researchers repeatedly conclude: *He is the heavy. She is the innocent.*

Because the male has owned and acted out his sexuality, his aggression and his autonomy, he has inevitably set himself up for being the target for all the vile accusations currently being hurled at him. Because he has not been able to see beyond the surface interpretations, he is a bottomless well of guilt, self-hate and confusion. It will be discussed and demonstrated farther on in this book that women are just as sexual, potentially as aggressive and even more independent of the male than he is of her, and that *actor-reactor* role playing enhances every masculine self-destructive tendency and reinforces all of the female illusions of being the innocent victim of exploitation and abuse.

In actuality, in the *actor-reactor* interaction ultimate power resides in the *reactor*, who is very much like a Skinnerian behavior modifier shaping the behavior of a pigeon in a cage. (Skinnerian psychologists influence behavior by determining which acts shall be rewarded and which shall be punished.)

In the male-female interaction of *actor* and *reactor*, the process of interplay is basically unconscious on both sides because of the intensive early conditioning process and therefore its processes need to be rooted out by making them conscious. They need to be put into perspective primarily because the *actor* role is such a lethal and loaded one. So long as he continues to play that role, he will be haunted by latent or overt feelings of being responsible, even if he has lost everything and wallows as a skid-row alcoholic or is a divorced, lonesome, desperate soul living in a one-room apartment while his ex-wife continues apart from him in the mode in which they lived when married. He will still be filled with self-hate and images of himself as having been the destructive one.

In less drastic instances, the role of *actor* still causes many husbands to engage in self-hating ruminations that run something like this: "I don't know how she puts up with me. She has the patience and soul of an angel."

By playing *actor* to her as a *reactor*, he has actually

given her considerable power and control over him. He looks to her to affirm his lovability. Often his evaluation of his behavior is tied to her reaction. If he is a success and she applauds, he feels validated. In some instances, even while the money he earns is readily spent, he still receives negative feedback for his low-level preoccupation with making money and the kinds of people he associates with in his working world, or for the fact that his ambition deprives the family of his involvement.

If he experiences failure, she may be supportive or she may react in a rejecting way, as many men have discovered when their women turned cold as their business failed or they were fired from their job. Whether she reacts with love and sympathy or with hostility and rejection, the point remains that his reaction to himself is often intimately linked to her reaction to him as an *actor*. This makes him extremely vulnerable.

Likewise, the traditional male sees it as his role to be the woman's protector, even though she is often in no danger and may not even desire "protection." He will risk health and life, for example, to battle another man who makes an offensive remark or a pass at "his" woman.

In the sexual arena, too, by being the initiator and the active one, if his performance falters and he gets no erection or fails to facilitate an orgasm for her, he floods himself with doubts and negative evaluations and looks to see if she will continue to care about him and be patient while *he* works *his* problem out.

By his lack of consciousness in these matters, he digs his own grave. The gun is surely loaded. By clinging to the role of *actor*, he sets the stage for his inevitable nightmare.

The female role of *reactor*, while allowing her to escape the punishment of being an *actor*, must ultimately be frustrating to her as well. The fact that she knows she can indirectly control and affect his reactions must overwhelm and at the same time revolt her. To see a man apologize and cringe in pathetic self-hate because he doesn't have an erection or because he lost money in an investment or was fired from a job must, on a deeper level, make it very difficult—if not impossible—for her to feel really good and loving toward him.

Furthermore, as the passive-submissive *reactor*, she has

had to deny critical parts of herself and has thus built up a reservoir of rage. The rage accumulates because, by adapting to the rhythm and identity of the man she is involved with, she is denying and crushing so much of herself. Inevitably, she will see herself as being exploited, someone who is there just to service his needs. In playing the role of *reactor*, she is constantly suppressing her identity to the point where she may no longer even know who she is. The resentment over feeling "pushed around" will build steadily and constantly. Finally, she either explodes in rage or manifests countless psychological and somatic symptoms that reveal her frustration.

The gender fantasies we have all been raised on of establishing a "happily ever after" relationship between Miss Passive-Delicate-Fragile-Emotional Female and Mr. Right-Successful-Rational-Dominant-Powerful-Strong Male are, from a look at their psychological underpinnings, an impossible dream. Still, it haunts most men and women and aborts their growth to the extent that they pursue it, certain that it can be found and made to work once they find the right partner.

For the man, the *actor-reactor* relationship lays the foundation for unending guilt and opens him up for the most hostile accusations. He can be blamed for everything, for, indeed, by being the *actor* he is responsible.

For other reasons, the *actor-reactor* interaction is lethal to the male. The *reactor* woman is out of touch with her aggression and consequently will not be prone to see her share of responsibility and negotiate in areas of conflict. She will tend only to blame, accuse, turn away in hurt or scream out in righteous rage. Meanwhile, he will be left to feel guilt-ridden and ugly. The statement "You have made me unhappy" rings primarily in the ears of the *actor*.

The aware, evolving woman understands that the rigidly controlling, dominating male is both destructive to her growth and a boring partner as well. Likewise, the self-caring, aware and growth-oriented man will realize how loaded, destructive and impossible is a relationship with a passive-submissive female *reactor* and will avoid and reject her for being lethal and destructive to his development as vigorously as a feminist would avoid the rigid *actor*, or, as he has so often been labeled, the "male chauvinist pig."

9. The "Macho Warrior" and His "Earth Mother" Wife

> He never found her, though he looked
>   Everywhere,
> And he asked at her mother's house
>   Was she there.
>
> Sudden and swift and light as that
>   The ties gave,
> And he learned of finalities
>   Besides the grave.
>
> Robert Frost, "The Hill Wife"

His underlying need is too strong, his anxieties and buried anger are too great. He cannot accurately see the woman he lives with.

He is the contemporary "macho warrior," self-contained, active, emotionally controlled, striving for dominance and out to stave off and slay the economic dragons. In the process he hustles, manipulates, smiles and claws his way to "material security" and the top of his sandpile.

In relationship to his "earth mother," he alternates erratically between sticky sentimentality and bursts of rage, withdrawn silence and hungry urgency, "set-me-free" demands and clinging dependency, and instant decisions and vacillating confusion. His manliness is in his erection, his ability to win, to provide, to be strong, unafraid, rational, certain and autonomous.

His "earth mother" wife is relatively faceless as she goes about the business of taking care of the house, buying and preparing food, waking everybody up and sending them off to bed, cleaning, shopping and reminding the family members of their responsibilities. Most of all, she reacts to the structure her "macho warrior" husband provides.

79

She has babies at a young age. A typical woman, she marries before she is twenty-two, while her husband is less than twenty-four. Within five years they have two children.

If he "lets her" or "wants her to," she takes a paying job besides her household functions. If he is a rigid, determined "macho warrior," however, he won't "let her" go to work. He'll say instead, "I want my wife at home to take care of the house and kids. Maybe that's not the way I'm supposed to think nowadays, but I know a woman can't divide up her time that way. Besides, I'm not going to come home after a hard day and help her scrub floors. I'm just not going to do it."

If economic necessity forces her to work, he feels ashamed and threatened. The shame is part of the guilt and self-hate that comes from "failing" as the *actor* who is responsible for the support but can't carry the load by himself. The threat is that she might become too independent and too worldly, and discover that she doesn't really need him, or that there is someone more interesting or "manly" available to her out in the "real world."

The "macho warrior"—"earth mother" relationship is a dream conceived in a fantasy heaven but lived out in a psychological hell. This interaction between him and her—she in her seemingly aggressionless, fragile, compassionate, self-denying, submissive, "nonsexual" role and he in his exaggerated aggressiveness, sexuality and intransigence in relationship to other men—can be seen in its purer form in some aspects of Latin-American culture.

The cult of Marianism, a movement within the Roman Catholic Church, has as its object the special veneration of the figure of the Virgin Mary. The "real woman," as she is pictured to be and as she behaves, is known for her infinite capacity for humility and sacrifice. No self-denial is too great, and there is no limit to her capacity for patience with the men in her life.[2] She is submissive to the demands of these men, be they husband, sons, father or brothers.[3] Beneath this overt submissiveness, however—a fact well known to the Latins—is an entirely different perception of them. Inwardly she believes that men are to be humored because they are *como niños* (like children) whose foolishness, stubbornness and lack of temperance must be forgiven because "they can't help the way they are."[4]

Furthermore, these "good women" do not enjoy coitus. They merely endure it when the duties of matrimony require it. When such a woman finds it necessary to even refer to sexual intercourse, as when speaking with a priest, a doctor or a trusted confidante, she describes it as *"Le hice el servicio"* ("I did him the service").[5]

Even her "macho" husband finds it necessary to reassure himself that she does not *really* enjoy sex. One Peruvian journalist illustrated the man's need to believe in the frigidity of "good" women by reporting typical male remarks such as, "So-and-so is a bad woman; once she even made love in the bathtub," or "American women (*gringas*) are all prostitutes. I know one who *even takes the initiative.*"[6]

For the "macho," the lethal aspect of this inter-sex dance is vividly seen in the popular, widespread image of the black-clad, mantilla-draped woman, "kneeling before the altar, rosary in hand, while she prays for the souls of her sinful menfolk." It is seen even more directly in the classic religious figure of the *Mater dolorosa*, the tear-drenched Mother who mourns for her lost Son.[7]

This Latin image is only an extreme variation of the American scenario, consisting of the impulsive, alcohol-prone man who runs around while his long-suffering, selfless "good woman" is waiting at home.

The "macho warrior" and his "earth mother" wife are alive and wearing many disguises in our culture. Family, friends and others are sentimentally moved when these beautiful young couples are embodied in the football player and his cheerleader girl friend, the military officer and his adoring French or Oriental wife; the construction worker or truck driver and his virginal, shy, wholesome, religious waitress or secretary bride; the energetic, "godlike" physician and his respectful, worshipful nurse-wife, who may even refer to him as "the doctor"; or the middle-management businessman, engineer or attorney who is ambitious, tough, dominant, rational, detached and unemotional and his demure, nurturing wife, waiting on him and supporting him in his struggles and battles with the world.

She has, at least temporarily, given up parts of her own identity for him, protecting his ego during lovemaking and rarely, if ever, confronting him or asserting herself directly on anything that would threaten his masculinity. She is "happy" to plan their social calendar, prepare the weekend gourmet meal for three other neighborhood couples, oversee the house, act as chauffeur for the children, run the errands and work at making herself attractive by regular appointments with the hairdresser, manicurist and dermatologist.

She is sufficiently amorphous in her way of being in the relationship for him to be able to perceive her passivity as mutuality and agreement, her accommodation to his rhythm as caring, her submissiveness as loyalty, her dependency as devotion, her lack of overt aggressiveness as fragility, vulnerability and helplessness and her sexual receptivity and accommodation as purity, adoring love and a sexual unworldliness.

In his perception of her sexually, he resembles the child who cannot really imagine his parents being lusting people who enjoy "doing it." For example, researchers queried Illinois State University students on their perceptions of their parents as sexual beings. One-fourth of those asked believed their parents no longer had sexual intercourse, and over 50 percent set the figure for sexual intercourse between their parents at once a month or less.[8]

Another part of the romantic, time-honored mythology about "his" woman that the traditional man clings to is that she is a mystery, ever changing and infinitely complex. Unable and in part unconsciously unwilling to see the psychological realities of the woman-person living with him, he chooses instead to see her as an unfathomable, emotionally unpredictable, Madonna-like "earth mother," driven to emotional extremes by raging hormones. In his mind, she is a devoted and fiercely protective mother, comfortably monogamous and satisfied to be in his shadow giving him background support in his worldly battles. He also sees her as somewhat of a saint with an endless capacity for understanding and forgiveness ("Sometimes I don't know how she's put up with me all these years; she's an angel") and self-denial ("She's content with so little"). What makes her even more spiritual and special in his eyes is that she has transcended the "grubby," animalistic drives and appetites that he feels rule and chain him. This makes him humbly grateful and even surprised that she would stay with him and still love him. In his eyes, this bewildering phenomenon is part of a cosmic master plan and mystery. And all of the qualities he sees in her—fragility, nonaggressiveness, childlike dependence and spiritual purity—validate his stance in the world as her protector and "macho warrior."

It has traditionally been part of his arrogance, and a tragic blind spot as well, that he has been unable to see and relate to her as she is rather than as he needs to believe she is, either separate or in relation to him. Of course, traditionally she has both consciously and unconsciously colluded with his need to avoid the total reality of her, as she suppressed significant parts of her identity in her relationship with him.

Traditionally, she did not express her needs for control or dominance overtly or directly. Her power came indirectly by withholding affection and sex, and through the guilt feelings he experienced when he saw her as someone who was easily hurt and damaged by him—a sensitive, fragile and helpless person. Because she reacted rather than acted and did not define herself clearly by asserting her needs and demands directly or by being openly aggressive, he could never be completely certain who she was, what she felt or really wanted and where she was going. Aggressive interaction of any kind was extinguished in her early conditioning. Therefore, hers became essentially a conflict-avoiding style. When issues of friction came up, her only possible response could be, "I don't want to argue (fight)." If he persisted, her tears would usually bring the encounter to an impasse.

This lack of overt assertiveness and aggression created the fantasy of a mystery. It reinforced his perception of her as spiritual and ethereal. Her non-confronting style and her vagueness allowed him to see in her what he wished. She was much like a Rorschach inkblot on which he could project his best or most negative fantasies. Occasionally she consciously reinforced this process. As one woman expressed it, "If he wanted 'nice,' I gave him 'nice.' When he wanted 'bitch,' I gave him 'bitch.'"

Her aggression has always been there, but because of its indirect, passive and hidden expression, he has not been able to recognize and deal with it. Professors Carroll, Smith, and Rosenberg, faculty members of the history and psychiatry departments of the University of Pennsylvania, studied the widespread phenomenon in nineteenth-century America of female hysteria and determined that hysteria was the result of cultural conditioning that socialized the woman into playing a weak, dependent role.

The hysteria would take the form of nausea, headaches, paralysis and so on. The most common form was the "fit," in which the woman writhed on the floor, tore her clothing, plucked out her hair and hit herself. These symptoms were attributed to "thin blood," masturbation or promiscuity, germs or sometimes simply the willfulness and evilness of the woman patient, who was seen as a vampire or pest. The underlying unconscious meaning of these symptoms was that through this "attack" she could vent her rage and dissatisfaction.[9]

Recent research comparing the psychological symptoms of the Anglo-American woman and her more passive-submissive Mexican-American counterpart as patients in psycho-therapy highlighted further these manifestations of repressed aggression. Mexican-American women were found to have four times as many somatic complaints, such as gastrointestinal disorders, and significantly higher frequencies of seventeen symptom categories ranging from crying spells to suicide attempts, withdrawal to the bedroom and staying in bed, eating difficulties, obesity, sleeplessness and temper tantrums.[10] Various researchers have observed considerable covert hostility on the part of the Mexican-American wives toward their husbands and have reported that since the hostility could not be expressed directly, it resulted in these symptom disturbances, which were sometimes as severe as catatonic symptomatology, psychologically interpreted as representing "frozen rage."

In contemporary American society the passive-submissive female frequently unconsciously becomes a "sickness tyrant" and then controls her husband and family with a wide and ever-changing repertoire of debilitating chronic symptoms. Or her repressed anger transforms into a bottomless well of complaints and she is seemingly incapable of being satisfied or happy.

When a woman transforms and begins to liberate herself, refusing to play any longer her self-denying "earth mother" role, allows her rage to emerge directly, reclaims her autonomous sexuality and refuses to remain in a dependent stance, her man often misinterprets these changes as being part of a psychiatric problem or a "nervous breakdown." He is convinced that she is "not herself," and encourages her to seek professional help in order to regain her "senses."

He has the picture in reverse. She *had been* "not herself" and is now "becoming herself." If indeed he is waiting for her to "come to her senses," he will be waiting for a long time. His rigid need to retain his unrealistic "macho" perception of her is backfiring. She is simply no longer being a figure on which he can project his rationalization of his own need to be *the* dominant, aggressive, sexual figure. He misinterprets her growth and sees it instead as emotional disturbance.

The "macho warrior" pays dearly for his inability to correctly perceive his woman or read the signals of the buildup of her dissatisfaction and resentment. Cook County Circuit Court Judge Margaret G. O'Malley commented on the behavior of some of these men who are suddenly abandoned by their transformed wives:

"I never used to believe it when a husband would come in after his wife filed and plead that he didn't want a divorce. I'd ask, 'Where have you been?' Now I realize they don't catch the signals until the point of no return."[11]

When this point of no return arrives and ends in divorce, "earth mother's" attitude changes considerably. She gets in touch with what has been buried or latent inside of herself during the marriage. What she says then must be paid attention to by any man not intent on impaling himself on his delusions of what "his" woman is really like.

Various researchers in Massachusetts interviewed recently separated or divorced women, who spoke with great honesty about their feelings.

"In separating from someone, you discover in yourself things that you had never felt before in your life," one woman said. "That's one of the things that really freaks you out. I've always used my mind to keep down anything I didn't like. And now I discover, wow, I can hate!"[12]

Another woman commented, "In many respects I really do hate my husband. But I don't want to think nothing but hate. You know, when I see him walking down the street, I don't want to think, 'I hope when you step off the corner you get run over.' "[13]

An attitude that would not fit the image of "earth mother" that many men have was expressed by one woman when she said, "My attitude toward men is—they are nice for friends, they're fine for sex. A good man is a guy who has his *own* money and enjoys sex. I don't want to take anything from anybody."[14]

Another ex—"earth mother" revealed, "There are times when I really miss my husband, and they're not flattering times—when a faucet leaks, a rat is in the garbage, taking a door off. They always know how to do it—I have to stare at it for an hour . . ."[15]

Other divorced women interviewed by researchers made similarly powerful remarks, such as:

1) "I don't know if I could accept responsibility of caring for a man. Men are big babies."[16]

2) "There are the horrors of loneliness—but the loneliness with him around was much more acute. I feel pride in making it on my own."[17]

3) "I'm more independent, more demanding than I used to be. I would have to trust a man a lot to give up my job again—this is my security."[18]

4) "It took so long to get myself back together. You can't put all your confidence, loyalties—eggs—in one basket."[19]

The "macho warrior" male, however, has yet to honestly acknowledge similar kinds of feelings. So he continues on in his blindly hopeful and urgent way trying to make the traditional "macho warrior"–"earth mother" relationship work.

A well-known professional athlete superstar saw an actress in a commercial on television and was very much taken by her. He arranged through friends of his in the television business to meet her. After a whirlwind courtship they were married, and the media gave this all-American dream couple extensive coverage.

One year later they were in the divorce courts, and his wife ungraciously informed a reporter that her soon-to-be ex-husband had brought a buddy along on their honeymoon and spent more time playing Ping-Pong with him than he did in his wife's company.

Clearly, she was impugning his masculinity in the eyes of the public, who probably believed there was something seriously wrong with him. After all, a "real man" would have been solely occupied with and jealously guarding his wife and would have had an ecstatic time spending hours in bed making love, interspersed only with sips of champagne and elegant meals, a few brief shopping sprees and moments in the sun or on the streets posturing for the envious world.

How many countless other "macho warrior" males have been hauntingly obsessed by feelings of inadequacy and self-doubt in similar situations because they did not experience with their women the kind of ecstasy and satisfaction they had expected on their honeymoon?

Because of their different psychological makeups, in the moment-to-moment process of being together the "macho warrior" man and his "earth mother" woman have precious little besides their fantasies of what ought to be to sustain an interesting, stimulating or pleasurable interaction. Many of these couples, in fact, could hardly make it through an afternoon alone together without feeling bored, yet they expect to maintain a lifetime of stimulating, enjoyable interaction.

The more gender polarized they are, in fact, in terms of his being "all man" and her being "all woman," the less of a psychological basis they have for relating to each other, because *they are opposite sides of a coin.* She is everything he is not, and vice versa. Consequently, they can only drive themselves into self-hating, hurtful and angry tailspins because they do not experience what they anticipated and were told by others they were going to. If indeed they remain together as a couple, the high-energy bursts of their initial romantic feelings will inevitably be transformed into deliberate, often painful efforts to be "nice" and "understanding" with each other. The relationship becomes a kind of stalemate, a painful, passionless compromise, as these couples try and force into existence what

cannot exist authentically and naturally under their gender
orientations and rigid role-playing interactions.

What is really often happening behind their closed doors
was suggested in the following account written by a
woman working in a model middle-class area of Los Angeles.

> For the past several years I have worked as a techni-
> cian in a pharmacy in the San Fernando Valley. The
> neighborhood is middle-class and the customers are
> smiling, polite, clean-scrubbed professionals. Most of
> them visually fit the clean-cut American stereotype of
> USC graduates with season tickets to the Dodger
> games. In short, they are some of the "nicest"
> families in the Valley.
>
> When I first began working at the pharmacy, I was
> struck by the fact that although the volume of work
> was heavy (filling about 150 prescriptions a day),
> there were only half a dozen prescriptions a day for
> antibiotics, antihistamines, or oral contraceptives. The
> remainder were for mild tranquilizers, antidepres-
> sants, codeine with aspirin, sleeping pills, muscle
> relaxers, amphetamines, and codeine cough syrup.
> The amount of codeine cough syrup dispensed was
> staggering and the only real rival to Valium and
> Librium; however, the customer rarely appeared to
> have colds or to be ill in any way.
>
> I then began to notice that the heaviest work days
> were invariably Mondays, especially the Mondays af-
> ter a long three or four day weekend. The refill
> business on Mondays often tripled our new business.
> Customers, both men and women, would begin call-
> ing as soon as we opened for Valium refills that they
> could pick up on their way to work; or with requests
> to call their doctor to ask for double the amount of
> their last prescription. When I mentioned this to the
> attending pharmacist, he laughed and said that the
> Monday "emergencies" were nothing compared to
> summer vacations.
>
> When vacations began in June, the Friday business
> picked up to the Monday level as families prepared to
> go camping, to Mexico, or to Europe for three weeks.

Husbands and wives with identical prescriptions got double amounts and joked about the necessity for having a "travel stash."

One Friday we ran out of Valium for two hours. One couple was so upset at not being able to get their prescriptions filled on the way to the airport (they were going to San Francisco for the weekend) that they decided to change their plane reservations to a late night flight, just in case the delivery man might be delayed in returning to the pharmacy with the new 10 milligram Valium supply.

I always ask unmarried or divorced people who deprecatingly label themselves as failures for their inability to achieve the romantic male-female ideal they obsessively strive for if they know any other couples intimately who do have the kind of relationship they so desperately seek for themselves. Invariably, they reply that it is difficult for them to think of even one. Clearly, these individuals who see themselves as "failures," along with many other frustrated couples who live in compromise relationships, are haunted by a fantasy which is constantly being reinforced by films, books, media, religion or the mythology they learned as children.

The sexual relationship is often the first to deteriorate into a non-satisfying experience for at least one of the partners, because its composition is that of a man focused on performance who is traumatized by a penis that is not instantly responsive and obedient, and a woman who approaches the sexual encounter with a relatively passive, receptive, reactive attitude, fearful and often unable to assert her needs and desires and often releasing her hidden anger by complaining about his insensitive touch or manner. "What do *you* want to do?" is her most typical answer to a question about her desires. Furthermore, the unexpressed resentment he must inevitably feel over the pressure to perform and her passivity, plus her resentment as she increasingly feels that she is being used mainly as a masturbatory receptacle, will also be reflected in their sexual experiences. Finally, his perception of her as special, different, fragile, even "sacred," and her perception of him as a man needing to be dominant, whose ego will be damaged by any honest feedback, will make both of them careful, fearful and inhibited about communicating honestly, to the point of rigid self-consciousness. This will further dam the sexual flow between them.

With growing problems in sex, the relationship, in order to survive, will probably change its focus from the bedroom to the kitchen and food preparation for the woman, and to the living room and munching and sipping beer in front of the television set for the man. On vacation, this will translate into endless rounds of dining at restaurants in search of ever more exotic foods, these excursions being interspersed with shopping sprees and time out for feeling ill after some of the meals.

At home, likewise, eating will become the primary, non-threatening vehicle for sharing. Its dynamic typically will be "she feeds" and "he eats." Her preparation of meals and having them on time, even when she is feeling harried and resents preparing them, will become symbolic of her "love" and involvement with him. In fact, when dinner is late, he may explode in rage because on a deeper level he unconsciously experiences this lateness as a rejection of himself.

Similarly, his enthusiastic eating of these meals will become symbolic of his communication with her and acceptance of her love. When he is particularly in need of proving something, he will eat seconds and thirds. Her willingness to continually get up and bring him food to nibble on without complaint will reassure him of her devotion.

People who wonder if they are caught in the deadening "macho warrior"—"earth mother" trap might use the following test. Imagine the relationship minus these eating rituals. Would it still be a pleasurable, playful, satisfying and interesting experience? The traditional relationship would probably not be able to stand this test.

In all other aspects of day-to-day living, "earth mother's" submissiveness, dependency, passivity, fragility and "purity"—the qualities he exalted when he first met her—will begin to grate, irritate and bore him. In fact, fatigue may set in whenever he's at home, as he feels himself drained by the constant need to be dominant and the lack of an energy-filled, honest and mutually responsible interaction. His energy will be sapped by his unconscious resentment, boredom and sense of futility about changing this pattern. Her "femininity," once a delight, will become instead a heavy weight.

Likewise, his dominant, performance-oriented, emotionally unexpressive, rational and hyperactive orientation will become an annoyance and an irritation to her, and she, too, will begin to feel resentment over the very qualities that drew her to him initially. She will begin to feel pushed around, invisible, taken for granted and exasperated by his inability to communicate.

The lethal aspect of this relationship for the male is that, because of his dominant, performance orientation, which makes him feel responsible for what goes on, he will probably see himself as the "heavy" when the communication and relationship break down. She, in turn, may be only too willing to corroborate this image of himself as being the responsible party when things go wrong. This interplay was well expressed by a recently divorced woman who was looking back on her marriage in a mood of warped sentimentality. She commented, "It's a little like the battered child syndrome. You never find a battered child that does not want to be back with its parents, because they are the only parents it has. I just have very much this feeling."[20]

It is easy to see how the "macho warrior" in these relationships, married to a traditional "earth mother," would be both chronically guilt-ridden and driven to distraction by his restlessness, boredom and a chronic sense of being inadequate. The higher the pedestal he has chosen to put his "earth mother" on, the more vulnerable he will be to self-hate in comparison with her and to shock, confusion and panic when she emerges as a person different from what he had imagined her to be when she no longer colludes with his fantasy image of her.

These relationships are also lethal for him because, in the end, he can only emerge as the pathetic one, feeling himself a failure, unworthy of love. The relationship that began with him as the dominant, influential force and with her as the submissive, helpless and childlike person will see her grow into strength and independence, while he progressively crumbles.

The greatest tragedy here is that many of her growth changes may come at a time when he is least capable of benefiting from them—or at a time when he is feeling most vulnerable in terms of his career and self-confidence. Consequently, when his wife announces she wants out, the impact on this man, in his forties, perhaps, and fearing a life decline, will be devastating.

Consider the woman who informed her husband that she wanted out after twenty-five years of marriage and five children.

> "She told him she had played the game by all the rules for long enough," her attorney said. "She figured that at the age of 46 she wanted out of her $200,000 house, out of the business—cocktail party circuit and out of a life-style that looked like nothing more than a well-oiled treadmill toward death. She was very determined about it, very much together. She gave custody of the children to her husband and moved to a commune in Arizona."[21]

The "macho warrior"–"earth mother" interaction only serves to reinforce and exaggerate the most self-hating and self-destructive aspects of his style. Her "purity" and "sub-servience" will intensify his sense of guilt and animalism. Her unwillingness to confront, assert and engage will make her look like the peaceful, self-denying one and make him appear to be the "heavy." In his desperate attempt to prove himself worthy, he will give vent to the most regressive, irrational and self-destructive parts of himself as he overworks, overeats, constantly competes to prove himself superior, isolates himself and develops a compulsively active style to keep himself busy and to prove himself ambitious and productive. It will be a relationship composed of extreme mood swings, denial of feelings, boredom, self-numbing through alcohol and excess food consumption leading to weight problems, nervousness and tension. The feelings between him and her will swing from sentimentality ("Aren't we lucky to have each other?") to hateful and murderous recrimination ("Why don't you drop dead!"), with very little that is real or pleasurable in between.

In abandoning this model of the "macho warrior"–"earth mother" relationship, a man will have nothing to lose but his fantasies and his guilt. His "earth mother" image of her, while temporarily reassuring, comforting and even exhilarating, ultimately dwarfs him and brings out his most self-destructive tendencies. "Earth mother" is a powerful, seductive fantasy, and the process of becoming unhooked from its grip is the greatest challenge he faces in the man-woman relationship. His potential, however, once he is unhooked, is incredible, for in the "macho warrior"–"earth mother" relationship he is a pathetically vulnerable, out-of-touch creature, functioning at the bottom of his human potential. Once released from it, he could move toward full expressiveness, and the honest struggle for growth, mutual relationships, joyful sexuality and a self-caring, fluid style.

As a released person with recognized feelings and needs and with an attitude of guiltless self-care, he will come to the male-female relationship expecting to be stretched by it, not to hide behind it. He will expect to learn from his partner, to share responsibility equally so that he avoids being sucked into the debilitating trap of constantly being the strong man—provider—protector—decision maker.

As a self-caring person, he will not be able to tolerate a relationship with a woman who lets herself be a trophy which he can show off to the world, a tagalong companion to his activities or a person who is not in touch with and expressive of her own autonomously originated sexuality, aggression and need for independence.

The acid test of any future relationship will be whether it frees him to be more creative and expressive than before, rather than constricting him and smothering him under the pressures of performance, lopsided responsibility and guilt. He will see through the romantic stereotype of the "macho warrior"–"earth mother" relationship that he has been taught is the sanctified one but which is, in reality, an involvement based on each gender's incompleteness. As a "macho warrior," he is psychologically but an unborn fetus who must see through the fantasies and stereotypes that have seduced, dwarfed and chained him in order to be born, lest he be destroyed in their devitalizing grip.

10. Sex Distortions, Misinterpretations, Myths and Stereotypes About Men

The seemingly unending quest for new information on sex, sex techniques, the physiology of sex and the latest "secrets" of sex appeal, arousal, control and performance testifies to a sub-liminal awareness that there is something missing, something elusive, something more or something wrong. Or it reflects the existence of some critical evasion, conscious or unconscious, that requires constant covering over and deflection by the illusion of search for the great aphrodisiac or sex liberator that will send us all to orgasmic heaven.

Books written on the subject of sex tend to fall into four major categories:

1) *Permission-giving books* that inform the reader that anything that feels good is O.K. as long as no one innocent is hurt.

2) *Technique manuals* that inform about the "latest and best ways to do it."

3) *"Plumbing" manuals* that blueprint the physiology of the sex organs and how the various parts of the body react and are affected during sexual intercourse.

4) *Clinical books* that describe and offer solutions for "sex problems."

As with hypochondriacs, whose restless, continual and obsessive preoccupation with their health drives them from doctor to doctor and from nostrum to latest "cure," all in order to maintain their belief that, indeed, they have a unique, mysterious ailment—a belief that allows them to evade other more threatening emotional issues—it seems that the eternal obsession with sex information facilitates the evasion of some very powerful and threatening psychological awareness. I believe that the awareness being evaded is this:

94

Every sexual response, no matter how seemingly insignificant, or under what circumstance, is a true statement of feeling and reaction toward one's partner, as well as being a revealing reflection of oneself as a person. Indeed, it is perhaps the most uncontrollable, powerful, clear and uncontaminated reflection of the overall feeling tone and quality of that relationship and of one's true self. It therefore always threatens to expose truths that one or both people would rather avoid.

Most "sex problems," I believe, arise from a situation in which at least one of the two people who are having sex is resisting or not totally involved but is unwilling or unable to get in touch with and communicate these reservations, resistances and negative feelings because it would risk uncovering issues and emotions that might upset the balance of the relationship or jeopardize the person's desired image. Unless one has totally depersonalized sexual encounters and transformed them into impersonal, mechanical ones in which the partner is simply an interchangeable object or outlet for sexual desire or tension, *each sexual response must be seen as pair-specific.* That means that each response is a unique and personal reaction toward one's partner. Just as one does not have the identical reactions toward any two people, neither are sexual responses the same from person to person. Rather, each is unique to one's partner at the time.

Specifically, the man who is impotent with his wife may be a premature ejaculator with a prostitute, be very slow in ejaculating in a new love affair, in which he feels insecure and needs to "stay inside" as long as possible for reassurance, and be in perfect control with a partner where the relationship is comfortable, mutual, caring, pleasurable and open.

Furthermore, with one woman a man might be detached and basically cold, while with another he will be aggressive, rough and urgent. With a third he might be clinging and insecure, while with another still he might be delicate and exquisitely sensitive in his touch and timing. Likewise, with his wife he might turn away and fall asleep almost immediately after intercourse, while with a new lover he may continue to reach out and touch and have the high energy provided by the adrenaline racing through his body.

For the alive man, aware of women as people rather than objects, *each* reaction will be seen by him as a unique reflection and expression of himself that is making a clear-cut statement about his feelings toward her and himself in the relationship and is at the same time a response to whatever *she* is communicating to him.

Evasion of the profound truths that one's sexual response conveys and the inability and fear of confronting the emotional and interpersonal issues that exist in a relationship has, I believe, resulted in a situation and cultural climate in which most people have focused on and become obsessed with "sexual problems" and "symptoms" rather than emphasizing the underlying interpersonal meanings and truths being expressed by each response.

The medical and psychiatric professions have been given the role of interpersonal and emotional launderers, and they stand ready with a host of diagnostic labels and syndromes to provide people sanctioned shelter from their inner experience. These medical rationalizations allow individuals to avoid the painful and disruptive process of confronting their psychological and emotional selves and avoid dealing authentically with their relationships by giving the threatening response an "illness" label. This label allows its owner psychological immunity, the special privileged and protected status and even the concern and deference one gets for being sick and "working on" one's problem.

Medicine, for example, by attributing the major or primary cause of the "problem" to a vitamin or hormone deficiency, fatigue, performance pressure, alcohol or even early trauma, provides permission for the evasion of what most people wish to evade, which is a here-and-now encounter with their deepest feelings and responses toward their partner.

A woman, for example, whose vagina is tight and resistant to opening up for her husband, even when there is no physical disorder, might be given the diagnostic label of "vaginismus." By turning over the "problem" to a physician, she removes the threat of having to take responsibility for the statement her body is making toward her husband, which is a powerful NO! One such woman, known to the writer, had been "tight" from her honeymoon on with her husband and had even submitted to surgical procedures, which still didn't completely alleviate her "problem." Toward the end of her marriage, when she began engaging in affairs, she was pleasantly surprised to discover how wide open and welcoming her vagina was to her new lovers.

Along with contemporary sexual liberation has come an ever-increasing incidence of "sexual disorders" such as impotence and non-orgasmic response in women. This is *not*, I believe, because sex has resulted in increased pressure to perform, but rather because it has become more difficult to evade the sexual encounter in a relationship and the truths it reveals. With increased sexual awareness and focus, underlying psychological and emotional truths threaten to surface. Consequently, medical rationalizations are welcomed as sanctioned evasions, and we hear of "impotence plagues," or the large numbers of non-orgasmic women who continue to be so during intercourse in spite of a more permissive climate.

THE MALE "NOT ME" PHENOMENON IN SEX

The traditionally conditioned male is so disconnected from the emotions attached to his sexual response that when he is not performing sexually as he believes he should be, he disclaims his response by denying responsibility. Specifically, he curses his penis for not performing, as he sweats and strains and informs his partner that *he* really wants to, even though something seems to be wrong with *it*. He is relating to his penis as if it were a piece of machinery that has become faulty but that has no connection with his feelings about or desire for his partner.

Because he does not perceive his penis as an expression of his feelings but rather as a separate mechanism with a will of its own, when it "malfunctions," his inclination is to get "it" fixed as quickly as possible. During those times of "impotence," in which a man has been described by Dr. Helen Singer Kaplan, author of the acclaimed book *The*

New Sex Therapy, as "almost unbearably anxious, frustrated and humiliated,"[1] he is open to any kind of advice or "cure," so long as it offers the hope or promise of *instant* recovery, be it vitamins, injections, hypnosis, sexual "secrets" from the East, pornography, sex paraphernalia or special medications. His masculinity is at stake, and he cannot afford the luxury of any process that will not immediately allow him to recoup his threatened image. He would probably even submit himself to surgical procedures if the physician promised to "cure" his rebellious penis. In general, he will be receptive to any remedy that allows him to avoid probing his inner experience and which might yield immediate results of the kind he feels he must have in order to reinforce his belief that he is the victim of a foreign malady. In that way he does not have to confront the possibility that his penis's reaction is *his* reaction, and that when it malfunctions, it is making statements that he does not want to or cannot explore and deal with. He will therefore experience a great sense of urgency for a rapid resolution of the difficulty.

The traditional male-female sexual interaction, in which the male has taken primary responsibility for the initiation and success of the sexual experience, has also meant that he will carry the burden of the so-called problems to a significantly greater extent.

This was the conclusion of three researchers reporting in the *American Journal of Psychiatry* on the distinctions between male and female invested partners in sexual disorders. Because the male has the greater responsibility in the role of lover, he also carries a greater burden of failure. Thus, it seems that men suffer as much psychologically from their partner's sexual difficulties as from their own. Women, on the other hand, appear not to "experience significant levels of conflict arising from feelings of responsibility for their partner's dysfunctional status," the researchers reported.[2]

At the suggestion that his "problem" might have some connection with his feelings rather than being physically caused (which only about 10 percent are, according to Masters and Johnson), he is liable to feel threatened, impatient and even enraged and to search for a doctor who will confirm his belief that, indeed, it is a medical problem.[3]

A thirty-five-year-old, recently divorced scientist came to my office for help because he had not been able to have an erection with his last two girl friends. He wanted me to "fix it." When I told him that I would be doing him a disservice by just helping him get his erection back quickly without his understanding and coming to terms with the feelings that were producing his reaction, he agreed to try psychotherapy. After three sessions and with still no erection, he became impatient and announced that he would see a physician instead, because he felt sure that he was suffering from an organic disorder. His whole orientation, life attitude and stance of being in control, approaching every problem cerebrally, not depending on others or acknowledging vulnerability or helplessness were being threatened. His anxiety was so great, in fact, and he felt so terrorized by his non-cooperating penis, which put his masculine image in jeopardy, that he could not afford the luxury of looking at himself as a person. Bizarre as it seems, he would have felt greatly relieved if he could have even linked his "impotence" to a serious disease. At least then it would not have been his "fault" or a reflection on his masculine image and he would not have had to take responsibility for his reaction or go about the painful process of becoming self-aware in order to deal with it.

"NORMAL" MALE FUNCTIONING

In light of the traditional processes of male conditioning, it is senseless, misleading and even destructive to speak of such a thing as normal male functioning, much less the super-stud image many men would like to have and believe they could live up to. The "normal" male on whom statistics are based, struggling to live up to the image and standards he has introjected, is a master of camouflage and evasion and also probably has a female partner who, out of love, conditioning or the desire to "build up his ego," has disowned her own sexual needs and rhythms to confirm his fantasies of sexual prowess by telling him what he wants to hear. So long as he provides her with security, she will provide him with sex and all the expressions of ecstasy he needs to affirm his masculinity. His being out of touch with his own feelings and sensibilities, coupled with a great need to believe, will make it possible for her to tell him anything he needs to hear. He doesn't want to know differently.

It is also interesting to speculate on the extent to which the sexual-superman image has been *unconsciously* reinforced by the woman. That is, by supporting his fantasies of being a wonderful lover, he will become uncomfortable, embarrassed, fearful of rejection and eager to redeem himself when inevitably he is no longer able to live up to the sexual-superman image, be it one month or several years later. Then, when she responds gently and lovingly to "his" problem, he'll become more attached and grateful for her "understanding." In effect she has become the powerful partner, able to control him by being "nice" when his self-hate and inability to live up to the superman image are causing him to anticipate ridicule.

THE MALE IN SEXUAL JEOPARDY

The traditionally conditioned male must be sexually in jeopardy because his entire early conditioning process creates the basis for him to become a psychological stranger to himself and his sexual responses.

1) His emotions are largely repressed. He is unable to read or express his feelings, much less act on them. This emotional estrangement makes it equally impossible for him to read his partner accurately. For example, there are many men who have lived under the illusion that their women were highly satisfied and orgasmic when, in fact, they were faking their responses to please the man. Often, even when the relationship was over, he harbored the delusion that she would return because "nobody can satisfy her like I can, and as soon as she finds that out she'll come crawling back."

2) From early boyhood on, his sensuality is repressed. Hugging, kissing, touching, stroking, being close and en-

gaging in body play were not considered masculine. Indulgence in them, in fact, made him suspect of being a "sissy." Consequently, as an adult he approaches sex as a goal-oriented activity, rather than a playful, sensual interchange in which the process of lovemaking is the major source of pleasure and satisfaction.

3) He is pressured by the continual compulsion to prove his masculinity through performance, and the proving *never* ends. It is final-exam time every time.

When he describes what for him was a great sexual experience, he tends to talk about how many orgasms he was able "to give" the woman and "how long" he was able to maintain his erection. The degree of his satisfaction is correlated to the success of his performance more than anything else. Sooner or later the performance compulsion will push him to participate or "try" even when he's not turned on, because, in his mind, a man is ready whenever a woman is. When his performance falters, the anxiety begins and a downward performance cycle is set in motion. Performers are winners or losers, heroes or bums, and "a miss is as good as a mile." Losing is inevitable sooner or later, and then he will be flooded with self-doubt and self-hate.

4) The more traditional the man, the greater will be his tendency to put "his" woman on a pedestal when he "falls in love," to attribute Madonna-like qualities and virtues to her and to perceive her as fragile, sensitive and to an extent an untouchable being. She is, in his eyes, beyond the bounds of the "animallike" impulses that he feels. He will greatly subdue any aggressive or even assertive impulse on his part, and he will be careful not to confront her specifically with information about what turns him on or turns him off for fear of offending or hurting her. He will also have great difficulty saying no if he thinks she desires him, even when he is not excited. In general, he will tend to paralyze himself with his self-conscious protectiveness of her and his overreaction to his own "animalism."

On the other side of the coin, he will unconsciously inhibit *her* sexual expressiveness by his indirect messages that convey his fantasy of her as pure, angelic and unlike all other women. Her own tendency to be sexually passive, based on her conditioning, will thus be reinforced, and she will be highly reluctant to be expressive, active and assertively sexual for fear of disturbing and disillusioning him in regard to this fantasy of her as ethereal.

When resentment or disappointment arises on either side, neither he nor she will be prone to talk about it. Rather, these feelings will tend to be suppressed and denied, and therefore matters will get worse.

5) He tends to choose a wife or long-term lover on the basis of "shoulds." The "right" woman for him is one whom his mother and his friends and business associates will approve of as being an appropriate partner who is "worthy" of being his lifelong partner. The choice is primarily a cerebral one, the woman who best fits the traditional image, and he will then try and force his body to respond with equal enthusiasm. However, his body may resist the non-sensually satisfying choice. This will be manifested by an uncooperative penis, which ejaculates too fast or does not stay hard.

He will not hear or understand the body messages. Instead, he will strive to overcome them. Soon thereafter he may be labeling himself according to some sexual diagnosis and begin a search for cures—magical stimulants, aphrodisiacs or a "treatment" to overcome his resistance. He may find the quality of his sexual experience rapidly deteriorating to bottom-line expectations, meaning being able to perform just often enough and well enough to save masculine face, no matter what artificial methods it takes to arouse him. He has once again sold out his inner self in order to accommodate role and image demands.

In summary, when masculine conditioning results in his:

a) Not being able to experience, express and deal with his emotions;

b) Not being able to confront "his" woman with his turn-ons and turn-offs, or clearly define his limits by saying yes or no according to his desire;

c) Feeling responsible for performance and the success of the lovemaking;

d) Being uncomfortable with prolonged sensual play;

e) Being unable to accurately read and act on his own emotional and interpersonal responses or to decipher hers;

f) Striving to live up to images and statistics of "normal" male sexual functioning set up by others;

g) Making love to a partner who reacts in a passive-submissive-receptive way and who will not be open and honest in sharing her inner experience because she sees it as her responsibility to build up his ego;

h) Being terrorized by underlying fears of "not being a man" or being a "latent homosexual";

i) Emotional isolation from others to the point that he will tend to develop an unconsciously inordinate dependency on the woman, thus transforming her into a mothering figure;

j) Needing to prove himself constantly in every way, *how can we even begin to speak about the "normal" or "healthy" male sexual response?*

NEGATIVE STEREOTYPING OF THE MALE

Owing to the traditional male-female interaction, in which he has assumed the role of *actor* while she has played the part of the *reactor*, the male has developed a built-in guilt reflex toward the woman, which manifests itself particularly strongly in sex. Since he sees himself as having to be dominant, in control and the sexual initiator, he will also tend to view himself as the responsible one and the insensitive "animal" whenever there are problems, while viewing her as the injured, though patient, understanding and forgiving party.

This built-in guilt reflex creates a bottomless-well potential for self-hating, "bad boy" feelings, which the militant feminists have played upon in their portrayal of the male as a sexual exploiter and chauvinist pig. He has, in fact, been accused of every heinous sexual crime and motive. Men may very well be the last remaining subgroup in our society that can be blatantly, negatively and vilely stereotyped with little objection or resistance.

Examples of such stereotyping by writers who, I am sure, would otherwise see themselves as liberals and humanists abound.

Gloria Steinem, for example, in a cover editorial for *Ms.* magazine, which discussed child pornography, wrote:

Children being undressed and sexually fondled by adult males. Men performing sexual acts on children. "Fathers" having intercourse with "daughters." These widely available, very profitable films and photographs are the subject of Congressional hearings and TV documentaries as America discovers child pornography, and condemns it as a sexual perversion. In fact, it is neither sexual nor a perversion. It is one logical, inevitable result of raising boys to believe they must control or conquer others as a measure of manhood, and producing men who may continue to believe that success or even functioning—in sex as in other areas of life—depends on subservience, surrender, or some clear tribute to their superiority. If that sounds farfetched, consider the facts of child pornography. And consider their echoes in our own observations, perhaps even in our own lives.

Who are the purchasers who feed their sexual needs and a nationwide, lucrative industry by buying books, films and magazines of the humiliation, the brutalization of children? *They are of course, men.** That fact is so taken for granted that it's rarely specified, nor is it a surprise that investigations have yet to turn up even a significant few female buyers. (Yes, there have been some women who help produce such pornography, but their need seems to be money or the approval of men they're dependent on, not the personal need for intimate, obscene power that creates the pornography market in the first place.)

... But how different are those obsessed, power-hungry purchasers of child pornography from the many "normal" men who are convinced of the need and permission to be violent, to conquer sexually?† Once the belief in a false superiority is inflicted on men in order to perpetuate a male-dominant system, surely the question is only one of degree; of how far the individual has to or will go in order to get the drug of male superiority to which society has addicted him.

And how different are the child victims of pornog-

* Italics not in original.
† Italics not in original. ——

raphy from the millions who have been sexually approached or molested or continually brutalized as children, sometimes by men in or close to their own families? How many readers of these words have had one such childhood experience themselves?"[4]

With a mixture of facts, half-truths, hyperbole, sweeping generalizations and the fiery adjectives of an old-time preacher or charismatic crowd manipulator, Gloria Steinem castigates, in wholesale fashion, the *entire* male sex.

Similarly, Susan Brownmiller, in her successful and widely discussed book, *Against Our Will: Men, Women and Rape*, stereotypes and indicts the entire male sex for being rapists, or latent rapists who get vicarious satisfaction and pleasure from the exploits of the actual perpetrators of rape. Never mind that men have literally killed each other over as slight a matter as an uncalled-for or derogatory comment toward a woman, or that convicted rapists in prison often are in grave jeopardy in relation to other prisoners.

Brownmiller goes so far as to assert that men perceive rapists as "heroes." In a chapter titled "The Myth of the Heroic Rapist," she first quotes Genghis Khan: " 'A man's highest job in life,' said the man who practiced what he preached, 'is to break his enemies, to drive them before him, to take from them all the things that have been theirs, to hear the weeping of those who cherished them, to take their horses between his knees, and to press in his arms the most desirable of their women.' " [5]

From this statement Brownmiller generalizes as follows: "This remains, I think, the definitive statement of heroic rape: woman as warrior's booty, taken like *their* proud horses. We owe a debt to Genghis for expressing so eloquently the direct connection between manhood, achievement, conquest and rape."[6]

Later in her book she writes, "Hero is the surprising word that men employ when they speak of Jack the Ripper. . . . Jack the Ripper became an important murderer and mythic figure precisely because his identity remained unknown. In other words, he got away with it."[7]

Articles have been written attacking the male sex for exploiting women in every sexual manner, from harassment on the job to forcing them into lives of prostitution on the streets. All employ a common stereotype. Men are exploitative, insensitive, destructive abusers of women.

There has been little protest because these hostile stereotypes coincide with male self-hate. This is even perpetuated by well-intentioned men. I attended a film program sponsored by a major men's collective ("men's lib" organization). The films dealt with the issues of masculinity. One particular movie stands out in my memory as a vivid example of subtle, insidious negative male stereotyping. It depicted a group of men together in a private men's club. All of the men were caricatured in cartoon form as penises and were engaged in various repulsive behaviors such as loud farting, belching, snorting and so on. In a word, they were portrayed as disgusting boors.

The audience, which was, I am sure, composed of "liberal" and "enlightened" men and women, roared with laughter and delight. Had any other subgroup been stereotyped in such a negative, hostile fashion, the outcry would have caused the film to be shut down.

Negative sexual stereotyping is even perpetuated in the form of psychiatric interpretation. For example, a recent article in a major magazine discussed men's responses to the emerging sexual assertiveness of women. One prominent California psychiatrist interpreted male resistance as meaning the following: "If I cannot dominate you sexually with my erect penis, then I will not be involved with you at all. I will control you by withholding that which you wish."[8]

The fact that men have traditionally expressed their sexuality actively while women have expressed theirs in passive-receptive ways has given men a psychological heritage of viewing themselves as the lusting, demanding and aggressive animal. Consequently, any negative label or interpretation which is pinned on the male is introjected and accepted as being valid. This self-hating propensity makes it that much harder for him to function in an assertively self-caring, growth-oriented way rather than in a defensive, self-accusing and destructive one.

For example, the man who is having a "problem" with his erections tends to interpret the underlying reasons in a negative way. Perhaps the "problem" is seen as an expression of his unconscious hostility toward women in general, his desire to punish his wife or a manifestation of his latent homosexuality.

Again, these accusatory, one-sided interpretations sometimes come from society's appointed authority figures in these matters. A professor of psychiatry at New York University School of Medicine coined the term the "new impotence" in describing the so-called contemporary male sexual plague. According to a published account, he and several of his colleagues "attribute impotence in these men to the changing and more aggressive sexual roles of women . . . they are already likely to be *hostile** toward women, have castration fears, or be latent homosexuals."⁹

In light of these negative interpretations he gives himself and also tends to get from the experts, it is not surprising that sexual "problems" would fill him with self-contempt and motivate him to "repair" his uncooperative penis as quickly as possible without allowing himself sufficient breathing space in order to listen and come to terms with the voice of his body.

To project the necessary image and to keep his penis functioning at its best in spite of anything else, some men even resort to self-abusive, outrageous "tricks" in order to maintain performance. For example, a man who claimed to have an excellent sex life and to have sustained it for over thirty years explained to a writer on male sexuality how he did it:

> The man's "trick" is to take a shower before having sex and before leaving the shower to rub adhesive cream for dental plates on his penis. It seems that this cream has anesthetic properties, for deadening sensitive gums, that also works to deaden the sensations of the sensitive penis. There is presumably a multimillion-dollar business in products such as Detain and Prolong that partially anesthetize the penis. I have even heard that cocaine on the penis deadens the sensations.¹⁰

---

* Italics not in original.

"IMPOTENCE" AND SEXISM

The word "impotence," aside from its intimidating impact in the way it implies a "sickness" or deficit in masculinity is also a *sexist and destructive* concept. It is destructive because it automatically suggests a medical or psychological disorder, and one that also contains an implicitly negative value judgment, despite assertions of professionals to the contrary. A man who labels himself "impotent" feels himself to have a serious problem, and it becomes impossible for him to perceive his response as a concrete expression of his emotions.

As I suggested earlier in this chapter, it is my belief that one reason why men have passively accepted the onus of such labels is that unconsciously it would be even more threatening for them to see their sexual response as a manifestation of their true feelings and to examine them and take responsibility for the messages being communicated.

In its widest ramifications, the causes of "impotence," when pursued to their root, might reveal that the nonfunctioning or resistant penis is merely the tip of the iceberg, a manifestation of a whole life on the verge of collapse because it was built on the psychological and emotional lies of compulsive masculinity. "Impotence" might be an unavoidable, visible announcement of the collapse of these defenses. Clearly, since men tend to base life decisions on their compulsion to prove themselves rather than on true personal needs, it is very likely that they have stayed in "good" marriages out of guilt, remained in an onerous job in order to be "responsible," fathered children to prove their potency and please their wives and society and in the process of all of this have built up considerable hidden resentment and frustration. Once they have committed themselves both economically and psychologically to the emotional lies of their lives, a resistant penis that threatens to expose and even topple this sand castle by precipitating a confrontation with frustration, anger and unhappiness would constitute a powerful threat. At the same time, a medical interpretation of "impotence" as being caused by vitamin or hormone deficiency, fatigue, alcohol, latent homosexuality or even "unconscious hostility" toward women would be far less threatening than the trauma of having to explore and reassess the psychological structure of one's life. The men are between a rock and a hard place, and the self-hate and torment associated with labeling oneself "impotent" is actually less threatening than inner exploration.

Were I to write slogans for a men's movement, one bumper sticker would read, "Your penis is years ahead of your brain." While I say this in a humorous way, I do believe that many men would have saved themselves the anguish of a decimated life in middle age had they learned to listen to, trust and act upon their body statements rather than denying and trying to transcend them. *The male who is in touch with his inner experience will come to realize that he doesn't "have sex," but rather that he "is sex," which simply means that his so-called sexual response is "his" response and as such is one of the deepest, least consciously controllable, most powerful, truth-telling expressions of who he is and what he feels.* It is not an encapsulated, emotionally unrelated experience, or the result of faulty plumbing.

Beyond just his penis response, he would need to read and trust his total body response in relation to the woman. That is, is he inclined spontaneously to move toward the woman and to cuddle after sex, to freely express emotions, to feel focused and interested in her as a person, or is he inclined to resist touching and other sensual contact as he finds himself wanting to turn away, while his mind wanders or he falls asleep almost immediately after intercourse?

FAKING ORGASMS

Furthermore, it is meaningless to try and assess the scope of "male sexual problems," as eminent researchers have done, when, according to recent reports on women's sexual response, the majority of women are nonorgasmic during intercourse and may even fake orgasm to "please" their men. One eminent psychologist who writes on feminine psychology reported that the majority of college women she interviewed perceived sexual intercourse as a way of either securing love or ensuring they would not lose it. Very few of the women interviewed reported obtaining orgasm. It is mind-boggling to surmise what the subliminal impact of all of this has been on men's responses. Surely, on some level they picked up the cues of a non-orgasmic response, and it is safe to say that a reaction, possibly "impotence," became inevitable.

It is therefore both paradoxical and sadistic to establish standards of male sexual functioning when the female partner has traditionally come to bed in a passive-submissive manner, resistant to verbalizing her real reactions, feeling obliged to massage his ego by feigning greater excitement than she actually experienced, while suppressing her own desires.

Indeed, a man who functioned from a motive of self-care, who could correctly read and then act upon his body's responses, could totally transform his consciousness, life-orientation and relationships. His body responses, rather than being viewed as symptomatic because they were not as they "should" be, would be seen as statements of resistance and would be welcomed as cues and clues to his inner world. He would choose lovers toward whom he felt spontaneously and naturally sensual and playful, awake, eager to touch and be touched, unpreoccupied with performance, open with his responses and feelings, comfortably able to set limits and toward whom his penis responded in congruence with the way he felt. In other words, he would choose a partner toward whom his organism was communicating a clear YES!!

THE DANGERS OF SEX THERAPY

In light of the above, some of what is called "sex therapy" today can be seen as perpetuating the mind/body split by treating the symptom, which is his uncooperating penis, without sufficiently exploring the statement of feeling it is making.

For example, a widely used technique by reputable, well-trained sex therapists for the "treatment" of "premature ejaculation" is the "squeeze technique." This involves teaching the woman to manipulate the penis in such a way as to control the man's ejaculation. The approach, which clearly implies that the "problem" is a mechanical one, is rationalized by interpretations such as the following one offered by the Masters and Johnson team. Dr. Masters expressed it this way:

> In the old days of the cat house it was hurry up, hurry up. The faster the girls worked, the more money they made. The males hardly had a chance to get their pants off. If a young man learned that way— and at one time most of them did—it carried over to his marriage.
>
> Today it often begins in the back seat of a parked car. Again, it's hurry up and get the job done. The back seat of a car hardly provides an opportunity for the expression of personality.[11]

A clinical professor of psychiatry at Mount Sinai School of Medicine, explained it in a similar vein. "Premature ejaculation is just a failure of reflex, like a child not toilet-trained."[12]

These interpretations, which do have a positive impact in that they remove the guilt, sense of responsibility and failure and the depiction of the man as a "bad guy" who is unconsciously seeking to deprive his woman, nevertheless reinforce the tendency of the man to disown the immediate statement being made by his body. For example, in this instance he would say to himself, "When I come fast it's because I learned it in the back of a parked car or was just never properly trained," rather than focusing on the feeling being reflected by his too rapid ejaculation.

As a rule, so long as a man's sexual response is different from time to time, and from partner to partner, it must be viewed as a statement of feeling and reaction. Only men who repeatedly and over long periods of time have the same sexual response, with different partners, can be viewed simply in terms of expressing learned habits and symptoms resulting from problems which are basically unrelated to the relationship.

Viewed in this light, even the most benign therapeutic orientation which communicates to the man that it's O.K. not to have an erection and that he's still as much of a man even when he is "dysfunctional" misses the critical point, which is that every sexual response is an expression and reflection of how a man really feels toward his partner and himself. In addition, he will be done the disservice of being deflected from an ideal opportunity for self-exploration and change, because when he is having "sexual problems," his motivation for help is usually at its highest, and once he is made to "feel better" and told that his "problem" is a learning flaw rather than an expression of himself, a fine opportunity for growth will have been lost.

One man, who had become aware that indeed his penis was an expression of himself and not a disconnected piece of plumbing, expressed the meaning to him of this awareness as follows:

> The faster I come, the less I care for the woman as a person. When I can barely come at all, it's usually because I'm clinging. For some reason I'm sensing that I care for her or am hooked into her much more than she is to me and I'm feeling insecure. In a way, I don't want to get out because I may never get in again. When I turn over and go to sleep right after I make love, it's not my chauvinist insensitivity. It's that I really don't want to be close to her because I don't feel involved in a happy, sensual way. Perhaps I'm bored, made love out of guilt or was just horny and I used her. I'd probably rather leave but don't have the guts to say so, so I escape by falling asleep. Once in a while, when I don't get an erection at all, or when the erection seems to come and go, that's no accident either. When I examine my feelings closely in these instances, I realize that I want to avoid that woman for some reason. Maybe I don't trust her or maybe it's because she's cold and cutting or even using me. If I were really in touch and honest, I wouldn't even be there.

In fact, it is a reflection on how depersonalized and how compulsively performance oriented the traditional man has been that he has always expected himself to be potent and a good performer, regardless of how he felt toward the woman he was with.

SEXUAL STEREOTYPES AND MYTHS

1. *Men have a "fragile ego."*

The stereotype that says that men have a "fragile ego" when it comes to sex and that consequently women shouldn't own up to their real feelings and should even fake their orgasms in order to protect his self-esteem is destructive to the man and could also be seen as self-serving for the woman. By attributing their reluctance to be honest in their responses to the fragility of the man's ego, women can avoid facing an at least equally basic fact—that in many instances the man is a source of security or hoped-for security and that if she were honest it might, to her mind, put the relationship in jeopardy.

Indeed, many men might feel hurt or threatened by a woman's honest statement of frustration, disappointment or resentment. However, if there is a loving attachment and genuine caring, the short-term discomfort and threat created by the confrontation would translate into long-term growth. Avoiding an honest encounter locks the man into his misperceptions and delusions and makes him more vulnerable to the sudden ending of the relationship later on, because he was never even told anything was wrong. Worse still, long before that contingency the phony statements of satisfaction will contradict the woman's nonverbal and body messages. This creates a crazy-making, double-bind situation resulting from the multilevel, conflicting communications. He may even become "dysfunctional" as a result and blame himself because his partner seems to be so sexually responsive while he is the one with the visible problem.

In general, the woman who fakes or withholds honest negative feedback, allegedly to preserve the man's ego, contributes to his emotional and interpersonal stagnation, reinforces his tendency to feel guilty and responsible when things go wrong and intensifies his tendency to withdraw emotionally as he unconsciously seeks to protect himself from the impact of confusing, contradictory messages that tell him verbally how wonderful he is while simultaneously giving him messages of rejection and anger on nonverbal levels.

2. *Men are threatened by and dislike sexually assertive women.*

In a time in our culture when individuals are increasingly striving to take charge of their lives and to assert themselves constructively, it is important to differentiate between assertion and hostility, demandingness, the need to control and threats and put-downs which may come disguised as innocent self-assertion.

Many recently liberated women in the process of change are also experiencing the breakthrough of long repressed rage and resentment. What they perceive as being simple, new-found assertion may actually be a mixture of assertion with hostility, challenge and threat. On the other hand, assertive caring, which is an honest statement of personal feeling and need, is motivated by the desire to increase intimacy. It will be revitalizing to the relationship because it adds new person-to-person dimensions and moves the relationship away from role-rigid, *actor-reactor* interactions.

As to women who are experiencing a new, increased sexual appetite, this is only threatening to men who still see a woman's desire as a mandate to perform. In fact, were he comfortable in allowing himself to be made love to when he was less turned on than she, with no feeling of *having* to get turned on, new dimensions of physical play could be experienced.

3. *Men use women as sex objects.*

Many women express concern over being used by men sexually and wonder whether they should wait a certain length of time after they enter a dating relationship before having sex in order to protect themselves against such "exploitation." *To my mind, there is only one valid reason for a woman to go to bed with a man at any time, and that is that she is turned on and doing it for herself, with her pleasure and satisfaction in mind.* Perhaps she might go to bed with him on occasion simply because he desires it and she wants to satisfy him, but in that case she will indicate that to him rather than pretending desire she doesn't experience.

Women who, in a new or ongoing relationship, feel used need to ask themselves whether, in fact, they are not themselves using sex manipulatively, as a ploy to get or hold on to a man or for bargaining purposes. If a woman is in bed for herself, it will not matter to her whether it is the fifth date or the first, or even whether the man is "using" her, for even if she never sees him again, she will have satisfied *her* desire and had the pleasure of an experience she engaged in for *her own satisfaction.*

The traditionally sexually reactive woman who does not recognize or take responsibility for her own appetites is the one most likely to feel she is being treated like an object, because, in reality, by not defining her needs, desires, likes and dislikes and by simply reacting to the man she *is* denying her personhood and, in fact, behaving like an object. Indeed, the self-caring, in-touch man would not continue a relationship with a woman who allowed herself to be used, because, aside from its being essentially a boring, degrading, and dehumanizing experience, it reinforces his guilt, his self-hate, his sense of being responsible for her satisfaction, of being a lusting "animal" and of owing her something in return for her "gift" or "service."

4. *Men are insensitive to women sexually. They only want to satisfy themselves.*

If I were to write a book on female psychology, I would include a chapter on the "wisdom of the vagina" as a counterpart to a chapter I wrote in my book *The Hazards of Being Male* entitled " The Wisdom of the Penis."[13] In it I would encourage women to read and act upon their own body messages and the ones they receive from the man. A self-caring, secure woman would then choose as partners only those men whose body language and responses signaled their genuine interest, and she would reject the insensitive, selfish man outright rather than complain or try to change him. His chronically insensitive behavior is making a clear and powerful statement of rejection. It is my belief that a man who is turned on, involved and experiencing genuinely loving feelings toward a woman will not react in insensitive ways except occasionally, when that insensitivity stems from innocent ignorance of her needs. In that case, remedy would come quickly as a result of an honest exchange of feeling.

In many instances in the past, a woman chose a man for his potential as a provider and security source and then was resentful because she did not get the sensual response that she desired. My interpretation of a man's cold, "insensitive" response in these instances is that he may be unconsciously reacting to and resenting the fact that he is being seen primarily as a success symbol and security source rather than as a person, even though he may have consciously invited this himself.

In a future time when men and women come together sexually to give each other pleasure rather than to complete or rescue each other, they will make love only for the joy of the process and will choose a person who excites them on that level primarily.

5. Men reach their sexual peak in their late teens.

This often repeated notion about men I believe to be primarily an artifact of conditioning rather than a biological phenomenon. Men begin to enter firmly into harness in their late teens and begin to deny feelings and drown out impulses. They also strive to live up to models of responsible husband-father-provider and to assume the posture of chronic proving while taking the role of *actor* to the female *reactor*, at the same time relating progressively more dishonestly to their inner life.

The decline in sexual capacity, therefore, seems to me to be a reflection of the enormous repression of emotion and self, coupled with the smothering effects of guilt, unconscious anger over their suffocation and the compulsion to accommodate their female partner while denying themselves.

6. *Men are not basically monogamous.*

I believe that the conditioning of the male creates in him a powerful ambivalence toward monogamy. On the one hand, he has a deep craving for a special female partner based on his early experience of mother as his lifeline and source of nourishment and comfort. This is coupled with other factors that cause him to hunger for one special partner, such as his intense emotional isolation from other men because of his competitive stance toward them, his fear of being open and vulnerable in front of them, his homosexual anxiety and the fact that men are not usually sources of nourishment and comfort to each other. Finally, his orientation toward "his" woman is usually a possessive, protective and guilt-laden one. All of these factors would tend to make him lean *toward* monogamy.

His push *away* from monogamy would result from early conditioning in which he learned to view sex as a game of challenge and conquest. His masculinity was validated by the number of women who would go to bed with him. Second, his emotional and sensual repression and a concomitant tendency to relate to sex in terms of goal (ejaculation) rather than process (the pleasure of sensual play) would tend to create boredom and rigidity with any partner. Third, if his wife or lover is the traditional reactive-passive-submissive woman sexually, she will be a monotonous, highly predictable partner and will also trigger his tendency to feel guilty and self-hating for feelings of imposing himself on her. Finally, unconscious resentment over the strictures of his role may reflect itself in sexual resistance. All of this would tend to pull him *away* from monogamy.

In general, powerful ambivalence rather than a clear-cut positive or negative feeling would seem to be the logical experience of the traditional man.

7. *Middle-aged men in sexual pursuit of younger women are unconsciously expressing panic over growing old and are trying to deny their age and prove their virility.*

I perceive the craving of some middle-aged or older men for younger partners to be, at least in part, an expression of an underlying awareness that they have lived an unauthentic, emotionally self-denying life based on guilt and the need to prove themselves and that they are on the verge of having thrown their lives away. They see in the young woman the fantasy and possibility of rebirth, a fresh start and an opportunity to experience the spontaneous, sensual and expressive excitement they have not permitted themselves in their compulsive pursuit of the masculine role and ideal. It is, in effect, a last-ditch attempt, albeit unconscious, to reclaim their lives.

8. *Men are*————*(Fill in the stereotype of your choosing).*

The male sex is heavily encumbered with negative stereotypes that remain unexamined and unchallenged. The time has come for him to reject the role of all-purpose whipping boy and to reclaim his right to function as a self-caring, growth-oriented human being rather than a mechanical robot.

The only generalization that seems to be valid is that male sexuality has been so encumbered by a conditioning process that destroys the potential for joyful, authentic, spontaneous sexual responsiveness that one can only speculate and create visions of what might someday be if the male freed himself of these powerful and destructive role bindings. In the meantime, it only adds insult to injury to speak of norms of healthy sexual behavior, since he is an organism motivated by guilt, performance compulsion, emotional repression, denial of dependency and a resistance to passivity, plus a tendency to put the woman he "loves" on a pedestal and not to communicate with her or even see her as a person.

The potential for men who can read, trust and act upon their organismic responses is mind-boggling considering the present orientation. A caring cultural climate would place its emphasis on growth and exploration rather than on the cataloguing, describing and treatment of symptoms and the establishment of misleading, destructive norms.

11. Filters That Distort His Communication and the Impossible Binds He Puts Her In

It is a relatively simple thing for a man to be non-possessive, non-sexist, non-judgmental and liberal when he doesn't care, when he hasn't hooked into the woman on a deeper emotional level—the hungry, lonely, love-craving part. However, something entirely different seems to emerge when he believes he's found the "only person on earth for me," the special partner he fantasizes will put his whole life in balance and will offset the struggle, the pain and the depressing aspects of his day-to-day survival rituals. That "something entirely different" that comes out often means that he regresses and does many of the posturing, manipulative, corny things he may have always despised when he's seen them played out in other people when they thought they were "in love." It all seemed so transparent then.

For many men this regression might simply involve washing the car before he picks her up on a date in order to impress her; spending half a week debating the pros and cons of various restaurants he might take her to; worrying about the clothes he'll wear, the color combination and even his hairstyle; thinking of ways to make more money so that he can buy her the things he thinks will "make her happy," so that she'll "love him" more; becoming suspicious even of his long-standing, close male friends who he believes might come on to her and try to take her away if he's not vigilant; watching her all the time and even wanting to "protect her" if another man looks at her in the wrong way or makes an offensive remark, or uses "dirty" language in front of her. With other women words such as "cunt" and "cock" come out casually and unselfconsciously. Around her he says "vagina" and "penis" or

119

maybe even "down there." Even with these cleaned-up words, he feels a little "dirty" using them around her.

When he's feeling insecure about her, which is most of the time, he uses manipulative strategies, such as being deliberate about when he telephones, calculating how many times she's called him since he last called her. He goes to concerts and museums he has little or no interest in because he thinks it impresses her, and he even wears a suit and tie on occasion, which he otherwise would never do except for work and ceremonial situations when he absolutely has to.

It is amazing how even the more avant-garde life-stylist seems to regress and transform from an enlightened, "you do your own thing—I'll do mine," "let's give each other lots of space," "no laying of trips on each other" into a clinging, jealous, mendacious, moralistic, irrational person who embodies all the regressive, conservative characteristics that he previously rejected as being stifling, destructive and archaic when he becomes emotionally involved, *particularly when he has attibuted to the woman all of the properties of specialness and of being the important person in his life.*

Often he even recognizes the regression in himself, hates himself for it and struggles to overcome it. He tells himself, "I don't own her. She can talk to, sleep with or go where she pleases." But the urgency and anxiety and possessiveness are still there, along with the discomfort and guilt for being that way and the great effort to deny, control and suppress these feelings. In the process, he drives himself crazy trying to put it all into balance, to see clearly, to make sense of the communication and to get a handle on the contradictions, conflicts, extremes and impossible binds that are generated.

The usually complex process of male-female communication is made even more complicated in today's age of liberation, of changing consciousness, role transitions and growth, particularly where breakthroughs in intellectual awareness have not been emotionally assimilated and integrated. This liberated orientation, then, all too often only adds one more warring level of contradiction, confusion and inconsistency to the already manifold levels of man-woman communication.

Traditionally, there are at least four levels of experience and communication, two of which are largely unconscious, one of which is partly conscious and one which is conscious and operates when a man becomes emotionally involved with a woman; when his usual defensive, distancing barriers and protection have been broken through and he feels magnetized and fixated by her and desires to have her as a soul mate, *the* woman to be close and intimate with and committed to.

1) THE FANTASY LEVEL

Most, if not all, men, before they get attached to "their" woman, have a fantasy of what that woman should be like. The most common stereotype includes her being very "feminine," meaning she should be "soft," tender, gentle, selfless, loyal, sexy, sensual (but only to *him*), uncompetitive, charming, beautiful, adoring, fragile, nurturing, sensitive and giving.

For the "hipper," contemporary man who sees himself as having transcended gender-role stereotypes, the "ideal" woman fantasy he looks for is even more complex. Unbeknownst to him, he may actually be searching for psychologically impossible combinations in one woman and may become very frustrated and despairing looking for her.

I asked a group of sophisticated single men, many of whom had been looking for the "right" woman for a long time or who had periodically thought they'd found her only to have become disappointed and disillusioned as the realities emerged and the relationship crumbled, to write out a description of their "ideal" woman, the woman they would be willing to "give up" their freedom for if they found her. The most striking thing about most of these descriptions was their unreal and contradictory quality. One man in his mid-thirties wrote a description which classically embodied this "impossible dream" quality of many of the men's fantasies.

She should be autonomous in such a way that she won't be the dependent, clinging type who is an emotional drain. Of course, she shouldn't be so autonomous or independent that she wouldn't need me or could do without me, because then I'd feel too insecure.

She should be in touch and comfortable with her sexuality so that she is sensually expressive and free and comfortable with experimenting and exploring so that we can have fun acting out our fantasies. That doesn't mean I want her to be an animal, some insatiable nymph, one of those demanding "give me my orgasm" liberated type women or even one who gets easily turned on to other men and might screw around on me.

I guess I wouldn't mind if she got turned on to other men, so long as she told me about it in a nonthreatening way and didn't act on it unless we had discussed it first. Even then, I would hope that if we agreed it would be all right that she still wouldn't ever feel the need to actually go to bed with another man, because our sex life would be satisfying enough.

If I desired other women, I'd want her to be the kind of woman I could tell that to and she'd accept that in me without feeling threatened or without needing to retaliate. If I had a transient affair or a one-night stand, I'd hope she'd understand that it had nothing to do with her and that it did not reflect on our relationship or my love for her.

I want her to be a woman of strength, able to deal with the real world, successful at getting what she wants, but without being a competitive, driven type or a "ball breaker," the way some women are getting to be. She'd be able to get what she needed and wanted using the velvet touch and the strength of her talents and abilities. And no matter how successful she'd become, I'd want her to retain that softness, vulnerability and emotional quality.

If her ambitions jeopardized our relationship—I mean if it required her to be away a lot—my ideal woman would put our love and our relationship first. I'm being honest about it even though it comes out sounding like a double standard, but I'd want her to be old-fashioned enough to be loyal, devoted and selfless to the point that our relationship came first.

In the same vein, she'd be compassionate, warm, sympathetic and supportive, but not in a mothering, smothering way. She would just have a deep, natural capacity to care.

In terms of her interests, I'd want her to be an outdoor type person, able to rough it, to participate in athletic things. She'd be a woman who was not spoiled, hooked on luxury, comfort and the good life, who could withstand some physical strain and even some deprivation, a "man's woman," so to speak, but definitely not a masculine woman.

It sounds like I want everything, but why shouldn't I hold out for the best in a lifetime partner—a woman who's soft and strong, sexy but still faithful, competent and successful at what she does but not competitive, needing me but not overly dependent, nurturing and compassionate but not smothering or even mothering—a complete person, and if I find her I'll *never* let her go.

Much like the woman looking for the impossible "dream man"—one who is ambitious, successful, dominant, powerful, brilliant, while also sensitive, artistic, sensual, domestic, emotional, gentle, faithful, who loves children and is understanding, patient and warm—the man in search of his "ideal woman," like the man who wrote the above description, is leading from his head and imagining a composite woman who is actually full of psychological contradictions and probably could not authentically exist. He may on occasion believe that he has found "the only one" when, in the throes of an adrenaline high of romantic energy, both he and she become for each other what the other wants, acting out the ideal part. This posture, however, will be impossible to maintain, and disillusionment and disappointment will inevitably replace the euphoria of the temporarily fulfilled fantasy.

2) THE PROJECTION LEVEL

Perhaps the most elusive and difficult aspect of intimate male-female relationships, when the emotional investment is high, is to be able to see the other person as he or she *is*, rather than as one would like him or her to be. For example, it is a fairly common phenomenon that the last one to know that a spouse is having an affair is the other spouse, and the last one to fully recognize that a child is mentally retarded or drug addicted is the parent. Denial of what one doesn't want to see is very common when one is emotionally involved. Consequently, the last one to see one's lover as he or she really is is the person who is "in love" with the other and whose vision is blurred by the power of his need and hunger. Anything that threatens the required perception will be blocked out.

In fact, the process of becoming attached romantically, and that high and magical euphoria which accompanies it, seem to involve a temporary unconscious suspension of aggression, meaning an inability to see the negative, the flaws, the bad habits, the distasteful characteristics, or to acknowledge boredom, anger and resistance when they come up and to maintain honest personal boundaries and limits. Instead, there is a strong propensity to fuse identities, to be increasingly unable to identify autonomous desire ("I want" as opposed to "we want") and to constantly rationalize incongruities and negative awarenesses in order to preserve the romantic projection.

This process of romantic projection (seeing in the other person what doesn't exist) and denial of reality often results in the positive interpretation of a behavior or characteristic at the beginning of the relationship that is viewed with repulsion or anger toward the end. For example, what is seen as fetching naïveté and charming innocence at the beginning may be seen as narrowness, ignorance and a boring provinciality at the end. Similarly, a bold, brash manner that is romantically perceived as daring and healthy assertiveness initially is transformed by the absence of the romantic vision into abrasive pushiness, insensitivity and egotistical self-obsession. Emotionality and carelessness about detail may be seen as "femininity," vulnerability and fragility at the start only to become irrational hysteria and irresponsibility at the end. Likewise, a woman's willingness to have sex soon after first meeting may be interpreted as her spontaneity, powerful attraction and freedom at the beginning, while in a turned-off frame of mind it may be seen as shallowness, cheapness, "something she does with everybody" or a reflection of her inability to say no. Smells, voice inflections, movements, idiosyncrasies that were found to be endearingly human at the beginning may also become unattractive and even repellent by the end.

Therefore, projection and the tendency to deny and distort perceptions in order to make them congruent with one's required romantic fantasy add a second level of potential distortion or unreality to the intimate male-female communication process.

3) THE REPRESSED, REJECTED AND UNEXPERIENCED CORE LEVEL

Involved in the conditioning process of becoming a "man" and behaving in an acceptable masculine way is the repression of important core psychological aspects of the male, which are therefore not experienced consciously. This core is encapsulated and denied, though it continues to operate in indirect, sublimated or covert ways, and searches for safe outlets for expression and satisfaction.

This repressed core is composed of the man's "forbidden" parts; his dependency craving, his vulnerability, fear and other emotions, his desire to let go and be taken care of and anything else inside him that might be equated with femininity or unmasculine behavior. The more powerful and threatening this core is, the more rigid the defenses against it will be and the more he will need constantly to prove his autonomy, ability to perform, rationality, unemotionality, lack of dependency hunger and other human needs.

When he gets romantically involved, much of this

repressed core may be unconsciously manifested in hidden and deliberately denied ways. That means he may become possessive, jealous, clinging, demanding of attention, dependent and emotionally volatile, all the while denying that it's happening.

In the instance of one couple whom I counsel in therapy, the man played the macho who repeatedly protested his need for freedom and independence. When she, in response to his protests against *her* dependency, encouraged him to take a vacation, weekend trips or even evenings out by himself, he refused. He told her that he knew that she didn't *really* mean it, and that he also *knew* that she wouldn't be able to handle it if he went off without her. When she insisted that her motives were selfish and that she really wanted also to go off by herself, he became visibly upset. It was clear that it was *his* dependency on *her* that he was protesting and denying, and that in reality she would have been more than happy to have time to go off by herself.

This denied, consciously unexperienced core plays a large role in the communication distortions, ambivalences, conflicting expectations and impossible binds he will create for her in the course of the relationship. The struggle is between the underlying needs hungering for expression in the face of a psychological defensive system that works constantly to deny expression to the core and, for the sake of his masculine image, to prove that the core doesn't exist.

4) THE MASCULINE SELF-IMAGE LEVEL

This level represents the conscious self-image, or the way he needs to see himself. When he behaves in a way that is contrary to it, he will rationalize or even deny that he's doing it. For example, he needs to see himself as independent, patient and in control of his emotions. When he is confronted, after an outburst over a meal served late, for example, with the fact that he is behaving like an irritable, demanding child, he will deny this with vigor. He might even scream out in fury, "I'M NOT ANGRY!!"

The culturally dictated role image calls for him to be rational, self-contained, controlled, independent, strong, fearless, productive and dominant. This, then, is the way he needs to see himself and wants others to see him also.

Because we live in a "polite," "nice" society, which means that honest encountering and confrontations seldom, if ever, take place between people, most individuals can continue to see themselves as they believe themselves to be even though others don't see them that way. Or they may actually succeed in projecting the image they wish to. Still, the masculine self-image is just another defensive layer filtering his communication in order that he can affirm his image. It continually grates against the repressed core.

5) THE "LIBERATED" LEVEL

For some men who are working to free themselves from sexist behaviors and orientations, another level may be added to the already highly complex, often "crazy-making" business of man-woman communications. I call this level the *denial of the role-image level*, or the "liberated" level, because, for the man who is idealistically aspiring to liberate himself, there may very well be a rigid and defensive denial of the "typical masculine orientation" within him. In other words, his is a psychologically defensive liberalism that can be recognized as such because of its rigidity, its "protesteth too much" flavor and extreme hostility toward those men who behave in any other way. These men acknowledge the validity of the accusations and victim-philosophy of militant feminism, and proceed to echo these man-hating strains themselves in the name of "male liberation." It is not an authentically humanistic, flowing, freeing up of role behavior, but rather a militant, rigid, holier-than-thou attitude, and it is noted that these men tend to relate primarily on a cerebral and ideological level to each other rather than on a playful, spontaneous, warm, and accepting one that they claim to espouse.

Their defensive sermonizing was the attitude that caused a female writer, Karen Durbin, to write, in an article for a national women's magazine entitled "How to Spot a Liberated Man":

> A woman I know . . . startled me the other day by suggesting that she found it less irritating to be with a male chauvinist than with many of the supposedly liberated men she meets. "I find these self-consciously liberated men slippery," she said, "and I don't like slippery people. Conversations with them always seem to end up with them telling me how to liberate myself. The hell with that. Maybe I'm feeling the way some black people did in the mid-sixties toward white liberals—'No thanks, I'd rather do it myself.' "[11]

What these women who find themselves more comfortable with the traditional "chauvinistic" male (whom they find philosophically abhorrent) than with the "liberated" man may be reacting to is that the latter may very well be engaged in psychologically defensive behavior that is emotionally unauthentic and therefore unpleasant to be around. The behavior is brittle, rigid, predictable, boring, bloated with pretension and "born-again" religiosity rather than pleasurable, spontaneous humanness.

In this sense, the defensively "liberated" man communicates through five filters or levels rather than four. Although this filter is a relatively new defense of the kind a religious convert might communicate through, it is as powerful as the masculine self-image level, because this type of man sees himself as a rescuer, a savior of the downtrodden female and the righteous opponent of society's male chauvinist pigs.

All of these levels which filter a man's communications tend to cause him to send out contradictory and confusing messages and also to create impossible binds in the form of either-way-you-lose demands. In the following pages I describe the classic binds which manifest the conflict between the way he needs to see himself and the periodic eruption of repressed needs and feelings.

THE ASSERTION-SUBMISSION BIND

If she's direct in defining her needs, her likes and dislikes and her limits, he sees her as demanding, pushy, shrewish and possibly even castrating.

If she's reluctant to define her needs and to express her likes and dislikes and tries to avoid conflict by giving in, he sees her as being passive and unexciting and tells her that they will get along much better if she would only tell him how she *really* feels, what she *really* wants and what she *really* likes and dislikes.

Either way she loses. If she's assertive, she's a demanding shrew. If she's submissive and conflict-avoiding, she's a passive bore.

THE INTRUSION-NEGLECT BIND

If she shows considerable interest in what he does, who he's with and where he's going—wanting to join him in his activities, to help with his work and so on—he perceives her as intrusive, suffocating and distrustful.

If she leaves him alone, steers clear of his activities, never questions him about who he's with, where he's been or what he's doing, he feels neglected and tells himself she doesn't really care about him, his work or his feelings about his life.

Either way she loses. If she tries to be an integral part of his activities, he feels intruded upon. If she keeps her distance, he feels neglected.

THE CAREER-HOMEMAKER BIND

If she has a career or job that she finds satisfying and pleasurable and is therefore emotionally involved with, he views it as competition for her energies and concerns, feels neglected, and may accuse her of being selfish, uncaring, rejecting and unfeminine.

If she commits herself and her primary energies to homemaking, he sees her as a drudge, a compulsive cleaner, a dull companion and a guilt-maker because she's always at home waiting for him and "makes him" feel self-conscious and guilty for being late and for not paying enough attention to her. He then accuses her of insulating herself from the "real world," of not developing herself, and encourages her to get involved in outside activities.

Either way she loses. If her primary energies go into her career, he sees her as neglectful, uncaring, rejecting and says she loves him less than her outside endeavors. If she devotes herself to homemaking, he resents having to shoulder all of the financial burdens and complains that she is a compulsive, nagging, demanding, boring drudge who's always making him feel guilty.

THE MOTHERING BIND

A variation of the "career-homemaker bind" occurs once the woman has children. If she makes the mothering role her primary one, she may become increasingly desexed in his eyes as he relates to her increasingly as a mothering figure and his sexual passions go into his fantasies, or perhaps even outside flings and lovers. Furthermore, the consuming nature of the maternal role cuts her off to a great extent from outside input, and in his eyes she becomes less interesting and stimulating to be with.

On the other hand, if she involves herself in a career that takes up a significant amount of time, she may be made to feel guilty for being a rejecting, neglectful mother.

Either way she loses. If her focus is on mothering, she becomes a less interesting, less sexually attractive partner. If she pursues her career interests after she has children, she is blamed for being an unconcerned, rejecting and uncaring mother.

THE SEXUALLY ACTIVE–
SEXUALLY PASSIVE BIND

He complains if she responds in a sexually passive-receptive-submissive way and chides her for lacking passion, being uninteresting in bed, and tells her that she is not really excited by him or that she is frigid for not participating more. He encourages her to liberate herself sexually and to become more exploratory and experimental.

If, however, she's sexually active, comfortable in initiating sex, expressing her needs and turn-ons, assuming a dominant as well as passive posture and, in general, being sexually assertive, he may read that as a demand and be intimidated and repelled by what he perceives to be her insatiable appetite and her "masculine" and aggressive ways. If she is assertive to the point that she complains about his need to control and his insensitivity to her, he may even accuse her of being castrating.

Either way she loses. If she is sexually hesitant, he reacts negatively to her conservative, puritanical attitude. If she is sexually direct, he feels pressured and defensive about her "demanding," unsatisfied and complaining attitude.

THE AUTONOMY-DEPENDENCY BIND

In everyday language this bind may be expressed as the "set me free—don't leave me" conflict. If she encourages him to have an autonomous life outside of the relationship, his own friends, occasional evenings, weekends and vacations alone, and if she also indicates her desire for the same, he becomes insecure, suspicious that she doesn't really care for him, does not really want to be with him, is preparing to leave him or is involved with somebody else.

If she builds her life around his, wants to be with him evenings, weekends, and holidays, refrains from developing a separate set of friends and desires an exclusive sexual relationship, he complains that she is possessive and dependent and that he feels smothered and engulfed.

Either way she loses. Supportive of maintaining their own identities and separate interests, she gets an insecure, suspicious and resentful reaction from him. If she wants them to share friends, activities and free time as a couple, he sees her as dependent, engulfing and possessive.

THE "YOU'RE LETTING YOURSELF GO"— VANITY BIND

If she downplays concern for her physical appearance, mutes her sexual attractiveness, spends minimal time and money on "vanity" aspects, he resents her for letting herself go, tells her that she's not as attractive as she used to be and wonders if this means that she's losing interest in being attractive to him or in how he sees and reacts to her.

If, however, she *is* attentive to her appearance and spends time attending to grooming, clothing, hairstyle, cosmetics, dieting, beauty sleep and so on, he reacts negatively to her emphasis on the superficial, her self-preoccupation and her "narcissism." In his darker moments he may even wonder why she's so concerned about the way she looks. Is she trying to make herself attractive to other men?

Either way she loses. If she is casual about her physical appearance, he accuses her of "letting herself go." If she is attentive to it, he interprets this as her superficiality and vanity or her interest in attracting other men.

THE "TELL ME HOW YOU REALLY FEEL"— "YOU'RE REALLY HOSTILE" BIND

In intimate relationships with men, women have been taught to avoid fighting, conflict or saying things that would hurt the male ego. He complains, therefore, that she won't fight, won't tell him what she's thinking or how she really feels, and that he never knows what's bothering her or what's going on inside of her. He encourages her to level with him.

If, however, she is out front with her reactions, shares her negative feelings, expresses her anger openly and refuses to falsify her responses in order to pamper him, he complains that she is hostile, undermining, rejecting, unsupportive, "unfeminine" and "a bitch."

This bind was clearly evidenced in a man of thirty-three who came for marriage counseling with his thirty-one-year-old wife of nine years. At the beginning of counseling he complained that she was too passive, did not stand up for what she really believed and that as a result he found her boring. After seveal months of counseling she became significantly more assertive, and as her long repressed anger began to emerge, he told her, "Now that you're feeling more secure, you jump on me all the time!"

Either way she loses. If she resists sharing negative feelings or expressing anger, he complains that they can never resolve any issues and that he doesn't really ever know where he stands because she won't tell him what she feels. If she is open in expressing the full range of her feelings and reactions, he becomes defensive, resents her "bitchiness" and accuses her of not really caring for him and putting him down.

THE "WAIT ON ME"–"DON'T FUSS OVER ME" BIND

If she is very attentive to him, anticipates his needs, looks after him and is doting and concerned in her manner, he complains that he is being "mothered" to death. He tells her she is being overprotective, and that he needs more "space."

If she treats him like an adult who must assert his needs, ask for whatever he wants, take care of himself, and if she keeps a comfortable distance and relates to him on an adult-adult, friend-friend level rather than mothering him, he sees her as thoughtless, unnurturing, unloving and insensitive.

Either way she loses. If her attitude is nurturing, he

feels he is being treated like a little boy. If she relates to him on an adult-adult level, he feels unattended to and unloved.

WALKING THE TIGHTROPE OF MAN-WOMAN INTIMATE COMMUNICATION

The man-woman communication process is fraught with "damned-if-you-do, damned-if-you-don't" binds, hazards, impasses and breakdowns whose roots are the following:

1) The traditional romantic approach to courtship, which is usually the original basis for permanent relationships. This means that initially, in the getting-together process, aggression and negative feelings are repressed and denied. In the urgency to be "nice," conflict is skirted, and an artificial emphasis is placed on "fairness" and "equality," which later erodes into undealt-with dominance-submission issues, denied turn-offs and fundamental man-woman rage. That is, in the early romantic phase the other person is magically transformed into a unique being who is of a different mold from the rest of that gender, and consequently the usual resistances, resentments and distrustful feelings that are initially inherent in intimate heterosexual interactions, because of the woman's learned anticipation that she will be exploited and dominated and the man's fear that he will be manipulated, trapped, engulfed and smothered, are repressed and denied in the desire to "make it work."

It is a relationship whose foundation to a significant degree is in mutual fantasy and image creation rather than in the reality of two people rooted in the same culture and with similarly learned value systems of everybody else. The aggression that is temporarily suspended, the assertiveness that is muted or denied, seep through continuously in elusive, indirect ways and generate the push-pull, "come here—go away," "I love you—I hate you" reactions which are the basis for the impossible binds.

As a rule, the more "romantic" the initial courtship mood, the more "perfect" the other person seems to be and the more "uncanny" the apparent mutuality, the greater the potential for crazy-making, double-bind communications, as the torrent of repressed aggression, assertiveness, turn-offs, denial of needs for dominance, power and control subsequently and in myriad indirect ways continuously contaminates the "loving" communication.

The sense of being off balance, the insecurity, the vague feeling of unreality, the pendulum swings between euphoria and despair, the sudden silences, the walking-on-eggs sensation, the constant reassuring and need for reassurance that the other one "really" loves you, the sudden unpredictable eruptions of rage, the tendency to premeditate and calculate ("Shall I call her again? I've called her three times in a row and she hasn't called me") and the fear of saying the wrong thing—all of which may characterize romantic interactions—are overt manifestations and outgrowths of this repressed aggression.

2) There is a basic masculine ambivalence about committed, monogamous relationships for the reasons previously explored in the chapter "Sex Distortions, Misinterpretations, Myths and Stereotypes About Men" (page 117).

This ambivalence toward commitment produces a tendency toward extremes in his reactions from day to day, going from euphoria and sentimentality to despair and rage as different responses are triggered. Consequently, he may be cursing one day the very thing he applauded the day before.

3) Few men and women have gone through the kind of individual development that has truly freed them to be self-aware, emotionally responsible people who are able to perceive themselves as the psychological captains of their ships and to a great extent create that which happens to them. Particularly in an intimate heterosexual relationship, there is a tendency to finger-point, to blame and to portray oneself as a disillusioned, betrayed and abused victim. Few relationships have the kind of foundation required for a comfortably transparent, self-caring attitude, personhood rather than gender-limited behavior and capacity for sensuality, which are required to keep a relationship playful, pleasurable, alive and in a state of growth.

Instead, the bottom-line security needs are the ones usually met, while the needs for growth and exploration are stifled and buried. An underlying cause, then, of impossible binds is the war between these security needs—to belong, to be loved and to "have someone"—and the frustrated growth needs, which are made up of a hunger to explore, to experience new relationships and to follow one's own rhythm and instincts without needing to get permission from the other. I believe these frustrated growth needs are in part responsible for the periodic flare-ups of rage which seem unconsciously designed to push the other person away, to create more space, to provide a justifiable rationalization ("It's your fault") for the desire to become autonomous for a period of time *without* permission.

Finally, in an age of liberation, predictable, rigid, prescribed role behaviors and reactions will be shaken loose and underlying emotions and responses will pour through. In men, the sameness in response and the narrow limits of emotionality and reaction are the result of role straitjackets which create "supposed to" and "should" orientations motivated by conformist impulses to act out appropriately the role of being a man. When people start to grow, to get in touch with feelings and to have the strength to reject archaic role harnesses, they inevitably experience the turbulence and ambivalence of free-traveling emotions and reactions. Their responses are now emerging organically, flexibly and fluidly from circumstances and experiences, rather than from role prescription.

Whenever role behavior and conformist pressure to live up to external images are in a process of release and reexamination, the people involved become pioneers in the uncharted territory of internal experience. They are becoming people first and roles second, which is a radical departure from the traditional emphasis on roles first and foremost and "damn the person inside the skin." While this transition to inner-directed response tends to be a frightening, upsetting and threatening process, it may also be the only legitimate soil for growth and development.

In summary, in an era of change for the alive, fluid person, there is a tripartite struggle between:

1) *Role-prescribed behavior*—the way a person is taught he "should" be;

2) *Individuality*—the pull of individual need and emotion, which is different from person to person;

3) *Visions of potential*—notions, fantasies or models of what might or could be.

An exclusive emphasis on any single one of these three is unbalanced and stifling. The role-bound person is rigid, predictable and boring. The totally inner-directed person becomes an offensive narcissist, and the one whose functioning is shaped entirely by visions of what might be lives in a dream-world that will isolate him from others.

The ultimate and ideal heterosexual relationship, freest of loaded messages, communications and impossible binds, is one in which both the man and the woman are fluid in behavior and are thus able to float between role-prescribed behaviors, inner motivations and visions of the possible in a conscious way that allows them to share their experience and work through those aspects and moments which create turbulence in a relationship.

DEALING WITH IMPOSSIBLE BINDS

As long as impossible binds and crazy-making communication are a built-in reality of male-female relationships, the inability to recognize and deal with them will result in intensification of self-hate, the perception of oneself as a victim and endless varieties of emotional problems, anxieties, frustration and despair over not being able to make a relationship fulfill its romantic promise and work the way one has been told it's supposed to work.

Surviving these communication hazards, therefore, requires:

1) Recognition of their omnipresent potential existence;

2) An awareness of the layers and levels in oneself that produce them;

3) An acceptance of their inevitability and a commitment to working them through when they arise, rather than fleeing toward a new utopia;

4) A constant emphasis on self-development and self-

awareness, because without such individual development
relationships tend to become rigid and destructive.

The culture seems to encourage young, romantic,
growth-stifling relationships and does not have the perspective required to teach younger people to avoid the traps.
To an extent, of course, older generations are threatened
by younger generations that seem freer and more sensual
and who reject the traditional role harnesses. Obviously,
the early acquisition of heavy burdens of responsibility,
such as children, mortgages, insurance and so on, creates a
cage which makes growth, exploration and risk taking extremely difficult, if not impossible.

The impact of impossible binds can be softened and
dealt with in a nondestructive way if the relationship is
composed of partners who:

1) Are committed to their own growth and willing and
able to experience the anxieties and assume the risks inherent in the process;

2) Genuinely and realistically know, like and enjoy
each other and have the trust capacity to encourage a mutual journey that is satisfying rather than self-denying.

Traditional relationships are often maintained by sacrifice, self-denial and selflessness, endurance and learning to
put up with deprivation and hardship. This interpersonal
masochism has been glorified by labeling it "maturity."
However, too often "maturity" becomes little more than a
mutual blocking of growth, expressiveness, transparency
and joy.

In a psychologically enlightened world, relationships will
be considered mature and constructive only as long as they
create an optimum environment for growth, physical and
psychological health, fluidity, openness and the kind of
mutual enhancement that brings the people involved to a
new and better place in the path of their development.
Once a relationship becomes predictable, rigid and constricting, it becomes a psychological tomb and perhaps
ought best to be abandoned.

In the context of a living, fluid relationship, "impossible
binds" will be part of the soil for self-awareness and
creative change. In the context of a rigid, predictable relationship, they are only another toxic and destructive element.

PART THREE

———————◆———————

HE
AND HER
CHANGES

12. Who Is the Victim?
Who Is the Oppressor?

In fact, most of the male characters come off poorly
in *The Thorn Birds*. A fairly typical sentence runs:
"She eyed his flaccid penis, snorting with laughter."
The ambitious men are silly and the steady ones are
inconsequential. Meggie's eight brothers die or disap-
pear into the woodwork. Women seem to live forever,
while every hundred pages or so another man is
burned alive or disemboweled by a wild boar or
drowned or unsexed by gunshot wounds. None of this
carnage is required by the plot. The males are punished because their punishment is what romantic fiction requires.[1]

—From a review of
The Thorn Birds, by
Colleen McCullough
(major best seller of 1977–78)

Much of the energy of the feminist movement is derived
from rage over being a victim. The male-female dynamic
is portrayed in the following way: He is the oppressor,
victimizer, abuser, user, exploiter, chauvinist, sexist pig.
She is the oppressed, victimized, abused, used, exploited,
maligned, passive, blameless, helpless victim.

A major article published in the early days of the
women's movement in one of America's largest and most
widely read magazines illustrates this well. Various activist
women articulated their perceptions of the male-female
relationship. Martha Shelly, a poet, expressed a common
attitude. She said, "The average man, including the average student male radical, wants a passive sex object—
cum–domestic–cum–baby nurse to clean up after him
while he does all the fun things and bosses her around—

while he plays either big-shot male executive or Che Guevara—*and he is my oppressor and my enemy.*"*[2] Radical activist Dana Densmore said, "No more us taking all the blame. No more us trying to imitate men and prove we are just as good. Frontal attack. It's all over now."[3]

There are other examples. Feminist Phyllis Chesler wrote a classic "victim" piece entitled "Men Drive Women Crazy." In it she attempted literally to prove just that.[4] And Kate Millett promulgated the idea that women were helpless because men controlled the basic mechanisms of society.[5]

A recent best-selling novel, *The Women's Room*, is written from a woman's perspective. The author, Marilyn French, has her heroine express an attitude frequently articulated by contemporary married women who are angry about their role. "She felt bought and paid for and it was all of a piece; the house, the furniture, she, all were his, it said so on some piece of paper."[6] In a recent interview, Marilyn French said, "All men are rapists and that's all they are."[7]

I personally noted an example of the extent to which such accusations can go during a panel discussion at the University of California, Los Angeles. The subject was human liberation. The speaker on behalf of women's liberation was an officer of the National Organization for Women (NOW). Part of her support for her contention that men exploited women was that women had traditionally been forced into having babies to satisfy the man's ego.

I was amazed to hear that. I thought of the beliefs most men, including myself, were brought up with: Women wanted to have children. Motherhood was their special form of fulfillment, just as jobs and careers were for men. It would be selfish, hostile and unmanly not to support a woman's desire for motherhood.

I thought of the many reluctant fathers whose wives had informed them they would leave them if they refused to father children. I also thought of many very young men, adolescent or barely older, whose personal growth was thwarted or retarded because of an unwanted, unexpected

* Italics not in original.

pregnancy. The woman concerned either refused to have an abortion or simply sentimentally expressed her desire to be a mother. The man got the message! It was his responsibility. He could not refuse to marry her and assume the appropriate, responsible roles of father and provider. Then there were the countless other men who fathered at an early age because they were busy building careers. They felt it was only fair to facilitate their wives' fulfillment by fathering a baby. Only a selfish man would deny her this, they had learned.

The notion of woman as victim is displayed in its extreme form in the catch phrase "Woman as Nigger." When one considers that blacks have lived through generations of rejection, hostility and humiliation, this comparison is ludicrous. Women have more often than not been placed on a pedestal and glorified for their birth-giving powers. These accorded them their special status: "ladies first." While it has become fashionable to reinterpret this phrase as a hidden, indirect put-down, its original, conscious meaning reflected men's belief in women's vulnerability and specialness. The history of the civilized world is replete with occurrences of men giving up careers, fortunes and kingdoms for the love of a woman, of men battling other men, often to the death, because of an insult to a woman's honor or because of competition for her love. Then they spent years afterward proving themselves worthy of her.

At its best, therefore, this depiction of the oppression and victimization of the woman by the malevolently motivated man is unbalanced, unfair and psychologically invalid. At its worst, it is harmful and destructive to the real potential in the man-woman relationship. It puts her self-righteously on the offensive. She walks her new road looking for implied put-downs and inequities, without a balancing emphasis on *her* contribution to the creation and perpetuation of these destructive gender games and on her responsibility in transforming them constructively. Any changes that result from such guilt-inducing accusations will only generate a kind of righteous hypocrisy.

As in the case of condemnation and guilt-making by religionists, the result is often repression and the hiding of the real self rather than genuine, meaningful growth. The man who buys this portrayal of himself as oppressor will thus be manipulated into repeatedly needing to prove he is not what she says he is.

In this regard men have been the victims of their own tendency to misperceive the woman and to dress her up in their fantasies. If indeed he kept her "powerless," it is most probably because he believed the often dirty, deceitful and difficult work of the outside world was beneath her and that only an inadequate man, willing to submit himself to hostile innuendo and direct put-downs from other men, would subject "his" woman to it unnecessarily. He has perceived her as fragile, easily hurt, possibly even destroyed by stress and insensitivity. Therefore it was his role to protect her. She was the keeper of the sanctuary, creator of their oasis—his place of retreat, pleasure and satisfaction away from the cold, harsh jungle. She was also the giver of life, and it was his role, the test of his manliness, to make and protect the best possible nest. Undoubtedly there were selfish reasons as well: She may have been his sole outlet for sexual satisfaction in a time when sex was not readily available, and he may have had concerns and anxieties about her being exposed to other men who might seduce her.

Until very recently, most men have responded to feminist accusations of chauvinism and oppression by passive or sometimes even direct and guilty agreement. Men so readily absorb guilt and responsibility because they are deeply woven into the fabric of the traditional man-woman relationship. He has learned that she is sensitive, giving, warm and loving ("sugar 'n spice 'n everything nice"). He is cold, selfish and a potentially brutish animal ("frogs 'n snails 'n puppy dog tails"). This perception emerges directly from the traditional *actor-reactor* interaction already described: The woman's role was a passive-submissive and therefore a non-responsible one, while the man initiated, structured and decided. Also, because he sees her as the physically weaker sex and as a woman like his mother, he views it as unchivalrous, unmanly behavior to place responsibility on her or to defend himself against her assertions and accusations with any kind of vigor. This would cut directly across his conditioned orientation. He validates his masculinity by protecting her. Consequently, even today, as she changes and emerges as a strong, autonomous person in her own right, he has difficulty perceiving this as real and responding appropriately. He is frozen in his protective pose, not out of a demeaning, oppressive motivation, but rather out of a tendency to see her according to his fantasies and needs.

The finger-pointing attitude, the accusations of oppressor-sexist-chauvinist, the blaming and victim posture used by some women deny their emergence as equally responsible people. It is the strategy of a child or a neurotic, manipulative irresponsible adult to attribute to others the failures and problems of life rather than to focus on one's own part in the creation of these problems.

As a therapist who often works with couples in marital distress, I have found that the least optimistic prognosis for significant, positive change is when one or both partners assumes a blaming attitude, while portraying himself or herself as an unfortunate, well-meaning and faultless victim. The point is that the assertion that men exploit women is as valid as the generalization that women manipulate men for marriage, security and money. For every chauvinist who "uses" women, there is a woman who uses wiles, coyness, helplessness and other "feminine" manipulations to gain her end and to goad him into proving himself the big man, the succeeder, the dominant, fearless, powerful protector. For every woman who is frigid because her man is insensitive and abrupt, there is a man who is abrupt and insensitive because his woman is frigid. For every woman who complains of being confined to kitchen and house, there is a man who is driven to exasperation by his wife's compulsive, annoying obsession with cleanliness and orderliness around the house. And for every man who patronizes prostitutes for the reason expressed by Jackie MacMillan of the *Feminist Alliance Against Rape* in Washington, D.C., which is that the "Johns" get their kicks from the feeling of power that comes from buying a woman and that the sex is often secondary,[8] there is the equivalent evaluation such as the one by a woman who was interviewed for a book on "Sex Objects" and who works in a massage parlor and takes "care of" men sexually. She said, "A man lying flat on his back, naked, on the verge of orgasm, looks ridiculously vulnerable and powerless; the masseuse has complete control. I think the women really get off on seeing men in that position." [9]

The following are examples of typical male life experiences. Who is in fact the victim here?

First, marriage. A man who wrote about a marriage that couldn't be saved stated:

> I went through the wedding mechanically, devoid of any emotion. I simply figured I was following a road that was meant for me to follow. But I was very conscious of Marie's emotions. She was euphoric, and I was happy to be able to produce that in her. She was very beautiful. Perhaps that gave me the happiness I needed. I thought maybe that was all I really was there for. . . .
>
> Our first baby was born. . . . It was a girl, and Marie was ecstatic. I felt her joy. I really did. It would have been hard not to. But I did not feel my own joy. There was a glow coming out of her, but I had the feeling that it had nothing to do with me, that anyone could have stood in my place. It seems to me that there was a game plan laid out long before I got there and I merely was pushed from spot to spot, like some checker on a board. Yes, I was happy I had a daughter, but I felt more of a numbness. Here I am. What am I doing here? I don't remember how I got into this spot, but I'm here, so I guess this is where I'm supposed to be. [10]

A divorced man talked about his experiences with women:

> Everybody is looking for a winner. They're impressed by position and status even if they're not being treated well. They evaluate a man by such things as his dress and his home.
>
> If you start saying you want freedom and space, they can't handle it. You can just tell that they wouldn't be there if you didn't have money. . . . It's really easy to get laid. Just go to a nice place dressed nice—everyone's looking for a well-off guy.

Regarding his job, he said that he really wanted success, but had found that it was a lot of responsibility and a lonely place to be. He felt that his woman (or any woman) wouldn't love him if he failed.

Society preaches that you must be this or you must be that. Success has nothing to do with human qualities. I found that it was empty. I couldn't feel a damn thing emotionally. I was numb. Everything was in order, but nothing—no tears, no real happiness, no real sadness either. When you can't find anything to be sad about, that's *really* sad! I'm getting so I don't want to do anything. I'm emotionally upset by humanity. Not that I'm an angel, but it's discouraging to see that there's only one place you can go. Everyday I almost feel like vomiting.

I've always had people crash on me, but I've never been able to crash on them. It scares the hell out of me. There's no one who cares enough. The only reason I'm here is to keep the whole damn thing up. I wonder why I can't sink. It's scary.

A Sunday-school teacher describes the way a father reacted to his son on the first day of class:

A father brought his little boy into my room for Sunday school. The boy was quite small, only three years old. He didn't know me and was visibly frightened at the prospect of being left there. He was crying and clinging to his father. Normally I would have taken over in such a situation. I would have had the parent tell the child good-bye. Then I would have held and comforted him and assured him that his parent would return right after church.

This father wasn't about to leave the child in my arms, though. He sat him on the piano stool and began to berate him for his crying. He spent several minutes demanding that the child not cry, that he act like a man. During this time, there was no touching or any type of comfort being given the child. He just sat there crying while the father carried on. Finally, he slowed down his sobbing somewhat and the father then insisted that he shake hands good-bye.

A mother compares the behavior of her son and her daughter and the reactions of onlookers in an emergency-care situation:

My daughter was three years old when she got her foot caught in the spokes of her sister's bicycle. Her foot was torn up and needed stitches. As the doctor was working, my daughter, who had to be held down by both myself and her father, screamed constantly. She was scared and it was painful, and she let us all know very clearly how she felt. She shouted at us very determinedly, "Stop that! You stop that stingy stuff!" And then she would yell that it hurt, over and over again. People in the other end of the clinic heard her and wondered what was wrong with the poor child. During the time the doctor was putting in the stitches, I stood at my daughter's head talking to her, trying to sympathize and reassure her that it would all be over soon. No one attempted to interfere with her reactions or mine.

A few years later my son, who also happened to be three years old, fell and cut his arm on a piece of glass. It was apparent that he needed stitches, so I took him into emergency. I have never told him not to cry when he hurt himself, but he seems to have developed a need for restraint in spite of that. If I'm the only one present, he is fairly free with his emotions. But if others are present, he is not. In the emergency room, to the strangers, he appeared to be a very "brave boy." He was impassive. He held still when they probed for glass. He held still when he was given a shot. He didn't cry out at all. The people in attendance were very complimentary about this.

But I could tell from the expression on his face that he was scared to death and was straining not to cry. I tried to let him know that I knew he was scared and that it was okay, that I would help him. I said something like, "This is really scary, isn't it? Jimmy, it hurts, doesn't it?" Right away I heard the people around me saying things like, "Oh no, he's not afraid. It won't hurt! My, isn't he a nice husky boy?" I didn't argue with them but continued to hold tight to my son's hand and to provide what comfort I could.

We were soon finished and went home. I wanted to share my concern with my husband, that here was our son at such a young age already trying to squelch his feelings and act strong and tough. I began relating the sequence of events, and as I told of Jimmy's refusal to let his feelings show, my husband broke in and said, "Oh, I like that!" I could literally see him puff up to hear that his son had lived up to and had proven his inheritance. It seemed useless for me to go on. I just said, "Well, I don't," and dropped the subject. I knew then that I was kidding myself to think the pressure to deny feelings didn't exist in our family.

As women emulate increasingly the style and orientation of men, they may also expect to experience similar payoffs.

Thirty years ago men were twenty times as likely as women to get ulcers. Today the ratio is two to one.[11]

A recent study on suicide in California revealed that the suicide rate for women rose forty-two percent during the ten-year span from 1960 to 1970, while the male rate rose approximately fifteen percent. Nancy Allen, a suicide prevention expert at UCLA's Neuropsychiatric Institute, who prepared the study, interpreted the findings. "In precisely those arenas where liberated women are making the most progress the male-female suicide ratios move toward equality."[12]

In line with that, a report from the Medical College of Pennsylvania by Robert Steppacher, an assistant professor of psychiatry, and Judith Mausner, associate professor of community and preventative medicine, showed that among women professionals women psychologists commit suicide at a rate nearly three times that of women in the general population. Likewise, the rate for female physicians is three times the rate of women in general.[13] Perhaps these professional women are experiencing the stresses, conflicts and "pay-offs" that many success-oriented men do, namely, isolation and loneliness, emotional overcontrol, and constant conflict between professional ambition, success demands, and the fulfillment of personal needs.

The research firm of Yankelovich, Skelly and White, conducting a survey for the American Cancer Society, found that in 1969 only ten percent of teen-age girl smokers used a pack a day or more. By 1975 the rate had increased to thirty-nine percent. From ages eighteen to thirty-five the percentages of women who smoke more than a pack a day rose from nine to twenty-five percent.[14]

Between 1960 and 1972 the FBI Uniform Crime Reports show that arrests for serious crimes for women increased 256.2% as compared to 81.7% for men. In violent crimes such as murder and aggravated assault it rose 119.7%, and for teen-age girls it increased 388.3% as opposed to 203.2% for guys eighteen years old and under.[15]

The fantasy and hope that women in politics would have a humanizing impact and possibly generate a different perspective and mood is proving false. Instead, their performance is almost identical to the men. Comparing ten women members of the United States House of Representatives during the 91st Congress with thirty males of the same congress, Frieda L. Gehlen, a sociologist at the University of New Mexico, found that:

"Female legislators are no more conservative, independent or ineffective than their male colleagues, but neither is there clear evidence that they are significantly more liberal, dependent or effective. They emphasize the traditional female concern of health, education and welfare only to a small extent. This study lends little support to those who would like to argue that all will be well or ill with the world if women become our key political leaders."[16]

The blaming stance even permits wives to behave violently toward their husbands—to the point of committing homicide and attributing it righteously and exclusively to self-defense. This is a lethal variation on the theme of woman as victim, a rationalization that now more than ever in our culture demands serious and objective scrutiny. In 1976, for example, *for the first time in the history of Chicago, more women than men killed their spouses.*

"With more handguns available today, and women much more independent, it isn't surprising we're seeing more of this," said a police captain.[17]

The portrayal of the man as top-dog exploiter living a privileged existence and the woman as victim is a lopsided, black-and-white interpretation of the age-old gender dance. In its extreme form, it creates a paranoid atmosphere. As a closed system, the "victim's" perception allows for no new or conflicting information to alter his or her perception of the other person. While this orientation may temporarily succeed in intimidating the guilt-ridden other, it also widens the psychological gulf, rigidifies the interaction and creates an increasingly self-conscious, defensive and latently angry mood on the part of the habitually accused.

Women have as much to be legitimately enraged about as men. They have been deprived of their autonomy, their sexuality and their aggression by gender conditioning. But the price they have paid is no greater than for men, who have paid the price of masculinity with their emotions, expressiveness, capacity for intimacy, passivity, dependency, vulnerability and so on. To pull out the threads and determine who has done what to whom is futile, destructive, and probably impossible.

The woman who reacts with rage and fury at men for their alleged abuses reveals her lack of perspective and empathy. She is also not able to see beyond the surface to realize that men have been trapped in a powerful way, and that behind their chauvinism and sexism dwells a self-destructiveness, self-hate, isolation and rigidity. Be he the dominator, the wife abuser, even the rapist, more than anything else his behavior is a testimony to the most profound form of self-contempt and the rigid inability to change his behavior to a more self-caring style.

The woman who plays on the mono-theme of male chauvinism is exploiting a cultural fashion that at present sanctions such a biased perception. It apparently pays benefits with no immediate cost. But a more constructive orientation, presuming goodwill and a mutual desire to work through destructive gender roles, would be for both women and men to focus on the part of each in creating and perpetuating gender games, manipulations, deceptions, distortions and exploitations. This would probably be less exhilarating than the orientation which allows each person to see himself or herself as the maligned underdog combating a virulent oppressor. But it would generate a genuinely humanizing atmosphere which would allow both men and women to grow beyond destructive gender rigidities. And that is what feminists assert their ultimate motivation to be, anyway.

13. The Liberation Crunch: Getting the Worst of Both Worlds

Two men were dining in an expensive Manhattan restaurant with three women they had met that evening at the fashion-show opening of a new disco where admission had been by invitation only.

One of the men, Len Rockwell, was a vice-president of an entertainment agency. Bob Reynolds, the second man, was a young writer of fiction who had published two novels with fair success but paid his weekly bills primarily by writing commissioned magazine articles.

Of the three women, one was an attorney for an insurance corporation, another was a fashion editor for a popular women's magazine and the third, newly arrived in New York, had a job writing copy for an advertising agency.

At the end of the meal—which included a drink before dinner and two bottles of wine—the waiter brought the check. He placed it by the two men. Rockwell was reaching for his wallet when Reynolds, sensitive to women's feelings about chauvinistic behavior in dating situations (having just recently researched an article on it for a singles magazine), casually said, "What would be the best way to divide up the check?"

There was an embarrassed silence. None of the women responded. Finally one woman said, seemingly on behalf of all three women, "We'll make it up to you later if we go somewhere for a drink." Rockwell, increasingly uncomfortable about what was going on, turned to Reynolds and said, "Let me get this one." He handed the waiter a credit card. The subject was quickly changed and the matter was never brought up again.

Harvey Gold, twenty-four, living in Los Angeles and working at a low-paying sales job in the garment center (having dropped out of a doctoral program in history), became infatuated with an attractive, outgoing young actress of twenty-three named Kathy. She had recently come to Los Angeles from a small town in Kansas, hoping to break into the film business.

Her impact on Harvey was instant and powerful. She had the natural, free, spontaneous and sensual quality he had always fantasized about finding in a woman. When he met her, he told himself that this was the woman he wanted to spend his life with.

Though he earned only $150 a week, he would regularly buy tickets to rock concerts that cost as much as thirty dollars apiece, would bring her little surprise gifts and on holiday weekends would take her to Palm Springs, San Diego and San Francisco. On occasions when she didn't feel well, Harvey would go to her apartment before and after work to bring her food and medicine and to run errands for her. It made him feel good to be protective of her and to let her know that she could depend on him. He wanted her to think of him as her best friend.

Secretly, however, he often felt hurt, resentful and insecure because Kathy rarely reciprocated by inviting him over for dinner, offering to help him clean his apartment or sew a button on a shirt she saw lying around waiting to be mended, which she knew he was less than competent in doing himself, and never bringing him any surprise gifts.

He never made an issue of any of this, afraid of seeming to be demanding, petty or, worse still, a "chauvinist pig." He knew from her enthusiastic support of feminism and her cutting remarks about the "sexist creeps" she met in the film business that she was very sensitive about the way men treated women. Also, she often quoted from articles she'd read in *Ms.* magazine, and in the car, while he was driving, she often sarcastically pointed out billboard advertisements that used sexist symbols to sell products.

Their relationship swung between euphoric highs and lows that were characterized by sudden, vicious interchanges. During one such fight, ignited by Kathy's forgetting to pick up concert tickets that were being held at a theater near the studio where she had acting classes, Harvey blurted out, "You don't really care about me, do you? I keep taking you to all of these concerts and expensive restaurants, and it hardly ever occurs to you to make me a meal or even a sandwich."

This comment enraged Kathy, who shot back, "I knew you'd bring that up someday. I was just waiting to hear that! You think you can buy my time and services with the few lousy dollars you spend on tickets or a meal? You spend that money for yourself, so you can feel like a big man. I never asked you to do it. But for me shopping and preparing dinner takes half a day."

When things quieted down, Harvey apologized for being so "demanding" after Kathy had suggested that they should consider breaking up if he thought she was so selfish, because she wasn't about to change to please any man.

Because Kathy turned him on sexually in a way no other woman ever had and he loved being with her, Harvey accepted the limits she set. He rationalized to himself, "You can't have everything. I can always go to a restaurant for a good meal, or to the cleaners to get a button sewed on, but a woman like Kathy is impossible to find."

The relationship continued until one of Kathy's beloved cats was found dead in the courtyard under the window ledge of her apartment. She had often told Harvey about the hostile remarks made by the building superintendent, an ex-merchant marine who had retired because of back injuries, regarding her three cats. He had unsuccessfully tried to get Kathy thrown out of the building because of them. Kathy suspected he might have been responsible for knocking her cat off the ledge while the cat was outside sleeping.

She asked Harvey to go with her and confront him, but Harvey refused. He had heard of the superintendent's explosive temper and paranoid personality, and he was frankly afraid. He confessed his fear honestly and told Kathy, "There's got to be a better way of dealing with this guy. Let's write a letter to the owner." At this Kathy began to cry and told Harvey she couldn't love or respect a man who was so "spineless" and "easily intimidated," and she wanted to end the relationship.

The wife of a forty-one-year-old physician who for ten years had quite contentedly played the role of the supportive "doctor's wife" suddenly transformed in her attitude. Almost overnight, with no obvious indications to her husband that it was coming, she told him she felt stifled and would not play the part of his "shadow" or "backstop," as she resentfully called it, anymore.

She asked him to move out, and soon thereafter she filed for divorce. On her behalf, her attorney asked for the house, custody of their children and alimony for eight years so that she could go back to school and become a counseling psychologist.

Because her husband typically worked a fifty- to sixty-hour week (which had been one of her chief complaints), and he knew he'd have to continue that pace now in order to support two households if she didn't come back, he did not contest the demands. Besides, he felt certain that she would eventually return and that there'd be a reconciliation. He moved into an apartment in a singles complex with a lawyer friend of his who had also recently separated from his wife. He considered this very temporary.

Less than a year later it became clear to him that his wife was not coming back. She had become emotionally involved with a younger man of twenty-nine who was a Ph.D. candidate in clinical psychology at the university where she was taking undergraduate work in psychology.

When her ex-husband found out about her affair and the fact that her lover often slept at the house overnight and that, according to the report of a neighbor, his ex-wife often prepared meals, paid for dates and bought gifts of clothing for her lover, he became enraged. He confronted her with this and threatened to stop all support payments. She responded to this threat by telling him that if he so much as missed even one payment, she would not let him see the children, and if he continued to withhold money, she would have her attorney press charges and have him put in jail. Furthermore, she told him if he harassed her in any way, she would get a court order stopping him from coming to the house at all. "I was ripped off of my identity for ten years playing the 'good doctor's wife,' and now that I'm enjoying myself and finding out who I really am you're not going to stop me," she told him.

The once demure "southern belle" wife of an investment counselor, always elegant and in the very best of taste in dress and manner, informed her wealthy husband that it was degrading for her to be asked to play hostess to his business friends and associates at their home. In the future, she informed him, she would no longer spend days arranging fancy dinners for those "materialistic boors." She told him that she found the constant discussion about stocks, bonds and real estate vile and would no longer be a party to it in any form. That meant she would not attend the numerous civic and "social" affairs they were invited to, which she found to be excruciatingly boring.

She told him that she would be spending her free time with people in the arts. "Business is your interest. You're turned on by it. I'm not. I'm interested in the theater, music and sculpture, so that's where I'm going to spend my time."

Michael and Roberta were high school sweethearts who married soon after graduation. Their relationship and the sexual excitement that were once so magnetizing deteriorated when Roberta decided to go back to college, and then to work for a graduate degree in speech and hearing. Meanwhile, Michael continued working the plumbing trade.

From year to year there was an almost direct correlation between her educational advancement and their marital strain.

Eight years after marriage, with two children in elementary school, they separated. Michael had a breakdown six months later after almost continuous drinking, and was admitted to a hospital.

Roberta told the psychologist who called her in after Michael had attempted suicide, "When I was about to take a job that had prestige and paid me almost as much the first year as it had taken him six years to earn, he began to say things that told me he felt angry and inadequate. I guess I picked up on that and couldn't respond to him sexually anymore, even though I tried. That made him feel even more inadequate. He blamed himself for not turning me on, even though I told him it wasn't his fault. Finally he wasn't even able to get an erection at all, and that's when he really fell apart. I had to leave him, or we both would have gone under. I couldn't stand to see him going from being a person who was so proud that nothing scared him to being somebody who seemed to be afraid of everything."

The twenty-eight-year-old wife of an electrician and mother of a six-year-old daughter told her husband she resented him for the pornographic films he'd been bringing home for them to watch during their marriage. Whereas she had once indicated to him that the porno turned her on, she now expressed the feeling that she had felt sexually exploited during all that time.

He had married her ten years before because she seemed to him to be the ideal woman. She loved homemaking, "desperately" wanted to be a mother and went all out to please him, even to the point where she went along with and seemed to enjoy his sexual whims and explorations, including the pornography, vibrators and experimentation with various exotic positions.

Soon after she told him never to bring home pornography again, she exploded in rage over the ways she said he had always expected her to cater to him. The list of tasks she now said she found demeaning included being responsible for his dry cleaning, laundering his shirts, preparing him a lunch to take to work and cleaning up after him. Then she dropped the big bomb. She told him she wanted a more open marital arrangement that would allow her to have her own friends and even date other men if the occasion arose.

The changes and demands at first enraged and then threatened her thirty-year-old husband, who worked in a business where he rarely had the opportunity to meet women, except for the few that sat around in the after-work bars, and they disgusted him. He pictured a life spent all alone if she left him, so he agreed to go along with her demands.

He began to do his own chores after work, packed his own lunch in the morning and even occasionally prepared his own dinner when his wife told him she'd be out late. He tried to develop a social life of his own, going out with the boys after work and trying to meet women, but found it boring and depressing. So while his wife explored her freedom, he found himself coming home each day after work.

He accepted what he knew was a painful and somewhat loveless existence, because he rationalized that the loneliness and the probable loss of his six-year-old child if the marriage broke up would be far more painful.

In most of these increasingly common situations the man found himself experiencing the dilemma, confusion and painful impact of being involved with a woman in the process of change while he himself had not yet been able to define his own new direction and respond in a self-caring way. Perhaps the rules and rhythm of the relationship were suddenly changed in midstream. Or he found himself in a situation where he was getting the worst of both worlds: He was still assuming the old responsibilities and pressures, being the strong man—protector—provider, but the woman he was involved with was no longer willing to play the roles that had provided him with the kinds of gratifications, satisfactions and securities that he had come to expect and depend on. In most instances he saw himself with no suitable alternatives or options. He was caught in the "liberation crunch," which means he still felt compelled to live up to the old model and pressures of the masculine role but without receiving the payoffs he had come to see as his reward for playing these roles. He was not only the "victim" of a woman who was behaving in hurtful ways, but also of his own rigidity, dependency, isolation and vulnerability which were now being clearly exposed. Consequently, he was not able to deal with the situation self-caringly and could only respond in helpless rage, or simple acceptance. Otherwise, he felt he would have to face the seemingly more painful experience of rejection and self-hate. In some cases, there were no apparent choices available to him at all as he found himself suddenly and inexplicably abandoned anyway.

The "liberation crunch" is occurring in endless variations everywhere today across the country, and it's not difficult to understand why so many men are threatened, traumatized and thrown into a state of desperation as they find themselves defensively clinging to a relationship that provides progressively diminishing payoffs. That is, while women begin to set new limits and write new rules—refusing to cater to the man any longer, rejecting the exclusive assumption of responsibility for household chores, insisting on establishing their own style and identity socially and in their careers, becoming sexually assertive and untying dependency binds—many of their men seem unable to relinquish their traditional role behaviors and ways of seeing and reacting to things. Consequently, the man continues functioning in the same style, still playing the old games by outdated rules, still feeling he must assume responsibility for being the performer, the provider, the protector and the stud. Since he has been portrayed as the guilty one, and labeled the male chauvinist exploiter and abuser of women, he now feels he must also be responsible for supporting the woman through her changes.

This situation often puts him in an increasingly untenable, unsatisfying and frustrating position. That is, he is still assuming onerous responsibilities and playing old roles without the usual payoffs, while his partner charts her new direction, increases her demands and throws off stereotypical role restrictions, informing him that he may no longer expect *anything* from her on the basis simply of her so-called obligations as a woman. While she has put him on notice that he should not count on her putting his needs ahead of her own and has made it clear that even the proverbial "barefoot and pregnant" is no guarantee that she'll harness herself, put up with anything stifling or even, for that matter, stay around, he still goes through his traditional posturings, trying to conform to the old masculine blueprints.

He finds himself unable to demand anything concrete in return, or to establish new limits and a balance that would afford him new payoffs and rewards to compensate for the loss of the old ones. Instead, because of his rigidity and the defensive essence of his masculinity, it seems impossible for him to shift gears and respond fluidly and self-caringly, and the price of being a "cardboard Goliath" becomes starkly apparent as he flails about trying to hold on and find some security and satisfaction in a relationship that has gone out of control and is increasingly frustrating and painful.

For most men involved with a woman who is throwing off the traditional feminine harnesses and restrictions, her liberation has meant nothing more than greater involvement with household chores, child care, and support for the woman in her new career and academic aspirations. In other words, it has only *added* to his pressures, responsibilities and burdens, and stretched him thinner, without providing any obvious benefits in terms of greater freedom, mobility, expressiveness, security and satisfaction, feminist rhetoric notwithstanding. What feminists describe as beneficial to the man in these changes is an ideal—a potential rather than the reality of his daily existence. For example, being forced into a more active participation as a father may be potentially rewarding. The fly in the ointment, however, is that he enters into new behaviors under compulsion rather than with any positive motivation of his own. He sees himself as without choice, and therefore changes to please her. There is probably no genuine, spontaneous pleasure even though he might tell himself there is.

In his anxiety over possible abandonment, his rigid self-definition, his lack of self-awareness and his inability to respond in self-caring fashion (by charting a new course that will enrich his existence, untie him from self-destructive response patterns and afford him new areas of satisfaction, pleasure and development) have become clear. He has instead defined his new role as accommodator to her changing rhythm. He is placating the energy of her new ambitions and the fury of her newly experienced resentments and demands, perhaps secretly marking time until she "comes to her senses" or falls on her face and gratefully resumes her time-honored womanly roles.

What would seem to be a glorious built-in opportunity for his growth and change also, were he fluid enough to take advantage of her new assertiveness, independence and overt sexuality, has instead become a nightmare characterized by fears of rejection and mounting frustration and paralysis. He is pinned by his own delusions of privilege and top-dogdom and his inability to shift directions.

He is trapped by his own unconscious defensiveness and corresponding inability to define himself as a person rather than a masculine thing. He has founded his identity and self-respect on his ability to perform, do his job, have his erection and assert his dominance. In the process he has isolated himself by making every other man his competitor and every woman an object and a witness to his exploits.

Faced now with a woman who no longer responds positively to his traditional style or, worse still, reviles him for it, he fears that to let go is to face identity annihilation. He has no recourse, therefore, but to accept, accommodate and adjust. As he does this, however, rather than pleasing her by giving her what she wants or what he thinks she wants, all too often he finds himself even less respected than before. To accommodate is to appear weak, guilt-ridden and pitiful, and ultimately to generate contempt in the other person. On some deeper level she may perceive correctly that his accommodation is motivated more by fear and rigidity than by love, goodwill or concern for her growth. Therefore, his accommodation rings false and repels her, even though on the surface she may respond with appreciation.

Listen to this comment from the authors of a recent book written to help women make their men more sensitive. Special attention should be paid by those men who equate their liberation in the eyes of the woman by their ability to show emotion and to cry. Say the writers:

> And so, somehow, you must decide how far you want to go in this journey toward sensitivity. An odd and troublesome little refrain we've heard again and again in our talks with some of the more futuristic social thinkers has to do with men crying. A man who feels free to weep when he hurts is taken to have achieved the ultimate in male improvements. "I want my man to get rid of all those macho trappings," a typical female dreamer might say. "I want him to feel he can cry in front of me without any sense of castration." We've talked pessimistically about this dream before, and now we ask you to consider it with cold honesty. Would you really want your man to weep frequently when things go wrong? Can you easily imagine him sniffling into a handkerchief, tears running down his cheeks? If the idea gives you trouble, then you already know something about yourself and him. You

know there are limits beyond which you don't want
him to change.[1]

At present the composition of the "liberation crunch" is
a woman in transition in a relationship with a traditional
man. In this situation all of the options seem to be hers. It
is up to her whether she chooses to play the part of the
traditional or the liberated woman. Meanwhile, his behavior is a reaction and accommodation to *her* choice.

The man who in moments of honest reflection asks himself, "What is in all of this for me? What am I getting, and
what can I expect in the future?" may find himself at a
considerable loss to answer positively or optimistically.
Her changes in combination with his rigidity have put him
up against the wall. If he persists in his old ways, he
stands accused of chauvinism and sexism. If he stretches
himself to take on new responsibilities without making
equal demands and throwing off parts of his traditional
harness, he will only find himself overloaded and strained
to the breaking point. If he lets go of the traditional masculine style completely, he may find to his terror that he is
becoming invisible, unsexy and unworthy in the eyes of
most women and even most other men, who turn away
from a man who is without money, a job, status and
power. The man who thinks he can avoid all of these
dilemmas by finding and becoming involved with an "old-
fashioned" woman is also placing himself in great potential jeopardy, as she may go into transition and change
and alter the rules at any time, when her underlying rage
over having to be passive and submissive is triggered into
consciousness and overt rebellion.

Equally untenable and disorienting is being involved
with a woman who knows what she doesn't want to do,
but not what she does want to do. In such a relationship,
for him to take a dominant role, for instance, is for him to
stand accused of being sexist. To cease leading, however,
may mean to see nothing happen at all. In a dating situation, for example, this may manifest as his deliberately
avoiding chauvinistic behavior by seeking suggestions from
the woman as to what to do for the evening, or waiting
for her to initiate or structure a date, or even a conversation, and to be frustrated because little or nothing happens

as she lapses into silence or passivity or quite honestly says that she doesn't really know what she wants to do that evening.

Another hazard of the "liberation crunch" is when he finds himself stretched in ways that entangle him in impossible binds. That is, while his woman partner may on the one hand vigorously assert her independence, she may at the same time resent him for not taking care of her. Or she may want power equalization and yet reject him if he is not more powerful than she. She may protest his macho style and his lack of emotional expressiveness and yet be repulsed by anything that smacks of his being effete, weak or overly emotional. She might protest his sexual aggressiveness that makes her feel exploited and like a "sex object" and yet not take the initiative and resist being sexually assertive herself. And while she protests the time and energy he puts into his career ambitions and his "masculine" interests such as sports, when he lets go of these masculine obsessions and begins to be readily available to her, she may find him boring, less attractive and too demanding of her time. The wife of a very busy attorney personified this bind when she cried to her husband that he seemed to have so little time for her, only to become exceedingly uncomfortable some months later when he began to talk about cutting down his work week to four days so that he could be at home more with her and the children. "I don't think I could stand your being around that much and watching me all the time," was her response.

The paradoxes and impossible binds for the male attempting to relate to a woman in transition in this "liberation crunch" were also well expressed and demonstrated by a twenty-two-year-old woman law student who was interviewed by one of my researchers on the question "What does the contemporary woman look for in a man?" The interviewee responded as follows:

> I want a man to be understanding, a good listener, a family-oriented person who is able to express himself and his affection and feelings. I want him to be compassionate, athletic and emotionally stable.
>
> I want him to be an all-around guy who plays many types of roles—father, worker, lover and so on.

He has to be a flexible person in his reactions and outlook on people.

If he earns less money it's O.K. But in a sense, I would not marry a man who made less money than me. For a marriage partner I want an achievement-oriented person, someone who is motivated to earn more money and be more successful.

I would not want a "loser." If he's a loser, then he doesn't have self-confidence. That means there is a lack of motivation and concern and that turns me off.

It doesn't bother me if he cries. I'd like him to be emotional because that would mean he is a very human person. But it would bother me if he was scared. I don't mind if he needs to make a decision and can't adequately judge and doesn't know the outcome if it's a really big consequence. But it's not O.K. for him to be whimpy. I also don't like a dependent man. I want him to be independent and confident in himself.

Along this line, the inherent contradictions and binds men find themselves in in trying to become less macho in their relationship with a woman were poignantly expressed in a letter written by a young man to a New York newspaper in response to an article that addressed itself to a question posed by a woman writer—whether women would be able to think of a non-macho man as sexy. The letter writer wrote:

I am by nature a gentle and non-aggressive 27-year-old man who often finds women turned off sexually by my tenderness and non-macho view of the world. I have come to realize that for all their talk, a lot of women still want the hairy, sexy, war-mongering, aggressive machoman of their dreams. So after several fruitless years as a gentle poet-man, I now turn myself into a heavy machismo when I go out with a woman. It works. *I* open the doors, *I* order the food and drinks, *I* decide which movie or play we will see. I keep my shirt unbuttoned down past my nipples and wear a gold chain around my neck with a carved elephant tusk medallion, and if the relationship is not working out, I make the first move and tell my companion that I'm sorry but we're through.

The sad thing about all this is that it *works*. After all those years of being naturally sensitive and gentle, and now I've got to turn myself inside out just to appear sexy. It's fun and it's nice, but I do wish I could just be myself again.[2]

AVOIDING THE "LIBERATION CRUNCH"

In the final analysis, the "liberation crunch" is not the result of women's anger or malevolence, but simply reflects masculine rigidity and the male's uncreative and reactive attitude toward the woman's changes. Trying to accommodate her new rhythm will only drive him crazy and unconsciously enrage him, just as her having been a *reactor* to him over the years created a pool of latent rage that finally erupted into the fury of feminism.

There is no psychologically constructive alternative for him except to develop a new blueprint for himself based on placing priority on his own growth into a self-caring, fluid, expressive person. To move in this direction he may require a support system composed of other men and caring women who will create for him the kind of supportive atmosphere that assures him that no matter what his growth involves and reveals, even if it threatens the status quo of his relationship with his woman partner as her changes threatened him, it is the only course he can self-caringly take.

Clinging to archaic models of masculine behavior will leave him a crumbled, anachronistic fool. Changing to accommodate to her changes will create rage in himself and contempt for him on her part. Changing to make himself a complete, expressive, transparent and emotionally intune, fluid person will give him a sense of well-being and self-care that will make it increasingly possible for there to be a genuinely caring relationship with the woman rather than one based on desperation, isolation and the desire for escape from her changes which are perceived as rejecting, intimidating and dangerous.

14. "Nothing I Do Pleases Her"; or, How to Recognize a No-Win Situation

Certainly one of the saddest manifestations of masculine vulnerability and rigidity can be seen by watching a man cling to a dying or already dead relationship. He hangs on desperately and tenaciously, despite the fact that he is getting little from the woman except indifference and rejection.

In fact, the relationship may have been deteriorating for a long time, and even he *himself* may have entertained thoughts of breaking free. Yet, when he is suddenly faced with the realization that his woman is involved with someone else or for other reasons is serious about leaving, his "love" for her and even his once flagging libido are reignited. In fact, there seems to be no more powerful aphrodisiac for a man than to be told by his woman that she wants out or is involved with somebody else. Perhaps the freedom created by a safe emotional distance and the excitement of the renewed challenge bring about a rebirth of his feelings of caring and sexual desire.

The same woman in whom he had lost interest, become bored with and turned off to is now a desperate obsession. Whereas earlier he may have thought her a ball and chain, once he is threatened with abandonment he perceives her as his lifeline and suddenly doesn't want anyone else but her.

Such was the situation for thirty-year-old David Rogers, a commercial photographer. He had been married to his wife, Terry, a shy, quiet, passive woman who had related to him in a subservient manner, for nine years. Intimidated by her minimal formal education, she would say very little at social gatherings, or even when she was alone with David. To her mind, he had all the answers, and was overpowering with them. Even when she disagreed with something or felt a conversation was boring or stupid, she said nothing.

Her husband never really noticed her moments of discomfort or resentment. He took it for granted that when she was unusually withdrawn that was just the way she was. In fact, he believed that's how most women were. He also accepted the fact that he would have to get his stimulation elsewhere, and he did, during his frequent trips out of town servicing clients who owned entertainment production companies.

His wife always remained at home, taking care of their two children. While she was forgetful about errands, often misunderstood his requests and got sick regularly, at least David knew she would be around to mind the house and children when he was busy working and playing. Evenings when he was home for dinner, conversation consisted mainly of his instructing her on better ways to do things and giving her lists of things to be taken care of the following day.

While he felt bored with the marriage, he rationalized that he couldn't leave. He had two children and a "good" wife who never questioned him about what he did during his trips out of town. He saw himself as having the best of both worlds.

He had become progressively uninterested in his wife as a person until one day she announced to him that she was moving out and that he could have the two children. She told him of an affair she was having. She said she was in love and would be taking an apartment in order to be free to be with her lover.

David became desperate. He begged her to stay, and told her he loved her no matter what she had done. Still, years of Terry's repressed anger came pouring out. She screamed at him about his indifference, the humiliation she felt when they were together with his friends and his treating her like a child and a "slave." She told him that she had known all along from the perfume smells in his suitcase that he had been having out-of-town affairs. She had said nothing to him only because she was afraid of him.

Now, however, she had had enough. She was leaving because she no longer felt anything for him. David cried and trembled in panic and guilt. He blamed himself for everything, apologized and promised her he would change. Anything she wanted he would do. He even called a psychologist—something he had always expressed cynicism about when he had heard that other couples were in therapy or marital counseling. When he repeatedly told her how he loved and needed her, she responded only with sarcastic disbelief. "You're just saying that because I'm finally doing what *I* want to do. But you're not going to stop me again."

The tables had turned completely. She moved in and out of the house several times over the following ten-month period, then finally left for good. The times when she returned, it was out of fear that she couldn't make it on her own because of financial problems. Each time, however, David accepted her back gratefully and hopefully. He grasped at any straw that suggested a possibility that they would get back together. During the times she returned to live with him, he even sat by quietly while she had lengthy telephone conversations with her boyfriend. David never stopped believing she would return to stay until she finally moved out of the city with her lover.

In another dramatic reversal, a forty-year-old, twice-divorced man who was a successful wholesaler of women's shoes came for consultation because he wanted to end a relationship with a woman he'd been living with for two years. According to him, no matter what he tried, he was not successful in getting her to leave. Since it was his apartment they lived in, he periodically packed all of her things in suitcases and boxes, offered her money for several months' rent and asked her to move out. She would become hysterical, at which point he would back off and let her stay.

When he came for consultation, he was at wit's end. "How can I get her out of my life?" he kept asking. At home he would insult her constantly, stay out late or all night and tell her about other women he'd been with. If she reacted negatively, he'd tell her to leave if she didn't like it.

One night he came home late and she wasn't there. At 3 A.M. she called to tell him she was at a girl friend's apartment and would not be returning. Within three days after that he proposed marriage, something she'd been asking for all along. She became suddenly the "most special woman" he'd ever known, as he now talked desperately to his therapist about strategies to get her back.

Whereas she had always called him at work—a habit toward which he reacted with annoyance—now *he* was calling *her* constantly at her place of employment, and *she* was putting *him* on hold and telling him that she was too busy to talk and would call him back later. While at first she had seemed somewhat receptive to his proposal of marriage, it now appeared that there was a lover in the picture with whom she was already seriously involved. In spite of this, he continued to pursue her with letters, gifts, phone calls, invitations and tearful pleas.

Many men in formerly traditional relationships with women they were sure of have experienced their recently liberated women going through profound changes. Often there were no other men involved. The message of feminism had connected, and they simply wanted to reclaim their autonomy.

Her previous attentiveness to every household detail became absentmindedness. Compulsive punctuality was transformed into a casual disregard for schedules. Her former reticence was replaced by aggressive pronouncements on assertiveness, freedom, "finding oneself" and "male chauvinism." The less involved the woman became, the more clinging her husband or lover became.

Often a man in this situation found himself caught in an impossible bind. The woman confronted him with complaints about his domination, preoccupation with success and sexist behavior. Many of the behaviors she castigated him for, however, were the same ones he thought had originally attracted her to him. If he tried to change to meet her demands and threats, while it may have temporarily placated her, she would be ultimately repulsed by his desperate hunger to please and his sudden willingness to give things up that she had been asking him to stop doing for years. He would be seen as weak and sniveling in her eyes. If he resisted change, she would reject him for his rigid chauvinism and "piggishness" and tell him they couldn't go on.

In many instances, I believe, a woman's transition into liberation comes after so much repressed anger has built up over the years that there is really no way to please her or to change in a way acceptable to her once these feelings are unleashed consciously. While it may appear that a realignment of the relationship is what she seeks, in reality the man may be facing a hurricane of these previously controlled and denied negative feelings, a force of emotion far beyond rational negotiation. Her feminist philosophy in these instances serves as the socially acceptable channel for this explosion of rage.

The man who fails to recognize this, who clings to the relationship in the belief and hope that the differences can be rationally negotiated and resolved, may find himself in for a prolonged period of humiliation and of being kept off balance as he grovels and gropes for the light at the end of the tunnel that never appears. Like a cowboy on a bucking bronco, he is hanging on for a little more time, but the end is inevitable.

Through all of this he continues to misread signals, to view things from a distorted perspective that allows him false hope. He is unable to see it for the hopeless situation it is, so he is stuck, unable to pick up the pieces and begin anew elsewhere. The false hope is apparently less painful than an acceptance of the reality.

Often such a man, involved with a woman who is going through profound changes, tries to accommodate by understanding and even supporting her feminist philosophy. Instead of pleasing his woman by doing this, however, he succeeds in alienating her even more. She reacts with suspicion and even contempt to these efforts, which she recognizes as being motivated by desperate fear rather than a genuine awareness, understanding and commitment to a non-sexist consciousness. The woman's resistance in these instances is, I believe, well founded. Only a masochistic, desperate and self-hating man could integrate without appropriate resistance all of the rage and guilt laid on him by an accusing feminist doctrine.

Contained in these turning points of change are important moments of truth. She is being united with her long repressed rage while he, in turn, is being reunited with his deeper vulnerability, dependency and the sham of his so-called control and dominance in the relationship.

The behavior of this man is also often an important il-lustration of the dangers of the masculine tendency to fo-cus on intellectual or rational messages rather than the emotional and nonverbal aspects of communication. He takes what he hears from her literally. Consequently, while he is working at changing in the ways he hears she wants him to, she may be already in the process of replacing the relationship with other relationships that have become more important to her. However, he can't see or believe this. Instead, he is preoccupied with understanding her, fig-uring the situation out, developing strategies, adapting to the changes, coping with the rejection and hurt and trying to bring back to life something that is beyond reviving. Partially, he resists seeing the reality of her rejection be-cause her pulling away puts him directly and painfully in touch with his lack of any other emotionally satisfying in-volvements or sources of support and comfort.

She, in turn, may be giving him just enough rein-forcement to provide hope, probably motivated by ambiva-lence about her newly experienced power and her insecurities about her ability and capacity to make it on her own as well as the desire to let him down easy and not be unnecessarily hurtful. She therefore maintains some at-tachment to him and he uses this minimal involvement to fuel his illusions about the possibilities and potential of a reconciliation. He, however, cannot recognize that she is not interested in maintaining a relationship that no longer feels good to her. Consequently, he gratefully, hungrily and blindly holds on to anything that will feed his hope that things will again be as they were.

If he is the average working man in our society—not the professional person or the independent entrepreneur—he is *particularly* vulnerable to her shifts and changes and will be prone to accept all kinds of humiliation and buffet-ing in order to hang on to the illusion of hope. Contrary to the woman's belief about men's "privileged" position, his is largely a slave existence in which the opportunities to meet and form new and satisfying relationships with women are extremely limited. If his work involves heavy labor, he is probably surrounded primarily by men. The only women he might be able to meet are those who come to the bars he partonizes. In his mind, however, no woman worthy of an enduring relationship can be met there. Because of his extreme isolation from social environments where he can meet women, a situation which becomes particularly aggravated as he gets older, slower, more caught up in routine and responsibility and less able to communicate in the self-assured manner he will need to initiate relationships, his desperation will be especially acute. From his point of view, if he loses her, it may condemn him to a life of painful isolation in bars getting drunk. He is truly a trapped being.

Once the spiral of alienation from his woman is set in motion, if he doesn't know when to get out and begin some personal reconstruction, he may be irretrievably, seriously and self-destructively caught. Therefore, he must be able to recognize the signs of a no-win situation and not allow himself to be sucked into illusions he would like to believe are real but which, while giving him temporary hope, only make the eventual crash more painful. He is part of a disintegrating relationship because he couldn't read or deal accurately with the signs earlier on. Now he can't get out, because he fixates on each crumb of "hope" and denies the larger picture, which contains massive indications of indifference and rejection.

Over the years I have observed many such men trying to talk themselves into believing the unbelievable, ignoring the obvious and evading confrontations with the woman that would allow them to see the realities of the situation. Certain behaviors on the part of the woman, particularly when they are bunched together, are evidence, I believe, of the demise of the relationship, or, at best, the continued existence of a relationship contingent on the accommodating and self-degrading behavior of the man. The following are some of these signs and indications that I have compiled from working with many men in this situation. The man who resists recognition of them may be looking for love where it no longer is and seeing potential for renewal where the ground has been leached of all its nourishing elements.

SIGNS FOR RECOGNIZING A NO-WIN SITUATION

1) It's hard to pin her down to specifics of any kind—a date, plans for future meetings, how she really feels, what she thinks or what she's been doing. If you press the issue and demand specifics, she withdraws, tells you that you're smothering her and suggests that perhaps it would be best to end things completely. Out of fear, you back off and let *her* establish the rhythm and nature of the interaction.

2) She makes dates and shows up late, with ever-changing excuses, or she forgets to show up at all. Of course, you're always there on time. Occasionally, when she forgets, she may have forgotten so completely that if you never mentioned it, the broken date might have escaped her memory altogether. Clearly, she is not "there" for you, and you are no longer central in her consciousness.

3) She does not remember the nuances or subtleties of your preferences, your habit patterns and issues of importance to you, while you, on the other hand, seem to remember *every detail* of hers. Whether it be a food preference, a seating preference, a critical matter you are involved in and have told her about she seems oblivious. Your feelings are constantly being hurt by this, but if you tell her that, she responds with annoyance over your "spoiled," "little boy" expectations. "If you want me to remember, remind me. I have other things on my mind. Don't expect me to think of everything. I'm not your mother," might be her response.

4) On occasions when she tells you that she really cares about you or even that she loves you, you have a sense of unreality, a feeling that it's too good to be true and that the bubble will burst momentarily, which it almost always does.

Indeed, if in a romantic moment on the telephone she indicates this love, if you follow up her statement with a request to be with her right away or even very soon, she almost always has an excuse for why that would be impossible.

5) Frequently when you are with her, she seems distracted, preoccupied and resistant to being touched. Rather

than feeling welcomed when you come close, you sense that you're intruding on her, even though she may deny it. If you ask her why she seems so distant and cold, she tells you that it has nothing to do with you. It's just the mood she's in.

6) When the two of you are together, you feel that you're giving out all of the energy, and that, indeed, if you did not take responsibility for initiating and maintaining conversation or deciding on activities, little would be said or done because she is relating to you in a passive, detached, low-energy way.

7) When in a moment of extreme frustration and exasperation you say, "Maybe it would be better for us to stop seeing each other for a while," her response is calm, casual agreement. She might say, "Maybe we should. I don't like the fact that I bring this out in you. I obviously can't be what you want me to be, what you really seem to need." You then retract your threat.

8) There is no sense of continuity in the relationship. Each time you meet, it's almost like starting at square one. You feel no development of solidity or momentum, and after each time together, no matter how good it seemed, you sense that there might not be a next time.

9) You are obsessed with thinking about her. You rehearse conversations with her in your head and premeditate strategies for holding on to or interesting her. While nothing else seems important except being with her, you're often too insecure even to telephone her without your heart racing, while questioning whether you really should call or whether you're just making a nuisance of yourself and driving her away. You've lost your spontaneity and balance, and it's been replaced by premeditation, an overly deliberate scheming and manipulation born of insecurity.

10) You're constantly showing off to her, trying to prove yourself worthy in ways you don't ordinarily do— talking about how much money you just earned, how well you handled a situation, how successful you've been at work and so on. This reflects your very low self-esteem when in her company.

11) You catch her in little lies and distortions of the truth. If you confront her with this, she always succeeds in

evading admission and may even make *you* feel guilty for not showing more trust.

12) You're anxious around her, and certain self-destructive habits intensify. You find yourself constantly reaching for cigarettes or alcohol, sipping coffee, spilling drinks, clumsily bumping into things, dropping dishes, scraping your car in parking lots and in conversation frequently putting your foot in your mouth. You drive faster, stop exercising and become more belligerent with men who you think are coming on to her. All the things that in your more balanced periods you control and know better than to do you find yourself doing.

13) Like a child, you find yourself constantly asking everybody for advice, information and answers to help you deal with her. Underneath, the real message that you give off is that you're looking for reassurance and want people to tell you that everything will work out all right.

14) You focus on and magnify any little sign that allows you to tell yourself, "She wouldn't have said or done that if she wasn't planning to stay with the relationship." Your search for such indications and clues is insatiable.

15) Many parts of you emerge that you usually hold other people and even yourself in contempt for, such as possessiveness, clinging, suspicion, insecurity, jealousy, manipulation and the never-ending need to prove yourself in front of her. You withdraw energy from other relationships and from activities and pursuits that are important to you. You even feel uncomfortable and distrustful around male friends when she's around, because you think they're interested in her and that she might find them more attractive than you.

You think every man is interested in her. When you see her in conversation with other men, it generates anxiety and suspicion in you, because you suspect she's establishing a liaison. When you mention this to her, she becomes enraged, tells you you're being paranoid and that she resents your watching her.

16) You're constantly the one doing the apologizing. No matter what the conflict, you are left feeling at fault. She seldom acknowledges that she has done anything to create the problem or to hurt your feelings. The responsibility for problems always seems to be yours.

17) You give up things that are important to you—activities, friendships, work—to be with her at *her* convenience. You might even move to another city just to be with her, even though she wouldn't do the same for you. You are somehow always available and flexible in regard to getting together with her, while she is always having a hard time figuring out when she can fit you into her crowded schedule.

The meetings, therefore, always seem to be structured to accommodate *her* schedule and desire, not yours. You feel unable to change that, because you sense that her motivation to be with you is less than yours to be with her, and that if you pressure her in any way, she'll sever the relationship and you won't be able to see her at all.

18) You accept progressively more outrageous behavior on her part and self-degrading behavior on yours. You go along with things alien and humiliating to you to the point that you might even consider supporting her boyfriends if she wanted to have them move in with you and her. In short, you'll do and accept almost anything if you believe it will make the difference between holding and losing her.

19) While you're constantly thinking of little ways to please her—gifts to give, places to go, surprises and so on—she rarely, if ever, does the same for you.

20) She encourages you to take more freedom, do more things without her, even to see other women. However, you can't think of anything you want to do or anyone else you want to be with.

21) Sex, particularly "good sex," occurs only when *she* wants it. Even then you may get a sense that she's not really there with *you*. When you're turned on and she's not, you're left feeling like a demanding, lustful animal, the insensitive, "horny" one, and nothing you do can turn her on.

22) No matter what she does or says and no matter how objectionable her behavior, you put her on a pedestal and excuse her, thinking she's the most perfect, sensitive and incredible woman in the world. Obvious facts to the contrary are ignored or disregarded. *Clearly, you are addicted to your fantasy of her.*

23) You're terrified of doing *anything* to displease or anger her. The relationship feels so tenuous to you that

you feel anything negative could trigger her into leaving you. Indeed, arguments often lead to a threat from her that "we ought to end things completely right now. I don't want to hassle anymore." You apologize.

24) Many times when others are around, you feel as if you weren't there, or even that you're an intruder. Specifically, she may begin to talk to someone and forget to introduce you, or not include you in the conversation at all, leaving you standing there uncomfortably.

25) She doesn't call you or want you around when she's feeling bad, even though you tell her you'd like to be there for her. She tells you, instead, that she needs to be alone when she's blue or depressed.

26) She seems to say the very things that make you feel hurt or rejected. For example, you speak of love and she says she's not sure there is such a thing—that it's all really just immature dependency. When you speak of intimacy and relationships, she philosophizes about how people are afraid of freedom and don't know how to give each other space.

27) Your mood swings are volatile in relation to her. When she says something reassuring, you're elated and energetic. Desperation, loneliness, anxiety and apathy set in whenever she is cold or in any way seems to indicate a lack of interest in the relationship.

28) No matter how much you pursue clarification, you're never really sure of where you stand with her. When you ask her how she's feeling toward you, the answer is either evasive or an angry "Stop asking me!"

29) She is always surprising you. She telephones just when you've given up or even resigned yourself to never seeing her anymore. Then, when you think things are becoming more solid, she doesn't call when you expect her to or are sure she will. There's constant unpredictability that keeps you off balance.

30) You're obsessed with her during the day and are constantly struggling against the impulse to call her, to talk or to tell her that you love her. When you do, she often puts you on hold, tells you she's busy, just on the way out or talking to somebody, and asks you to call her back in a few hours. You don't want to ask her to call you back, because you sense that she won't, so you say yes.

When you do call her back, sometimes she's not even there.

31) She seems oblivious to your down moods. When you're hurting, she doesn't seem to notice your pain.

32) You're constantly having to explain what you *really* meant. Or you're interrogating her about the *real* meaning of something she said. Either way it's as if there is always some tension and distrust, a sense of walking on eggs that you'd like to avoid but can't seem to.

33) You rarely laugh around her spontaneously. Instead, discussions with her tend to be heavy, intellectual and grim in their intensity, as you are seemingly always and endlessly discussing and analyzing "our relationship."

34) She's always telling you she needs time, freedom and space to be alone, to collect herself and to think things over. She rations out the amount of time you can see her, and the amount of time seems to progressively decrease.

35) She considers your endless gropings for affection and reassurance to be infantile, and she tells you they make her uncomfortable.

36) Your intuition tells you that you're not central in her life, that she doesn't love you and that the relationship is doomed—and YOU'RE RIGHT! To fully accept this is very painful, but to continue to deny it will be self-destructive.

15. The Feminist Movement Can Save Your Life

It is both surprising and not surprising that the male would resist or even feel threatened by the emergence of the woman as a total person. *Were he self-aware and self-caring, however, he would not only welcome the emergence but would insist upon it while setting into motion equivalent life-preserving changes of his own.*

He has nothing to lose from feminism but his guilt and his fantasies of what women supposedly are. The guilt is a built-in inevitability because of the way he related to the traditional woman, struggling constantly to live up to the model of the ideal man, the dutiful and faithful husband, the responsible father, the successful career person and the sexual performer. In the process, he was always feeling himself falling short or in danger of doing so. When his life became more frustrating and painful than satisfying and pleasurable, and when he fantasized changing his life-style or the direction of his aspirations, he often found himself trapped. To leave or change or let go would mean to betray, inconvenience, hurt or let down those who counted on him, because in his mind *he* was ultimately responsible for everybody. He was strong. She was weak and dependent. He was unbreakable. She was fragile. He could take the stress and self-denial. She couldn't. His lot, therefore, was to suffer in silence and to take it like a man.

From a psychological perspective, in the traditional marital interaction he was daddy and his wife was the child. She expressed her femininity by being dependent and essentially unsexual except as an expression of "love" to him. Her love was as much a love born of need, a child's love, as anything else, and was based largely on her belief in his strength and protectiveness and not on him as a real person. She feared and avoided conflict and confrontation.

180

When it occurred, her response, because she was unable to assert herself directly, was usually a tearful, hurt one that subtly or directly laid the blame on him. As the "daddy," he saw it as his role and obligation to make the decisions, provide for everybody, take major responsibility for fighting the battles and so on.

Indeed, the closer his relationship came to being an "ideal marriage," the more it resembled this father-child model in its dynamics, and the more suffocating and destructive it had to become for him. However, from his masculine viewpoint there were no acceptable alternatives. To avoid or reject these roles and responsibilities would be to impugn his masculinity. Therefore, he went along with the program no matter what the price to himself. The guilt and self-hate for letting go or failing at these role demands were his constant shadow and chain, and in his imagination avoiding them far outweighed the possible benefits of any alternatives.

If men could see beyond feminist blaming and rage— rage that inevitably builds up in any party to a relationship who chronically assumes a passive-submissive role —the feminist movement could be regarded as simply a movement describing a new attitude. Primarily, it represents an insistence by women that they function as a whole people, rather than feminine gender stereotypes. They are saying, "We refuse to relate like children anymore."

By doing this, the woman is shattering the man's fantasy of her as the weak, ethereal creature, the balancing opposite to his self-perceived animallike, selfish and destructive nature. It is hard for him to believe her when she communicates to him that she is not who and what he thinks she is.

He has come to need this fantasy of her in order to justify his own rigid, destructive style. Though it alienated him from other men, he saw himself as doing his performing, competitive and often destructive dances primarily for her. It is indeed disorienting and painful to have one's system of rationalization and justification pulled away, for now he too is faced with the psychologically threatening task of having to become a whole person rather than remaining a gender stereotype.

The best part of the old-style, traditional, *actor-reactor*, man-woman relationship was the fantasy, the initial burst of elation, the sense of magic and salvation that occurred upon meeting and joining. It felt to him as if he had been rescued from isolation and meaninglessness. The moment-to-moment process of the relationship, however, as it evolved in this dominant-submissive, daddy–little girl, "macho warrior"–"earth mother" interaction had to transform it into an increasingly deadening and unsatisfying experience.

The feminists would have us believe that men's satisfaction in these traditional relationships was in the control they supposedly had. He was the authoritarian thriving on her dependency and helplessness and her "need" for him. However, his was the kind of "power" and "control" that a parent gets in knowing a child won't leave as long as the child is unable to function and survive autonomously in the outside world. In marriage it is an expensive, exhausting form of control, contingent on the woman's remaining a child and relating in childlike fashion. The price for this is that he is endlessly under pressure to perform and drained constantly by responsibility. It is the sick parent who is distressed by a child's growing into maturity and autonomy. The healthy parent welcomes the easing of burdens and the pleasure of relating to the child as a capable adult person.

There are aspects of the way in which feminine changes have taken place that caused some men to react with resistance and justifiably with a sense of threat. So often what has been portrayed and labeled "men's lib" in the media, which in the minds of many people is a counterpart to feminism, amounts to a harried man rushing home from work to help with household chores such as vacuuming, washing dishes and cleaning or baby care. While there is nothing inherently wrong in the man's sharing in these responsibilities, compare that image of liberation with that of a woman emerging as an independent, assertive, sexual person who is redefining her role and her life to meet her needs for growth. In other words, while women's liberation has been depicted as a joyful, energetic freeing up and casting off of sex stereotypes and the onerous responsibilities that accompany them, "men's lib" has been depicted as the *addition* of responsibilities and onerous tasks to an already laden and pressured life and little else. No wonder the average man has resisted and reacted defensively.

In other words, what has been commonly described as "men's lib" is not liberation at all, but merely accommodation to women's changes. *What this means is that once again he is playing daddy, only this time, unlike in the traditional relationship where he got nurturance and support, the payoffs are almost nonexistent.* Changing would simply allow him to hang on to the relationship a little longer.

Authentic liberation means assertion, freeing up, breaking through gender barriers and refusing to continue playing self-denying and self-destructive games. It does not mean accommodation. For the man's liberation to be defined in terms of being a reinforcement and support for the woman while she goes through her changes is for him to be once again placed in the role of "strong man." His first assertive step must therefore be to reject that role with the realization that she is strong in her own right—indeed, *stronger* than he in many ways—and to transfer the focus of his energy toward finding ways that allow him to free up his own life from lethal and non-gratifying patterns.

Feminism was not born of or propelled by accommodation, but rather by a rejection of accommodating attitudes. The liberated woman is refusing to play nursemaid, housekeeper or "earth mother" anymore. It is time for the man, therefore, to reject the role demands on him to play superman: the unneeding, fearless, unemotional, independent, all-around strong man. Liberation for him would mean a reentry into the world of playfulness, intimacy, trusting relationships, emotions and caring, and a priority on fulfillment of *his* needs and *his* growth.

Until now, for many men the message of feminism has simply been that he has been a "bad boy," who must stop being a chauvinist. Nowhere has he been clearly informed or figured out what feminism *could* mean to him, i.e., no longer having to take responsibility for the woman. Furthermore, he could now also expect from her as much as he gave to her. It is no longer necessary for him to be exclusively responsible for courting, paying, performing, providing and deferring. In short, he no longer needs to put her on a pedestal, to hide his true self from her and to behave like a drone buzzing around a queen bee.

Clearly, the woman's role *before* feminism was psychologically disastrous for him. Because she repressed her autonomy, the burden of responsibility and decision making was placed on him. He was under constant pressure to produce and to be right. Her dependency may have engulfed and smothered him, but he couldn't acknowledge it. That would have meant being unmanly. Because it made him feel guilty to reject responsibility for her well-being, he could have no other relationships that might detract from the commitment to "his" woman. Nor could he walk away from an unsatisfying job, because she counted on him. Whatever resentment he felt about all of this he had to repress or deny. To control these feelings, he behaved in an even more mechanical, detached way. This only brought him further criticism, as he was then attacked for not being sufficiently involved and human.

It was clearly a no-win situation. To be a man, he had to take on burdens that eventually overwhelmed and deadened him. If he rejected them, however, he felt guilty and considered that he was a failure. Alcoholism, television, work, cars and watching sports became his distraction and salvation. All were largely dehumanized activities. Often, too, he was chided for overindulging in them. So while her dependence on him may have given him a sense of "control," since he saw her as helpless and was therefore convinced that she would never leave him, from the psychological vantage point he paid a heavy price.

The woman *before* feminist emergence denied her sexuality. She was to be sexually expressive only to a point, which meant satisfying her husband, and only in response to the overtures he initiated. The combination of his lustfulness and her denial of her own sexual need transformed the sexual experience into a gift that she granted him. It gave her tremendous power, although at the cost of her potential pleasure. She could control him and grant him sexual gratification in return for his courting her handsomely, taking responsibility for her, marrying her, giving her what she wanted and so on.

Theirs was, therefore, the relationship of a sex-hungry man and a woman who was all-powerful because she didn't need what he seemed to need so badly. To get it he would pay as high a price as he was capable of. He did so with gratitude and fear that the prize might be withheld or withdrawn again at any time if he stopped performing successfully. In this respect, if he was married he was trapped. She could withhold sex and he could do nothing except humiliate himself by trying to seduce or otherwise persuade her. Once he had married, if he chose to "cheat" on her or leave her, the price was often the loss of most of what he had worked for.

That time was not so long ago. Until recently, most men made lifetime marriage commitments because they hungered for regular sex. Often they married while they were still unable to see the woman as a person beyond her vagina. Then, it was too late. After the wedding he often found himself again in the pathetic position of having to beg for the very thing he had paid so dearly for. Clearly, the dynamic couldn't have been uglier or more degrading for him. Although she many times gave him sex, it was with a passive unenthusiasm that turned it into a distasteful experience, and may even have caused him to become "dysfunctional" in response to the uninvolvement on her part. Then *he* would be flooded with feelings of inadequacy and terrifying doubts about his masculinity. In this old-time man-woman interaction the feminists are rejecting, the man was a source of security who was reinforced and rewarded with sex according to his success. *He married a sex object. She married a standard of living.*

The fantasy of the woman Madonna, someone who is sexually "pure," is also being rejected by the feminists. As a result, he need no longer feel himself to be the hungry animal lusting after a woman who grants him a gift of love because she does not *need* sex. Recent studies on female eroticism, in fact, caused researcher Julia R. Heiman to conclude, "When the smoke clears after the last battle of the sexes, I suspect we will find that men and women aren't as different as we thought—not in needs, not in desires, not in sexual response. Jong's fantasy of the 'zipless fuck' is, after all, what males have yearned for and joked about for years: a sexual encounter with literally no strings attached—neither physical ones, such as zippers or girdles, nor emotional ones, such as feelings of guilt and anxiety."

Heiman continues, "My research finds, indeed, that women like erotica as much as men do, that they are as turned on by sexual descriptions, that their fantasies are as vivid and self-arousing. . . . The experiment also tested the cultural assumption that women are slower to become aroused than men. It is possible that they are merely slower to *admit arousal*."*[1]

Using a series of erotic and romantic tapes, researcher Heiman wrote, "We found, first of all, that explicit sex, not romance, is what turns people on—women as well as men. . . . One erotic tape . . . was especially sexy to women, the female-initiated, female-centered story. . . . I was fascinated that both sexes preferred the female initiator."[2]

The woman before feminist emergence also denied her aggression. Consequently, she resisted dealing directly with conflict and fighting on her own behalf. If she saw herself as injured or neglected, or if she sensed her husband's resentment or anger, she responded with tears or demonstrations of having been hurt. She presented herself as sensitive, fragile, weak and easily injured. In contrast, he was portrayed as the insensitive and hurtful one. He was ultimately responsible and therefore had to apologize. Fights had to be his fault, because she did not release her anger or aggression directly. She simply reacted to him and gained her power and control by acting helpless and maligned.

She gained her power indirectly also by making him feel guilty. Or she developed a repertoire of symptoms such as "nervousness," worry and fear. If he "misbehaved" by coming home late, looking at another woman, forgetting a birthday, making a hurtful remark and so on, she punished him by withdrawl of affection. The conflict, the differences, the causes of the difficulty were rarely dealt with or worked through directly. Nothing could ever be resolved, therefore, and there was little he could do but feel guilty and accept her demands.

In other, more damaging ways the repression of ag-

* Italics not in original.

gression was destructive to males. It is my belief that the
resentment and rage a wife felt toward her husband over
being "controlled" and "exploited" she displaced onto her
son, toward whom she would overreact with excessive dis-
cipline, control, defensive overprotection and a punitive
blocking of his sexuality and aggression. She reacted
to her son as she might have wished to react to her husband but could not. The result of this, I believe, may partially explain the astounding disproportionate rates of
problems experienced by young boys in comparison to
young girls. Autism, hyperkinesis and stuttering all show
rates several hundred percent higher for boys. Childhood
schizophrenia is almost 50 percent higher.

According to government statistics in the early 1970s,
admission to state and county mental hospitals for behavior disorders for boys in the five- to nine-year-old group
was sixteen times greater than for girls.[3] Boys outnumbered girls five to one in this age group for admission for
adjustive reactions.[4]

For residency in state and county mental hospitals, boys
outnumbered girls by approximately ten to one for behavior disorders, and five to one for adjustive reactions.[5]

Psychologists Janet Hyde and Benjamin Rosenberg recently explored the myth of the demure little girl. With a
broad sampling of females of all ages who were asked if
they considered themselves tomboys when they were
growing up or, for the young girls, at present, over 60 percent said they either were or had been tomboys. These researchers found that "tomboyism is not so much
abnormal as it is typical for girls." The image of the
sweet, passive little girl sitting at home by her mother's
side was, they concluded, a false stereotype.[6]

The woman before feminist emergence denied her assertiveness. When asked by the man what she wanted, what
she liked or disliked, where she wanted to go and what she
wanted to do, she frequently responded with a vague "It
doesn't really matter," or "Whatever you want." She
would go along with his choices but often react later with
boredom or even resentment.

In the matter of sex, also, she rarely asserted herself. It
was hard to determine what she really liked or disliked.
She saw it as her job simply to please him. She waited for

him to initiate and orchestrate the experience. Her resistances emerged as physical symptoms—headaches, fatigue, cramps and so on. Or she responded simply in lukewarm or passive fashion, which was also a powerful message of rejection. They were her indirect ways of saying the no she could not take conscious responsibility for.

Because she did not initiate sex or assert herself sexually, a "bad" sexual experience was blamed on *his* ignorance, insensitivity, poor timing and so on. In this regard he was caught in a bind. She would not clearly define her likes and dislikes, nor would she initiate sex. Consequently, he was groping in the dark, and when things went wrong, it was not possible to remedy them. She would not give him feedback or take responsibility and he could only blame himself.

Overall, with her autonomy, sexuality, aggression and assertiveness repressed or consciously hidden, he was living out a part of a gender nightmare which he believed he was supposed to enjoy. After all, he was the master, he was told. The moment-to-moment reality of the situation, however, had to be excruciatingly unsatisfying, crazy-making and boring. He knew something was wrong, but there seemed to be no workable clues or ways to change things. It was a situation beyond his control.

Feminism has been a trauma for some men only because they have reacted defensively, trying to accommodate to the woman while being castigated for being exploiters and chauvinists. These were accusations he could not see beyond. While she was busy defining her new role, he was busy trying to adjust to it rather than redefining his. While she reexamined and rejected aspects of her roles as wife and mother and passive-supportive figure, he was unable to challenge the preconceptions and presumptions of his roles as father, husband, active dominator and so on.

Perhaps the single most valuable contribution of feminism has been the way it has chipped away at men's fantasies about women. Today it is the destructive woman, consciously or unconsciously intent on controlling, manipulating and exploiting men, who feeds on his regressive, pathetic desire to see himself as the dominant superman. In return for these false ego strokes, he assumes responsibility for her. As a result, his emergence out of the gender nightmare is aborted, and he remains a posturing caricature.

This hostile attitude was well expressed by one woman who responded with the following comment to a survey on attitudes and experiences regarding the roles of men and women in our society. She wrote:

"[If men learn that women are superior] we'll be stuck with a lot of sniveling little boys clinging to our skirts. It's better to let them think they're king of the castle, lean and depend on them, and continue to control and manipulate them as we always have."[7]

A man is in jeopardy if he fails to realize that the "fragile," "passive" women of today is not "feminine" but repressed, and may well emerge as the angry woman of tomorrow who will turn the tables on him at a time when he may hardly be prepared or equipped to adapt to the changes. Such is the price of refusing to recognize what is.

The man who grasps the psychological meaning of feminism will be the man who can liberate himself from the destructive compulsion to perform and to assume all responsibility. He will be free to create a life-style that puts a focus on his own development as a person. This will mean an end to the all-consuming obsession with success, which has produced in him a defensive, distrustful stance toward the world such that all of his energies go toward protecting and proving himself. He will live not by the symbols of masculinity but by the measure of whether his life feels good and brings him in closer contact with himself and other people. Gone will be the days and the relationships that have drawn him into endless penis waving, muscle flexing and wallet flaunting in order to prove that he is worthy of love and respect.

Indeed, should the feminist movement falter, should the impetus toward female liberation be slowed by the regressive pull of old-time manipulative feminine role playing, men, out of the most self-caring of motives, must insist and facilitate woman's transition to the point where she relates and functions as a total person who is equally responsible, sexual, assertive and autonomous. The growth of men depends on the growth of women, and vice versa, in order for the sexes to experience the full potential of themselves and each other. To fall back into the sex-object, success-object way of relating may be a temporarily anxiety-reducing, even seemingly pleasant seduction because it is familiar ground, but the price will be the continuation of the destructive gender fantasy which perpetuates the annihilation of each other's full personhood.

PART FOUR

HE
AND HIS
CHANGES

16. Self-Destruction Is Masculine, Getting Better Is Feminine

It is a core factor in the tragic paradox of masculinity that the attitudes and patterns that break a man down are uniquely masculine, while the processes required to move him in the direction of reintegration and growth are feminine.

The traditional man does not come to therapy until he has reached an insurmountable crisis and exhausted all other remedies. He is usually in a state of desperation when he arrives for help and, understandably, he wants instant relief and concrete results. No matter that his crisis is merely an end point, a rupture caused by years and years of repression and unawareness.

After working with large numbers of men over a long period of time, one can predict with fair accuracy a man's initial response and the length of time he will remain in therapy. The more "macho" he is in his orientation, meaning that he is:

1) Strongly rational or problem-solving oriented;

2) Threatened by the acknowledgment of weakness, fear, vulnerability, the exposure of his inner life or the fact that he can't solve his problems himself;

3) Competitive toward other men and compulsively needing to prove himself superior and able to control and dominate situations while projecting an image of self-containment and strength;

4) Impatient and suspicious of any process that has no clear-cut path or timetable and promises no specific results;

5) Needing to project a totally masculine image while defensively denying anything in him that might be construed as "feminine" or "homosexual"; and

6) Fearful of depending on and trusting somebody else,

204 THE NEW MALE

the quicker will his anxiety, resistance, resentment and
overall defensiveness build, causing him to back away
from the therapeutic process. In fact, if there were surgical
procedures or drug therapies available that could bring
women back to their terrified husbands or lovers, restore
erections instantly or create success, most men would forever close themselves off from the exploration of their
emotions and their life experience.

Typically, the more "macho" his orientation, the more
resistant will he be and the more delicate will be the
process required to bring him around to a commitment to
the arduous and unpredictable process of growth.

A thirty-one-year-old bus driver came for psychotherapy
because his twenty-nine-year-old wife had become involved
with a fireman she had met while working as a hostess in
an all-night coffee shop. She told her husband of her intention to move out and file for divorce proceedings, though
financial insecurity was causing her to postpone an immediate move. After his initial shock he retaliated by dating
several women and was impotent with each. His wife had
always passively accommodated his most idiosyncratic sex
fantasy or experiment, even though she found it distasteful, and so he had never had any potency problems with
her. He had treated her like a sex object, never even aware
of her growing resentment and lack of genuine responsiveness. His experiences with his dates, coupled with the
prospect of losing the woman with whom he felt sexually
secure, terrified him. So he came for psychotherapy.

He entered the office looking very depressed. He rumi-
nated openly about suicide. He was filled with regret and
self-hate over what he had put his wife through sexually.
He described all the things he had done to try and get her
back—threats of self-destruction, violence toward her
boyfriend, withholding financial support and fighting for
custody of their child. Nothing swayed her. He looked to
his therapist for an "answer." After only forty minutes of
the first session, when his therapist said he could offer no
quick or easy solution, the patient stated, "I don't think
I'm getting anything out of this. I knew I would be wasting my time," and he left.

In a similar instance, a man in his mid-thirties who had
been abandoned by his wife six months before and had

since been having difficulty getting erections came for therapy because he had found a woman he felt he might want to marry. He had not yet risked sexual involvement and came for therapy to prepare himself so that he'd be sure not to fail. He was afraid that if he couldn't perform, her image of him as a man would be destroyed and she would end the relationship. He was even concerned lest she somehow find out that he was seeking help. This would mean that he had "clay feet," and she would lose her romantic feelings. Further, he sought immediate assurance that his employer would never find out he was seeing a psychologist, because he was up for a promotion and feared he would be labeled "unstable."

He came, as many men do, looking for psychotherapeutic magic. He wanted his impotence "cured" as quickly as possible. He announced defensively that he knew many women who had gone to "shrinks," and he didn't see any real changes in them. However, he didn't know what else to do, so he would give it a try. He said, however, that he didn't want to waste time talking about his past or himself. He wanted a solution to his "sex problem."

When his therapist didn't immediately pursue a line of questioning focused on sex, he became antagonistic. He asked if the therapist performed hypnosis or could teach him fantasy imagery that he could use to stimulate himself when he was having trouble. When the therapist said he didn't feel that was the best solution the patient asked to be referred to a urologist. "Maybe I have a physical problem," he said.

A twenty-five-year-old man, a bank-management trainee, came for psychotherapy because his wife of two years was openly involved in an affair with a young attorney who lived directly across the courtyard in their apartment complex. His wife informed him that she needed a month to think things over and to decide what she should do and would be taking her own apartment. Her husband pleaded with her to give him a chance to change in order to get her back. When he asked her to be specific about what she didn't like about him, she told him that his temper was a major cause of her leaving.

He took her contention literally and came for therapy.

He announced with great urgency that he only had one month to change and wanted to know how to get rid of his temper. When his therapist asked him if his temper was a lifelong problem, he replied that he had always thought of himself as mild mannered until about a year ago. When his therapist responded that perhaps his temper was a reaction to something in the relationship, the patient retorted, "I don't like my temper, either. I think she's right. Just tell me what I can do about it." When his therapist told him that they'd have to explore his angry reactions in greater depth, the man asked for a tranquilizer prescription to hold him over in the meantime. He couldn't risk the possibility, he said, that it might take longer than a month to overcome *his* problem.

The bind faced by any therapist working with these men in their time of crisis is that by the time they come for help they often feel that the stakes are too high to engage in any time-consuming process. If the therapist accommodates the patient's urgency with some expedient procedure that might bring about a temporary change and a reduction in discomfort, the patient is likely to terminate. The usual comment is, "I think I can handle things from here. I feel much better." The hard job of growth and self-awareness has been aborted. If the therapeutic process is allowed to proceed at its usual and slower pace, the patient's anxiety, impatience and resistance often become so great that he leaves to seek out an alternate solution. Either way he never really learns about himself, and the problems are bound to recur.

A twenty-five-year-old marketing manager with one of America's largest computer corporations came for help because of the panicky feelings he experienced whenever he had to make a presentation at a staff meeting. He was intensely competitive, and was concerned that if he didn't overcome his problem quickly the other salesmen might soon be passing him in the climb up the corporate ladder.

Realizing the urgency of the situation (several important presentations were scheduled for the next few months), his therapist used the behavioral technique called systematic desensitization. This is a form of relaxation training and requires the patient to lie on the couch with his eyes closed as he pictures himself in the process of preparing for and giving his presentation.

Shortly after beginning his first session, the patient became noticeably tense. His therapist asked him what he was thinking, and he replied, "Nothing." After another twenty minutes of obvious discomfort and an inability to focus, the patient fearfully revealed his fantasy that the therapist might attack him violently and homosexually. Asked to explore this further, he began relating experiences with his father and early memories of being insulted, punished, hit and called a sissy when he performed poorly at a task. He related this to his experience during a sales presentation where he imagined his peers making fun of him if he made any mistakes or did not appear polished.

Had his therapy remained confined only to symptom relief, specifically the elimination of his "stage fright" or nervousness while making a presentation, the underlying dynamics that were the actual cause of his anxiety would never have been uncovered. He might have experienced temporary relief, but the problems caused by the deeper feelings would have intensified. Increasingly, his energies would have gone toward protecting himself against these anticipated assaults.

Because men define themselves by denying the existence of internal and emotional factors that threaten or contradict their masculine image, they will avoid an approach to their problems that is probing or psychological in nature. The idea that there is something inherent in their masculine orientation that might be a factor in creating their problems will provoke hostility and a defensive reaction.

At a talk I gave in a conservative business community in California, sponsored by a chapter of the American Association of University Women, many men were present who would not ordinarily have come to my lectures. They were there only because they traditionally accompanied their wives to this once-a-month meeting for married couples.

The majority of the men in attendance were between the ages of thirty and forty, and many were in the midst of developing their management and business careers. A half hour into my talk, the tension level in the room was unusually high as I elaborated on the subject of masculinity and the "hazards of being male." Several men were nervously shifting about in their seats, looking down at the floor or at me in obvious resentment. After the presentation was over, a conversation with the husband of one of the women who had arranged for my talk revealed his concern that one of the men would lose control and become physically assaultive. He had planned a strategy, as he stood in the back of the room, in the event that this happened.

The "macho" male, resistant to psychotherapeutic help, is often still unconsciously reacting to his painful and destructive relationship with his father, who had been rigid, punitive and emotionally withholding when he was a young boy. Entering therapy with a male therapist, who is seen as an authority figure, threatens to reproduce the father's hostile reaction to any exposure of the patient's inadequacy, fear or weakness.

A thirty-two-year-old man, a compulsively achievement-oriented accountant who was completing law school at night while holding down a full-time job, was ridden with anxiety and feelings of inadequacy. He described his relationship with his father this way: "My father never felt that I did anything right. He has never shown in any way that he cares for me. I never told him how I felt inside, because he would have gotten angry and thought I was weak."

In a more pathetic instance, a professional counselor who was a quadriplegic victim of the Vietnam war went for therapy because of severe strain in a relationship with a woman he hoped to marry. He sought out a female therapist because he said that he could never trust a man who might turn out to be like his father. "He was so cold, so violent. He never showed any feeling except violent anger, and if my brother or I showed any feelings at all he would beat us. He beat us into holding everything inside. I can't do that anymore. He'd never understand this."

There are numerous vicious circles that operate in the father-son relationship that perpetuate and intensify the emotional strangulation that takes place from generation to generation. A father who has incorporated as a positive value his own compulsive self-denial as he stoically takes on stifling and frustrating roles passes on his own emotional repression and self-punishing orientation to his son. He erupts in explosive defensiveness when his son displays any of the emotion he himself has expended much of his psychic energy to control and deny. He is much like the puritanical mother who reacts with extreme punitiveness to any overt expression of her daughter's sexuality, the impulses she has fought against and denied in herself.

The paradox of psychotherapy, one of society's approved ways of getting better emotionally, is that the process itself, if analyzed according to its dimensions, is essentially a feminine and unmasculine enterprise. Consequently, it throws a man up against the very things in himself that he fears most. It is understandable, therefore, that most men are inclined to ridicule the process of therapy and to view it as a rip-off, an expensive price to pay for a shoulder to cry on or a waste of time engaged in primarily by unstable women. The male view of it as a "feminine" activity makes sense when one recognizes that a person who enters therapy is consciously or unconsciously engaging in the following "feminine" or "unmasculine" behaviors:

1) Asking for help and acknowledging that one cannot do it by oneself. This is tantamount to crying uncle, and any man "worth his salt" will resist that to the very end.

2) Exposing one's weak side, one's helplessness, vulnerability, confusion and pain. Men have learned that to do this is foolhardy because it may lead to destruction. At best it will result in humiliation and rejection.

3) Depending on someone else for a sustained period of time. Dependency is acceptable only for women. The dependent male is a "sissy."

4) Acknowledging that one has emotions and that a rational, problem-solving, goal-oriented approach is not enough. To be emotional is to be feminine. Giving in to this unknown and threatening entity, in the man's mind, may lead to being overwhelmed and losing complete control.

5) Suspending the masculine desire for action, immediate answers and a concrete approach that will produce specific, rapid results.

6) Spending money on something that is intangible. Psychotherapy is a process that is nonmaterial. One can neither eat, wear, drive or play with it. In his mind, such frivolous spending is a wasteful, feminine extravagance.

7) Experiencing and working through the blocks to intimacy. The possible feelings of affection and warmth that might arise would be upsetting, particularly if the therapist is a man. Worse still is the prospect of any homosexual fantasies or desires arising in the process.

8) Confronting and suspending his competitive need to prove himself superior and to "defeat" his therapist. In that sense he had to give up his inclination to be "one up."

9) Recognition that life decisions and long-held cherished values may have been based on distorted and destructive premises and motivations. This is a particularly threatening realization for someone who has committed himself to the belief that he must always be right. In other words, by probing his inner experience he is confronted with the frightening possibility that the lie will be given to that which he has tenaciously clung to as being the correct and best way.

It is not surprising, therefore, that women have traditionally made up the bulk of most psychotherapists' practices. The reason for this is not the one feminists have put forth, namely, that women have more emotional problems and are vulnerable to more psychological distress. Rather, men have by and large unconsciously boycotted psychotherapy because it is essentially a "feminine" activity. The men who in the past have willingly gone into analysis or therapy are, I believe, primarily those whose gender identification is softer, less masculinely defensive, and allows for more of their "feminine" parts to be available and acceptable to them.

Masculine resistance to therapy is a tragedy more because of the implications than anything else. The efficacy of psychotherapy is still a matter of debate. However, the implied statements men make by resisting it are the crucial aspect. Quite simply, they are tacitly indicating that asking for help, depending, giving up control, being emotional, acknowledging fear, weakness, vulnerability and so on are all unacceptable. The only masculinely appropriate alternative is to battle it out on one's own to the last vestiges of one's strength. There are *no* other non-implicating alternatives. Such is the nature, paradox and tragedy of the masculine attitude when it comes to change and growth.

17. Feed Yourself!

Ike was fifty-nine when his wife, Ruth, went into the hospital for the removal of a malignant brain tumor. The doctor leveled with him. "She may not live more than a year, and it's going to be a very, very difficult time. The chemotherapy will make her nauseous, weak and forgetful. She'll need a lot of your attention and help."

Ike was despairing when he related this to his ex-daughter-in-law, Sally, who called him after the surgery.

"I know why I left my husband," Sally said to a friend of hers while describing her conversation with Ike. "When he really sounded the most upset, it was about food. 'Who's going to prepare my meals? Ruth's the only one who knows how I need to have my food cooked.' I had to reassure him," Sally continued, "that he would still get fed properly and wouldn't starve. His son was the same way when we were married."

A forty-three-year-old woman was married to a cement worker who had the habit of behaving in a seductive way with other women in front of his wife. It never failed to enrage her, to the point where she would threaten divorce, even though this behavior had been going on for years.

Theirs was a traditional "earth mother"–"macho warrior" relationship from the start. When they were married, she was virginal, religious and passive-submissive in her reactions to him. She spent much of their first two years together designing menus and preparing special meals, in between keeping the house immaculate and the clothes cleaned and ironed. Her husband, Acker, would come home tired and often slightly high on alcohol and would sit in front of the television set with his dinner. Periodically he would call out, "Another beer, honey, please!" That constituted the bulk of his verbal communication.

From the first year of their marriage he had shown his resentment toward her by regularly finding fault with one of the dishes she prepared for dinner. He'd always leave some food on the plate, and then later complain that he was hungry. When he was really upset about the food, perhaps because it was over- or undercooked, he would go over to the pot on the stove and spit in it or feign vomiting.

Each day she woke early to prepare him a lunch to take to work. On the days she was angry with him because she had caught him staring at a woman or he had been particularly offensive in his reaction to something she had prepared for dinner, she would punish him by not preparing him a lunch. Not knowing how to prepare it himself, Acker went to work without any. His co-workers would tease him. "Sheila and you been fightin' again, huh, Acker? Why don't you start treating her right and you won't have to starve!"

It always embarrassed him to be lunchless, so by evening he was contrite. He knew that if he irritated her any more, there'd be no lunch the following day and he'd have to face the gibes of his co-workers again.

Julie, a thirty-year-old woman, also submissive in her response to her engineer husband, though very successful in her professional work as an economic analyst for a government agency, had married her husband ten years before.

Now, ten years later, she found herself in a sexless marriage, sleeping in a king-size bed with an invisible line down the center, demarcated by her husband. She was not to trespass it when they were in bed together unless he gave her permission.

Her strict Mormon upbringing had made an affair a frightening, out-of-the-question idea, until quite suddenly and unexpectedly she found herself with an adolescentlike crush on a co-worker, a recently divorced man her own age. She was overwhelmed with anxiety when, after a morning in bed with him at his apartment, he asked her to leave her husband and move in with him. She sought the help of a psychologist to deal with her guilt and confusion.

She related the details of her marital relationship. She

described the rigidity and emptiness of a life which revolved around her husband's six-day, twelve-hour-a-day workweek, with his Sundays spent tinkering with his boat or sports car.

The idea of leaving him, however, left her guilt-stricken. "I can't do it," she said. "He counts on me completely, and he'd be helpless if I left. I wake him in the morning and get him going. I put out his clothes for him and buy him new ones when he needs them. He doesn't know how to shop or cook or even do dishes. He'd be eating out of cans and wearing the same underwear until he'd have to throw it away if I wasn't there. I really think he might die without me," she said in guilty, anxious tones. "I just couldn't do that to him. He depends on me for everything."

A report on the plight of America's two million widowers, published in the *U.S. News & World Report,* indicated that American widowers have a much higher rate of mental breakdown, physical illness, alcoholism, suicide and accidents than do widows or married men.[1]

Helena Lopata, a professor of sociology and director of the Center for the Comparative Study of Social Roles at Loyola University, writing on widows and widowers, described how the division of labor in the family has meant that husbands become totally dependent on their wives for most activities pertaining to the home, and even for their own maintenance, except for a few "male" tasks. In addition, the woman has been assigned, or has taken upon herself, the function of maintaining the couple's social interactions, not only with her family and other couples, but even with her husband's family.[2]

Many widowers are incapable of adequate self-maintenance. They go to pieces when their wives die, as they find they can't turn on a gas range, operate a washing machine or even buy their own food or clothing. They also tend to become socially isolated, because they don't know how to maintain social relationships outside of work without their wives to act as intermediaries. For some, even making a personal telephone call becomes a terrifying experience.

The phenomenon of helplessness, which is plainly visible

among widowers, also exists among many married men. Their relationship to their wives becomes progressively more regressive, the man transforming into a demanding child and the wife emerging as the mothering figure, the feeder and the wiper.

The blossoming of this deadening, draining dependency often occurs early in the relationship. One desperate twenty-four-year-old man had a wife of two years who was restless, busy liberating herself and putting increasing emotional distance between herself and him. In a moment of despair when he thought he might lose her altogether, he told her, "You give me life. Without you I don't really enjoy anything."

It was obvious why his wife, in the interest of self-preservation, began secretly dating other men. In two years' time the relationship had gone from being a very erotic, spontaneous one with frequent weekend trips to one in which weekends were spent in their newly purchased home, with him doing yard work, making repairs around the house and working on his car. Sex occurred on a predictable, twice-a-week schedule, often during commercial breaks on television.

They rarely saw other couples unless she initiated it, which she did with decreasing frequency, because he always looked so bored when they went out. His wife could see the tomb she was being enclosed in. She was only surprised that he couldn't see it the same way. She couldn't understand how he could claim to be happy. It didn't please her to hear that *she* was his happiness and that *she* was his best companion. Without her, he'd tell her, all that would remain for him would be barhopping with co-workers, shooting darts, getting drunk and trying to pick up a woman in order to get laid. "I already have the best," he'd tell her, thinking she'd be flattered. Her reaction, however, was resentment and revulsion at his childlike dependency and predictability.

Once most men become deeply involved with a woman, they steadily abandon their own tastes and sensibilities and progressively relate to her as a mothering figure in charge of feeding, clothes selection and home decoration. Worse even than little boys, who at least choose their own friends and create their own social life, these men tend to turn the responsibility for social arrangements over to their wives. Then, after resisting sharing in these decisions, they passively endure what she plans, all the while complaining of boredom.

Eventually this social withdrawal extends to a resistance even to making phone calls, whether to members of his own family or a "friend" or to make a doctor's appointment. Sending off gifts, thank-you cards and birthday greetings also gets assigned to her. At best he signs the card, and often only after repeated urging.

In a regressive social withdrawal, he becomes practically phobic about initiating or involving himself in any social experience by himself, except perhaps for going to a sporting event or to a bar for a drink. (Many men won't even do that.)

He is setting the stage for extreme vulnerability and isolation should his relationship with his wife change or end. It is a dramatic reversal from their courtship days, when he felt that decisions as to where to go and what to do were his responsibility. Once the relationship has taken on a permanence, however, he regresses to this passive, detached state. Some men even begin to believe that they would starve, walk around in filthy, tattered clothing, stare all alone at television in a dirt-infested room after nursing a beer in a seedy bar if it were not for her.

It took one man almost three years after his marriage had ended to realize that he disliked most of the clothing he'd been wearing, which had been selected by his wife at *his* urging. He also found his household furnishings, most of which his wife had originally picked out, uncomfortable. During the course of his marriage he had come to believe, as many married men do, that his taste and judgment in these matters were crude and even embarrassing. Perhaps it started when he picked out a shirt or suggested an upholstery fabric or some artifact or painting. His wife's reaction may have communicated to him that he lacked taste and that he was lucky to have her, because in this regard she could save him from himself. He accepted her reaction as truth, because it jibed with his own image of himself as an aesthetic clod. He stopped trying to develop his own tastes, to the point where he really had no conscious opinions on these matters. After a while he didn't trust his judgment and he didn't really know what he liked.

In so doing, he had given up a large part of his self and his potential. Many of these areas of responsibility—food preparation, decorating, social planning, clothes selection, even parenting—had been defined to him as feminine when he was growing up. A "real man" would be suspect if he showed great interest or sensitivity in these areas.

A less conscious reason for turning over these matters to the woman was that it created a basis for communication. It gave them a way of connecting. Not to give her these responsibilities might push them toward the very threatening realization that they had little in common, little to say to each other or to share and enjoy together. Without this structure they would have to relate person to person as one would expect to do in a friendship, rather than as mother to child. Indeed, many who choose each other for marital partners or for living together (because he sees in her "earth mother" qualities and she sees in him qualities of protectiveness and dominance and a source of security) would not be compatible enough to choose each other as friends. That is, they do not truly enjoy each other's company as play companions. To look closely at all of that is a frightening prospect. It is easier to polarize and behave in rigid, gender-defined ways.

Growth is blocked, then, because growth requires relating as person to person rather than by prescribed roles. To move in that direction might reveal that there was nothing to fill the vacuum. In addition, once he has invested his primitive dependency needs in her and feels simultaneously compelled to affirm his masculinity, he cannot risk jeopardizing the balance of the relationship, lest his perceived source of life be withdrawn. His unconscious resistances to change, therefore, become very powerful. The man who scorns "men's lib" or is glad his wife is not a feminist may be merely hiding his own dependency needs, revealing his fear of change and possible abandonment and the loss of the precious breast.

The relationship in these instances becomes progressively less sensual and playful. Its focus gradually moves to the kitchen and the dining room. She feeds and he eats. To prove her love, she prepares special "goodies" at mealtime and encourages him to eat several helpings. To demonstrate his acceptance of her love, he eats even when he's not hungry or doesn't really like what she has prepared. In restaurants she regularly shovels food from her plate onto his, or leaves some of her food for him to finish. It is interesting to note how rarely one sees the reverse—the man pushing food onto the woman's plate—unless it involves a special dessert treat. Then, in a temporary role transformation, he becomes "daddy," giving his "little girl" a fatherly token of love.

When he's angry with her, he rejects or insults her food or precipitates a fight at the dining table and stalks away. When she's angry with him—if she's bold enough—she won't prepare anything at all, or will simply throw something together haphazardly, serve it late, over- or undercook it. That becomes her way of punishing him.

Even when the mood in the house seems to be pleasant, he may suddenly be transformed into an angry child when he comes home in the evening and dinner is late, or if he asks for something from the refrigerator, which he could easily get himself, and she doesn't immediately meet his demand or, worse still, tells him to get it himself. Each minute that he waits for the food seems to him like an hour, because it is unconsciously translated to mean rejection. Each request becomes a test of her love. The greater his underlying insecurity, the more frequently the testing occurs.

Often she prepares meals even though she's too tired and doesn't really want to, simply because she is afraid to upset him. Even illness may not be a satisfactory excuse for warding off his resentful response to not being fed. After all, his mother always managed to have food on the table, sick or not. If his wife "really" loved him, she'd find a way also.

He eats the meals she prepares for him even though he may not be hungry, because not to do so would mean symbolically to reject her love, aggress upon her, hurt her "fragile" feelings, upset the "earth mother"–macho interaction or possibly turn her off to the preparation of meals in the future. He can't afford to get her angry or have her remain angry too long, any more than a child could live with that in his mother.

Without the rituals around food there might be little other ongoing basis for verbal communication. The oft-repeated feminist contention that men have controlled women by keeping them in the kitchen could be looked at in the opposite way. That is, women have controlled men by reinforcing the processes that caused the men to feel that they could not survive—or could barely survive—without the women there to prepare the food.

Feeding him, together with all the other mothering activities she performs, becomes the major basis for the traditional relationship. Even though he may be less physically active than she on a daily basis, he usually eats much more than she. Again, this is a replay of his early childhood experience. Mother was always too busy feeding others to eat herself. She was the food preparer and server. Her son was constantly pulling at her for an extra something to eat. When she provided it, he relaxed and felt loved. When she didn't, he felt hurt, tense and angry. Part of being a "good boy" was also being a "good eater," the one who never left anything on his plate.

The obsession with dieting which is so common in these marriages can also be seen as having some of its roots in this interaction. When food is the major basis for sharing and communicating, weight problems and an obsession with eating become inevitable. The huge market for diet books is thus created.

Diet and an obsession with calories and weight become a never-ending, insoluble problem, because the eating rituals are critically needed to sustain the interaction. Such couples cannot afford to downplay or eliminate the eating focus for too long a time. Going out to eat, discussing what will be eaten or was just eaten, preparing special things to eat, are too important to the maintenance of the relationship. Like the couple who are having "sex problems" because of a lack of genuine interest, passion, playfulness and pleasure in each other but are afraid to deal with these feelings and therefore intellectualize and abstract this "problem" by attributing it to physiological ignorance or faulty techniques and proceed to buy books to study up on the subject of sex, the "earth mother"–macho couple become involved in an endless pursuit of the perfect or magic diet. It can never be found, because each new diet must eventually be undermined in order to preserve the relationship.

If the overweight man looks to the woman to help him with his dieting, an impossible bind is created which will subvert his best intentions to lose weight permanently. Since her way of showing love has been to feed him, and eating has been his way of accepting her love and feeling loved, dieting throws this interaction off balance and the relationship into a crisis if the diet lasts too long.

Socially, he becomes progressively more withdrawn as he responds mechanically to her announcements about what they'll do or whom they'll see on the weekend. As part of his masculine posture, he will groan and complain, while she plays out her mother role and chides and warns him to be civil and to try and make an effort to be friendly. He welcomes this unconsciously, because by himself he would have no social life and no friends. Her social arrangements, despite his complaints, save him from confronting the total emptiness of his interpersonal life.

The social life of his own creation at best involves talking to his next-door male neighbor, discussing the latest in gardening equipment or automobile maintenance. Nothing really intimate is shared, and "He's a nice guy" becomes the extent to which these men can describe each other. Often even these truncated relationships break down when one of the men becomes disappointed, bored, angry or sees the other as just "an asshole!" or a "jerk!"

All this was perhaps viable *before* feminism. Today, however, women are owning their feelings of resentment. This is the inevitable result of having played passive-sub-missive-receptive "earth mother" and being drained by his little-boy demandingness, his pouting when food was late or not prepared to his liking or a sock misplaced, at the same time his once frantic sexual appetite turned into mechanical, perfunctory, even grim efforts at lovemaking. She is actively making changes, refusing to play some old roles and sometimes abandoning the relationship altogether.

The result of having given up these significant parts of himself confronts him. He doesn't want to live, or is afraid to live without her as a feeder, a buffer against people and an all-around protective, caring figure. On his own he finds he is only a compulsive work machine. He has lost so much of himself that he can only envision a life of loneliness, canned food, dirty underwear and an unkept apartment.

This primitively dependent way in which many men tend to relate to the woman in their life is *the* invisible obstacle, *the* single most powerful block to their growth. It will abort any significant, genuine, self-caring change in the man. The rapid and powerful movement toward growth and change by many women during the last fifteen years came about because female dependency on the male did not have the kind of primitive tenacity that the male's has on the female.

Her dependency need for him existed primarily to the extent that the economic marketplace appeared to her to be an intimidating battleground. The nature of her need, however, was not the primitive one of being fed, cleaned, dressed, provided with human contact and so on. For many women the unfamiliar economic world was even an attractive one in its way, an area of masculine privilege that she wanted to participate in.

For most men, however, the woman *is* perceived as a lifeline. It is not surprising, therefore, that the abandoned man often becomes deeply depressed, even suicidal or violent toward the man he blames for taking "his" woman away. "I don't want to live without her anyway," was the way one man expressed it after mutilating a man who was having an affair with his ex-wife.

It is also not surprising that so many women today are initiating the breakup of these relationships. It is a self-preservative response designed to protect them from having their lifeblood drained by the man's tendency to fixate on them as a mothering figure. The woman has become exhausted playing the ever-flowing breast. If she is anything but a masochist or a frightened manipulator holding on to him as a meal ticket, she must inevitably reject him for her survival's sake.

Samuel Wallace, an associate professor of sociology at the University of Tennessee, in his book *After Suicide*, interviewed in depth twelve women who had been widowed by suicide. The thread that tied together the narratives of these women was that their husbands were men who had a never-ending need for care. These women originally had a seemingly equal need to provide that care. Their lives revolved around this care-giving, with increasing isolation and the exclusion of others as the marital relationship became more intense. The man's dependency progressively dominated the whole marital life space.

Wallace states that at first these women continued to live with their husbands. "They threatened, they complained, and they suffered, but they slept in the same house and usually in the same bed. They lost their friends, their neighbors, their families, their children, their financial and emotional resources and still they continued to care."[3]

Then something happened which caused seven of these women to reverse their pattern and to break from their men in what Wallace describes as a "social dying." It preceded the eventual suicide.

This study by Wallace is particularly significant, I believe, because it is only an exaggeration of the state of most marriages in which the woman is cast in the role of "care-giver," at first appearing to thrive on it but ultimately being engulfed and drained by the demanding dependency and the increasing isolation from outside influences. When she finally becomes overwhelmed and makes a break for freedom, he is flooded by terror and depression and behaves desperately and self-destructively.

The possibility of alienating or offending her with his changes, his movement toward liberation and away from stereotypical masculine role playing is an intimidating and powerful obstacle to his growth. He is much like the young child who is fearful of expressing his anger or independence directly toward his parents for fear that they will reject him and he will be left to starve.

He is caught in yet another impossible bind. To change in a way that might result in rejection is threatening because it might lead to abandonment. To change in a way that meets her demands will not really deal with the important issues of his life, and while he might temporarily appease or please her, she may be ultimately alienated and repelled when she sees through his façade of "goodwill" and recognizes its underlying motive, which is the fear of losing his lifeline. Not to change at all is also to risk losing her.

Until he can find the resources within himself and among others, both men and women, to nurture and sustain him through transition periods which may upset the balance of the relationship he is in, he will lose *whatever* direction he goes, because he is pinned by his primitive dependency. In this light it is understandable that many contemporary women are resisting intimacy with men altogether. Their choice too often seems to be between a rigidly masculine sexist who is controlling and unemotional in his attitude and an accommodating male who is changing for fear of rejection and abandonment.

To remedy this difficult situation there must first be a male awareness and understanding that the primitive fixation on one woman for his nurturance is psychologically destructive and a dangerous, untenable choice. Then he must begin the hard work of bringing himself up again.

First, he must experience the anger and fear that underlie the dependency grip that is strangling him. While the woman is *not* to blame for his fixation—since her psychologically controlling role is as unconscious and automatic as his reaction—the resentment is nevertheless there and must be experienced directly. Just as the woman needed to experience her anger and rage initially in order to free herself from her narrow role, he needs to experience his. However, to experience these feelings, including the intense need, the fear of loss and the anger, is deeply threatening to him, because it contradicts everything he has learned to cherish as part of his masculine image. Still, growth, I believe, will be aborted without it.

Once this is experienced and worked through, he must avoid the temptation of a repetition of investing his total self in one woman while systematically cutting himself off from all other intimate ties. Instead, he must establish a new relationship rhythm, working through the defenses that block him from getting close to more than one person at a time. Typically, competitiveness, fear of vulnerability and homosexual anxiety have kept him away from closeness to other men, while various forms of sexual games have blocked him from having friendships with women. Intimate ties with caring people of both sexes must be nourished and nurtured if he is to have the safety and security required to emerge as a person rather than as a gender stereotype.

Next, he will have to reown all of the basic survival skills and aesthetic sensibility that he has traditionally believed belonged to the woman or thought he was incapable of handling. Feeding himself is the symbol of these changes, because food has been the primitive glue that kept him fixed to the regressive and destructive "earth mother" relationship. A non–"earth mother"–macho relationship will be based on the pleasure of each other's friendship rather than on being taken care of in childlike fashion. He will come to her to expand himself as a person rather than to be mothered.

To be fed by her, to eat at certain prescribed ritualistic times, to feel angered when meals are late, to be fearful of not eating because doing so might upset her, to see himself as incapable of choosing and preparing exactly what he wants to eat by himself when he wants to eat it will be viewed by the free men as humiliating and self-destructive. Therefore, while the pleasure of sharing in the preparation of food with her can still be retained, he will self-caringly reject a relationship in which the woman's basic and primary posture toward him is one of feeding and taking care of him. It brings out the worst in both of them as he becomes increasingly a demanding, clinging, insatiable and guilt-ridden boy, while she assumes the part of the long-suffering, all-giving "earth mother."

Feeding himself will also be a symbolic launching place for freeing himself from other forms of childlike dependency. Most important, he will need to choose and maintain his own relationships, whether she shares in them or not. Choosing only individuals that both he and she are comfortable with tends to reduce the level of these relationships to the lowest, least threatening and unstimulating common denominator.

Further, the tendency of the man to relate to his woman intimate as the sole close relationship, and to lay on her the responsibility of being the social director who decides what they will do and with whom, systematically thwarts and blocks the development of his own social sensibilities and makes him self-destructively vulnerable. Should the relationship with his woman ever be in jeopardy, he will tend to accommodate and cling, rather than move in a self-caring direction, because to lose her is also to witness the collapse of his social world.

Along with the "feed yourself" attitude will come the rediscovery and reclaiming of his own taste in clothing and grooming styles. To give these up is tacitly to affirm that his judgment is inferior and that she knows best. There will be much pleasure in exploring and learning what feels and looks good to him.

He would also need to discover what makes his environment feel good. A Los Angeles psychologist recently described the experience of selecting and decorating his own place to live. "It is like exploring a larger part of something of me I have never explored before; I have always lived with the assumption, one I grew up with, that as a man I wouldn't understand how to make a place 'feel at home.' Now I am making the decisions, exploring what *I* want, trying to find what feels comfortable. I don't think these things can be classified as female, but I think that is how many men perceive them. I have admired men who seem to have more of a feeling for doing these kinds of things."[4]

Once he has resumed all of the basic dimensions of self-care, feeding himself in his own rhythm, selecting and caring for his clothing, creating his own environment, selecting and maintaining his own relationships regardless of whether the woman in his life shares or approves, he can then relate to his woman on a basis that can produce the highest form of the male-female relationship. They can become playmates who assume the burdens and responsibilities for life equally, who come to each other not out of the motivation of regressive dependency and the inability to survive separately, but out of the drive to enhance their lives, to be exposed to new dimensions of experience, to be challenged and stimulated, and without feelings on his part that he needs to cling to her for his life's sake, to feel responsible for her or frightened of alienating her. In short, they will come together to facilitate each other's movement toward a spontaneous, authentic, playful, expansive and exploratory attitude toward life, rather than the rigid, serious, isolated and conservative attitude that describes the posture of the "earth mother" and the "macho," the nurturer and the demanding child who is seeking to be fed both literally and symbolically.

18. The Recovery of Male Sexuality: From "Serious Sex" to "Playful Sex"

Of the impossible binds that ensnare and ultimately paralyze and destroy the male by confronting him with paradoxical and insoluble dilemmas, perhaps the cruelest is the area of "sex." I put quotation marks around the word "sex" because I believe that the traditional way the word has been used is misleading, psychologically erroneous, damaging and in many ways crazy. Consider these statements and questions:

"How's your SEX LIFE?"

"I don't like SEX."

"Do you have less of a SEX DRIVE than he/she does?"

"What is the normal number of times a week to have SEX?"

"Sometimes I'm too tired to have SEX."

"How do you feel about SEX?"

These create, then reinforce and perpetuate a depersonalized, split-off orientation toward this experience. The implication underlying these usages is, "There's ME, and then there's my SEX LIFE." My "sex life" and "sexual functioning" have a life of their own.

The language used to describe sexuality and the nature of most discussions about this subject continually perpetuate this orientation. A man who is sexually involved with a woman might acknowledge, if he stopped long enough to look at it honestly, that he was bored with her conversation, did not particularly find attractive the sound of her voice, her smell, the look or motion of her body, nor did her touch even feel good to him. *Yet that same man would feel threatened, anxious and defensive if he were not sexually aroused by and able to perform with that woman according to the standards he had established for himself or accepted as being masculine.*

217

He might even allow himself to stand accused of being an inadequate lover or, worse still, labeled impotent if he were to have erection "problems." In effect, he has separated his sexual response from his emotional, sensual and sensory experience. He expects to perform sexually in spite of himself. Even though the separate components of attraction are missing, he feels he must maintain high levels of sexual excitement and performance.

The way men have continued to function sexually with this orientation is by depersonalizing the experience. They are not having sex with someone they are tuned in to and aware of as a person. Rather, they are "having sex" with a "thing," "making love" to an "object," and there is no genuine awareness of their own or the woman's internal experience. In fact, this may very well be necessary. Were they suddenly and totally aware of their real emotions and sensibilities in the here and now toward their partner, they might experience severe disruptions.

"Having sex" with their woman, therefore, becomes much like masturbation. The woman as a person does not really exist. Rather, she is an orifice, a challenge and a proving ground. Indeed, many women complain that they are simply receptacles for the depositing of the man's semen and feel that they could easily be interchanged with other women. The language of the men confirms the truth of this. For example, they might say, "When the lights are off all women are the same," and describe a woman as "a piece of ass."

Because he is not tuned in to her as a person, he may also delude himself into believing that his "sex life" with a particular woman is "great," even though she herself might not be enjoying it at all but refrains from telling him to avoid conflict or to "protect his ego."

Before the female sexual awakening of recent years, men were able to maintain their sexual illusions and delusions and a depersonalized orientation in which they saw the woman as an object because, indeed, many women colluded with this and allowed themselves to be seen and used that way too—as objects for the man's pleasure. Partially, this was the result of their conditioned inhibitions, resistances and distaste, which caused them to distance themselves from the experience, and partially they were bartering their bodies for support and security. The man and the woman were, indeed, "having sex" rather than having each other.

It was not a genuinely human sexual experience for her, or for him. The only times he might be jolted into an awareness of her as a person with feelings and sensibilities were when she would protest during sex, "You're hurting me!" or "Not so hard!" This might occur as he tried to penetrate her while she was still unlubricated and he did not know or care that she was not ready. The overall dehumanization between the man and the woman was often expressed in nonverbal ways by the fact that after the initial romantic phase they rarely kissed or made direct eye contact while making love.

Today he is confronted with a new and intimidating dilemma. Many women will no longer collude with the man's denial of their personhood. They are refusing to pretend satisfaction and to serve merely as a sexual outlet for him. This has placed him in a crisis situation for which he is unprepared, because he must now relate to her as a person and not a thing, and he is not ready for this.

The conflicts and dilemmas this presents are anxiety-provoking. Will he continue to function as a performing machine, only now with a new and more demanding program which requires him to perform according to more elaborate prescriptions involving mastering the specifics of her body, accommodating her likes and dislikes and bringing her to orgasm? This often translates into meeting her needs rather than his own. Or will he be able and/or willing to risk becoming a person himself, insisting on the right to his own individual rhythm and the honest expression of his responses, sensibilities, resistances and emotions? In this case, he will surely become an erratic performer, sometimes "better," sometimes "worse," but always changing according to his varying inner states and reactions. He will be sometimes erect, sometimes not; sometimes aggressively lusting, sometimes passive; sometimes affectionate, sometimes cold; sometimes fast, sometime slow. Will he be able to be all of these without fear, guilt, apology or a sense that his masculinity is in jeopardy?

Because many men still don't or can't experience or

express their humanness, yet feel pressured to become ever more skillful performers, some are turning off to "sex," particularly within sustained relationships, and are withdrawing into self-protective detachment or humiliating themselves with lies and the kinds of evasions that have previously been part of the woman's avoidance repertoire—"I'm tired," "I don't feel well," "I'm preoccupied with things at work" and so on.

Male backlash by means of such passive resistance, withdrawal and lack of interest is already under way. Popular and professional articles are describing the decline in male interest in "sex." I believe it has nothing to do with "sex." It does, however, have everything to do with the fact that he is confronted with impossible binds: the combination of extremely demanding expectations and standards he has been taught are attainable if he is man enough, with a psychological conditioning which makes these expectations and standards impossible to attain. Therefore, like the schizophrenic child who withdraws because he is confronted with unresolvable, damned-if-you-do, damned-if-you-don't binds, he walls himself in, assuming the stance of nonparticipation and non-emotional involvement.

A new breed of negative permission-giving psychologist-writers is predictably emerging, telling men that it is all right for them not to desire sex at all. The following quote is from a recent book on male sexuality by a psychologist who for five years headed the men's program and was co-director of clinical training of the Human Sexuality Program at the University of California, San Francisco.

> Sex is not the most important thing in the world and it is not necessarily good for you. Only the individual can decide how and where sex should fit into his life, if at all.[1]

SEXUAL ROOTS

Rather than retreating and giving up one of the most joyful and pleasurable ways a self-aware, healthy and spontaneous man and woman can play with and enjoy each other, we need to examine the binds and processes that have produced the destruction of the male's sexual humanness. To do this we must examine the roots of male conditioning and sexual attitudes and transform them, releasing men from their grip and creating a new set of attitudes, perceptions and ways for him to experience himself.

The major reason sexuality has become a decreasing source of anxiety-free pleasure for traditionally conditioned men is that the elements that make sexual intimacy pleasurable, satisfying and comfortable have been systematically extinguished in him through the processes of his early conditioning.

1) Sensuality: Parents rock, hug, caress, stroke, cuddle, lick and engage in body play with little girls. Fathers especially, but often even mothers, fear that to indulge their sons in this way beyond an early age is to risk turning them into sissies and homosexuals. Therefore, boys respond negatively to such behavior, and the young boy who desires and seeks out this kind of interaction becomes suspect and arouses the concern and anxiety of his parents.

As an adult lover, however, sensuality is expected of him. But the early repression of his sensuality dwarfs his capacity for such physical sexual play. After the initial romantic phase of the relationship, in fact, it is not uncommon for husband and wife or lovers to "have sex" with a bare minimum of sensual touching.

The impossible bind here is simply that the very sensuality that is repressed in him as a boy, that would have defined him as a sissy, is both demanded of him by his adult woman partner and required in order for *him* to enjoy *himself* fully and playfully.

2) Emotionality: The capacity for accurate recognition and communication of feelings is a prerequisite for good sexual relatedness. Like sensuality, however, emotions are repressed and largely forbidden to him as a growing boy. Sensitive boys are seen as girlish or sissies. Free expression of his emotions as a boy puts his maculinity in doubt.

As an adult lover, however, he is told he must express his emotions, which often he cannot recognize or communicate, and be sensitive to and able to read correctly his woman's emotions. His inability to do so makes the sexual experience a limited and mechanical one, and causes him to both depersonalize his partner and, at the same time, be an unknown quantity to her.

The impossible bind here is that getting in touch with and expressing emotions threaten his masculinity. To remain in a state of repression, however, is to continue to function mechanically and without an awareness of the emotional reality of the interaction with his partner.

3) Expression of needs: He learns as a boy that the less need he acknowledges and the more self-contained and independent he is, the more masculine he is. The words "I need" become two of the most difficult and threatening for a man to say. When he does have needs, he tends to deny them.

As an adult lover, his inability to acknowledge and communicate needs makes him a silent partner who accumulates considerable hidden anger and frustration because he feels misunderstood and insensitively responded to. He expects his needs to be read without his having to acknowledge or express them. When they aren't, he becomes resentful. At the same time his partner becomes confused and put off by his childish reactions to hurts she never knew she perpetrated.

The impossible bind here is that to express these needs is to feel unmasculine. Not to express them is to remain frustrated and unknown and to build a considerable amount of hidden anger.

4) Aggression toward women: Early in his conditioning as a young man he is taught to see the female as fragile, emotional, vulnerable and easily hurt. Especially if he loves her, therefore, he will tend to feel protective of her.

As an adult lover, this repression of his aggression toward her places him in impossible binds. It will make it very difficult for him to be honest about his resistances and his dislikes and even to say no to sex. He will also be unable to express his negative reactions to the ways she touches him, smells, sucks, makes love and so on for fear he will hurt her feelings and possibly injure her emotionally. In general, he fears that to be assertive in any of these ways may destroy her, cause her to withdraw or to reject him.

Furthermore, his own defensive overreaction to his aggression will cause him to be overly self-conscious and inhibited in bed, treating her like a fragile flower and going to extremes in order to be gentle and sensitive. He may even reserve his more spontaneous, aggressive, "animalistic" impulses and reactions for encounters with prostitutes or for affairs where he feels sufficiently free and detached to be himself.

The impossible bind here is that aggression toward the woman makes him feel guilty and fearful of losing her love, while suppressing this part of himself makes him an inhibited, dishonest lover.

5) Passivity: Because passivity is feminine, he loses his capacity to lie back, do nothing, allow himself to be made love to, give up control and the need to dominate, be the receiver and periodically turn the lead over to his partner, and thereby share the responsibility for the success and rhythm of the sexual encounter.

Worse still, the need to control and dominate eventually turns the sexual experience into a job. When the experience is unsatisfactory, unless he can blame it on fatigue, illness or *her* lack of interest, he has no way of escaping the conclusion that a complaint or failure is his fault.

The impossible bind is that he cannot let go of his need to control and dominate because it threatens his masculinity, yet holding on to it eliminates the possibility of having a flowing experience, one in which he can move easily and comfortably between active and passive behavior.

In summary, his early conditioning has severely impaired or destroyed most of what is required for sustained pleasure in the area of sexual involvement in a relationship. The one motivator acquired from his early conditioning that does allow him sexual excitement is challenge. Consequently, if he meets resistance from the woman, if she is a new partner, if she communicates unavailability or, in a longer-range relationship, if she manages to keep him off balance and uncertain as to whether he might lose her to someone else, he may very well retain a high level of excitement. But in a relationship where challenge is not present, there are no techniques, no words of wisdom, no magic elixirs that can make "sex" a genuinely pleasurable form of play in a sustained, caring, person-to-person relationship, short of reclaiming these lost capacities, sensibilities and awarenesses.

"SERIOUS SEX" vs. "PLAYFUL SEX"

His compulsion to perform and the repression of his humanness and personhood have resulted in his being involved in what I term "serious sex." "Serious sex" I define as sex which is goal oriented, laden with imperatives, "shoulds," standards, evaluations, performance pressures, measurement and so on. It is this orientation to sex that inevitably produces "sex problems," which are accompanied by the onus of ugly medical diagnostic labels.

In "serious sex" one or both partners are working hard *at* "sex" rather than playing pleasurably. It is depersonalized and discussed with the terminology that suggests that "sex" has a life of its own ("I like sex," "I'm good at sex," "I'm getting tired of sex," "Sex is good (bad) for you," "I don't feel like having sex right now" and so on).

Its terminology is depersonalized because it has become an experience which is separated from the self and from an awareness and acceptance of the continual changes in a person-to-person relationship. In "serious sex," static, mechanical compulsion replaces fluid human interaction. It results in the man examining his "sex life" with questions that characteristically begin with the word "How":

1) How often?
2) How long?
3) How many (orgasms)?
4) How was "it"?
5) How to do "it"?

Symptoms inevitably arise in "serious sex" when the realities of the relationship do not coincide with the external standards. That is, by turning "sex" into a separate entity, an experience with a life of its own, replete with externally imposed measurements and expectations, "sex" will inevitably be thought of in terms of "good" or "bad," "healthy" or "sick," and the man will see himself as "functional" or "dysfunctional." His penis will be seen as "working" or "not working." Whenever he fails to live up to the expectations and standards which he has set for himself, he will view himself and will also be seen as having a "sex problem." His inclination will then be to do something about "it," to overcome "it," to remedy "it." As soon as possible he will want to "fix the penis" in order to regain his masculine self-esteem.

If he remains in the relationship with the woman with whom he has a "problem" and never successfully "fixes it," never rises to the standards of performance he was using to measure himself, his self-confidence as a man may be forever crippled. He will be pathetically grateful if he is still accepted and seen as worthy of "love" by the woman in spite of "his problem." His self-hate will lead him to constantly anticipate rejection and he will have to face the repeated humiliation of experiencing, explaining and trying to cope with and overcome "his failures."

In his search for a "cure" he may initially pursue magical solutions such as special diets, vitamins, prayer, concentration, exercise, autosuggestion, fantasy and so on. If these fail to "help," he may turn to a physician for hormone injections, pills, hypnosis and occasionally even new and bizarre surgical remedies, such as plastic implants.

The recovery of his capacity and potential for sexual pleasure will therefore require a movement away from the "serious sex" orientation toward the one of "playful sex." In the absence of neurotic or other kinds of emotional problems, the questions he might ask himself in order to recover his personhood and break the stranglehold of "serious sex" while entering the realm of "playful sex" would be in the nature of:

1) Are my senses turned on to my partner? Does her smell please me or do I need her to perfume and deodorize herself in order to come comfortably close to her?

2) Do I find the look, motion, rhythm and grace of her attractive? In other words, does it please and delight me to watch her as she moves?

3) Do I enjoy the taste of her and the flavor of her body as I kiss, lick or suck her?

4) Do I enjoy listening to her speak and am I stimulated by the conversations we have? Specifically, does the timbre and quality of her voice please me? When she talks, do I find myself readily and enjoyably concentrating and listening to her? Do I focus in on and feel good about what she says and the way her words convey her perception of people, situations, experiences and life? Or do I find myself getting bored with her conversation, does my mind wander when she talks to me and do I resent her outlook and way of seeing things?

5) Do I enjoy touching her and being touched by her? Does my body experience a relaxation, comfort, openness and responsiveness when we make physical contact? Do I enjoy the feel of her skin when her body is next to mine and the touch of her hands as she caresses me? When she strokes and hugs me, does my body delightedly pull toward her or do I find myself avoiding her, tensing up, touching her as little as possible and pulling away from her when she reaches out and touches me?

6) Do I feel playful around her, free to be myself regardless of whether I have an erection? Or is sexual involvement with her a deliberate and serious business in which my major focus is on techniques, timing, "right" places to touch, erections and so on?

7) When I sleep beside her, do I find myself turning away from her and avoiding contact, or do I seek out the closeness of her body?

8) When we're making love, do I comfortably and effortlessly delight in the foreplay or do I want to get right into the act of intercourse? During intercourse, do I enjoy staying inside her and maintaining that contact as long as comfortably possible for both of us? Or is my primary mo-

tive and emphasis ejaculation? Do I tend to come quickly and do I have to make great and deliberate efforts to avoid ejaculation because my honest desire is to come and then to pull out and break contact? Or is it easy to control myself because I feel comfortable and close to her?

9) After I ejaculate, do I find myself wanting to turn away, withdraw and go to sleep? Or do I still enjoy the closeness, the hugging and the feel of her body next to mine after the orgasm?

10) Do I feel expressive, open, readily and trustingly transparent, comfortably able to be fully and honestly myself and able to share my internal reactions and responses with her spontaneously, be they positive or negative, strong or helpless, confident or frightened, affectionate or angry? Or do I find myself guarding and censoring what I say and withholding important reactions?

11) Do I feel I must always be strong, dominant, unafraid, in control of myself and unneeding in any way in order to retain her love? Or do I feel that I can be vulnerable around her, sometimes weak and a failure, confident that it will not affect her love and respect for me? In a larger sense, do I feel that she is seeing me as a person rather than as a symbol—specifically, a provider—protector—performer—security blanket?

12) Does she relate to me in an open, assertive way, or is she basically passive-submissive-receptive toward me so that it is difficult for me to see or understand what it is that she really likes or dislikes, feels, thinks and wants?

13) Can I comfortably confront her with things I don't like, expressing my anger and resistance honestly, confident that I will not be made to feel like a "heavy" or a bad guy for being honest? And do my negative expressions incite her to destructive forms of retaliation and punishment such as pulling away and turning cold?

When I share negative reactions, does she assert herself in return, engaging me actively in conflict resolution in order to work things out constructively? Or does she react in a way designed to communicate that I am guilty of being destructive and insensitive by becoming tearful, falling apart and accusing me of being hostile?

In other words, does our relationship tolerate negative interchanges and will she stay in there with me and fight things out in a constructive way until matters are comfortably resolved for both of us, or does she have a tendency to lay the blame on my shoulders?

14) When she confronts me and gives me negative feedback, is it in the spirit of closeness and to enhance intimacy, or do I experience it as motivated by an underlying desire to hurt, humiliate, control or triumph in the relationship?

15) Do I feel that she really sees me as I am and loves me for that, or do I feel she or both of us need to play out a fantasy, create images for each other and be unreal in order to keep the "love" going?

16) In general, do I find joy and pleasure in being next to her and am I readily playful with her? In simple terms, does she make me feel good about myself, my life and the experience of living, and do I do the same for her?

The primary motivation and pleasure in "playful sex" is the nearness of the other person. There is only minimal concern or focus on erections, orgasms, techniques and timing. It is the *process* of being close, not the end point of sexual tension relief that is the primary goal.

This is not to suggest that in short-term relationships or non-emotionally involved encounters sexual interaction cannot be pleasurable. However, sex motivated primarily by tension release ("horniness"), flights from loneliness, curiosity, challenge, the desire to please or the need for reassurance that one is lovable or attractive is more or less a depersonalized experience and it is usually not of great significance who one's partner is. It is particularly important, therefore, not to measure, evaluate or define oneself in terms of one's performance and responses in these kinds of sexual experiences.

"Playful sex" will be ever changing and reflective of the relationship and mood changes of the people involved. At different times it may be accompanied by sadness, silliness or seriousness, exploration, confrontation, reminiscence, reflection on feelings and so on. The act of intercourse itself will occur with a minimum of deliberate intention. "Sex" itself will never be evaluated or measured except as it reflects the state of the relationship and the way the partners are feeling toward each other.

In "playful sex" there is nothing to prove. There is no emphasis on techniques or premeditated positions. When the "sex" is "bad," the *relationship* rather than the performance of the sex act will be examined with a view to improvement.

In the best of "playful sex" one discovers who one is and what one's sensual and playful potential is. It is, I believe, a part of the highest form of male-female interaction. It is physical play between two people who accept, love and trust each other. As opposed to "serious sex," in which there is deliberate effort, self-consciousness and a censoring of feeling and fantasy, "playful sex" is expressive, flowing and easy.

The tragedy in the past is that many men have measured their masculinity and attached their sense of self-esteem and self-worth to their performance in "serious sex." They expected to be great performers, to reach and maintain certain levels and standards *regardless* of their feeling toward the woman. When the "sex" was poor, when they were "impotent" or ejaculated "prematurely," they accused themselves of inadequacy, rather than focusing on how their response reflected their feelings and the state of the relationship.

Undoubtedly, "playful sex" and the capacity to function on that level require a man to be self-aware and capable of expressiveness, because in "playful sex" he *is* his sexual response, and the limits and potential of the experience are *his* limits and reflect the extent to which he is a person in touch with and capable of feelings, sensual responsiveness and so on. Such a man will not be controlled by externally imposed standards which pressure him to function at a certain level. He will recognize those standards as erroneous and destructive to himself.

Nor will he expect himself to be a good performer simply because he married the "right woman," or is involved with a woman *everyone else* tells him is "perfect" for him. In the past many men became involved with the "right woman," who earned him the plaudits of the world because of her looks, education, background, financial standing and so on, but he may have found his own personhood atrophied and his emotions numbed by this interpersonally forced and emotionally dishonest interaction. There were the instances in which he functioned within the orientation of "serious sex." He was making love with a woman who fitted an intellectual model of the person he felt he "should" be with. He married on the basis of this, and when his emotions and his body resisted, he struggled to deny and overcome his responses, labeled himself negatively in the language of a medical diagnosis and tried to overcome and "correct" his deeply rooted resistance by describing it as a "problem."

This orientation, so typical of most men's relationships, created the basis of much of the sexual agony men have experienced in the past. They navigated in response to external pressure, and tried to live up to the appropriate masculine image: the standards, rules and expectations established by social pressure. Consequently, they had to constantly deny their real responses and remain in a relationship where the bond was fragile or even nonexistent. Eventually they were destroyed by the numbness, or the situation exploded in their faces and ended, as so many of these relationships do, in cold hate.

The liberation of male consciousness in the "sexual" area will mean trusting his responses. The only negative self-evaluations he will make of himself will be self-chastisement for the compromising and denial of his sensibilities: his resistance to recognizing the real nature of the relationship and to assuming responsibility for becoming a self-aware person whose intimate relationships could be governed by a desire to be with a partner toward whom he moved easily and delightedly, and where the relationship was playful and the hunger was to know and be known.

The man who lives in the self-caring consciousness of "playful sex" will never again measure his performance harshly or allow himself to be labeled diagnostically. He will respect and delight in the awareness and full communication of his body's responses, recognizing them as one of the truest expressions of himself.

19. To the Woman Who Asks, "What Can I Do to Help?" (Will She Be There to Hold the Net?)

While many relationships begin with the fantasy of the man as the protective partner and the woman as the weaker and vulnerable one, a turnaround in this interaction often takes place. Sometimes it occurs almost immediately after the relationship takes on a permanence and commitment. In this reversal the dynamic becomes one of woman helping man. *She* becomes the tower of strength, the stable element in the relationship, and *she* is now busy trying to help *him* straighten out his life—be it the overcoming of a drinking problem, regaining a lost erection, learning to relax and minimize stress, watching his diet, recuperating from a major illness or weathering a job crisis. He becomes the leaner and she seems now to be holding him up.

Such is the condition increasingly emerging as a result of the newly evolving relationships between a woman in the process of liberation and growth and a man who is threatened, confused and flailing fearfully about, trying to cope with, adjust to and perhaps even change in rhythm with her changes. As she becomes more of a complete person—assertive, sexual, autonomous—he is revealed to be *anything but* the strong, protective partner she might have originally imagined him to be. In fact, the more she lets go of some of her feminine poses, needing him less and less for all of those reasons she needed him originally when she was still committed to playing the dependent, submissive and vulnerable role, the more she can begin to see him for who and what he really is. Rather than being strong, he can be seen as rigidly tied to narrow behavior patterns, out of touch with his emotions, activity-driven, interpersonally blind and naïve, hooked on obviously body-destructive behavior patterns designed to numb and keep him going,

231

hardly the stud he was once touted as being and, more than anything else, threatened by change.

Thus, many caring and well-meaning women, aware of their own need to change and to grow, while still wanting to maintain their relationship with their man and perceptively sensitive to the self-destructiveness and impasses reached by him, are now asking a new variation of the old woman-helping-man-to-cope theme, namely, "How can I help him to change—to become a more liberated, satisfied, fulfilled, relaxed person?" It is an important question indeed, and its ramifications and unconscious implications demand clarification lest old traps cloaked in new, well-meaning liberation disguises are fallen into anew.

The processes and meanings of the word "help" from a psychological perspective are complex and laden with myriad motives, often the least of which are genuinely loving and caring ones. Helpers need their helpees, and often become as committed to the maintenance of the interaction and thus the problems and illness of their helpees as the helpees themselves.

The link between the helper and the helpee is a psychologically complex one, particularly in the area of emotional problems. Being a "helper" allows one to remove the focus from oneself—for example, the wife who is "helping" her husband with "his" impotence or the woman who despairs because she had married three times and each time had the "misfortune" to marry an alcoholic whom she "tried" to help and failed. It was easier to focus on solving "his" drinking problem than on her attraction to and the gratification she received from repeated involvements with such self-destructive men, and the ways her behavior might have reinforced their patterns.

Likewise, the woman who seeks to "help" her husband or lover to change in a given way, seeing that as her benevolent role, is more than likely also going to be consciously or unconsciously committed to controlling the limits of his changes. It would only be natural that she would not want him to change to the point where he realized that he no longer needed her. Or that his relationship with her was a manifestation of his problem and therefore it would be best for him to get out. Nor would she want him to become so self-caring that he began to indulge his

interest in other people, women and men alike, to the
point that he would spend increasingly less time with her,
nor so in touch that he became aware of *his* anger over
playing certain of his required roles in which she had an
investment, such as the dutiful, responsible, monogamous,
predictable lover-husband, provider and strong man—roles
often born of the feeling of guilt and the compulsion to
prove oneself masculine. Once he was self-aware and self-
caring, he might refuse evermore to assume those roles as
he became increasingly more individualistic, unpredictable
and resistant to such lifeless, compulsive, ritualistic behavior.

The very orientation of woman "helping" man, in its
traditional meaning, may no longer be viable in an era of
change, growth and liberation. In fact, the helping pose
may always have been a potentially or actually contami-
nated and psychologically loaded one. Surely it is a
charged one in the context of male-female intimacy, because each has a powerful stake in the kinds of changes
that will take place in the other, namely, that the changes
should be comfortable, attractive and enhancing to the
status quo. Alas, the changes that men may have to go
through may prove not at all to be the kind that an involved woman would approve of or be happy with, just as
her liberation changes were/are often disorienting and
painful for him.

The common stereotype of a "new" man is one who can
cry and hug his son. However, for too long being a socialized man has meant being a well-oiled, predictable, compulsive, controlled performer-machine. He blocked out
and denied a host of emotions and impulses in himself in
order to fit "comfortably" into harness and to play out the
accepted and approved masculine image. The man who
becomes suddenly and genuinely self-aware would have to
confront and deal with the long denied responses, with the
boredom, stultification, numbness and meaninglessness of
his programmed life. He might have to experience
suppressed rage over the ways he had denied himself, such
as by reporting dutifully home each day, refraining from
and feeling guilty about joyful, unabashed sensual responses to attractive women, cutting himself off from close
relationships with men and from a transparent orientation

that says, "This is who I am and this is how I feel!" All of these have long been repressed and denied because of unconscious guilt, mother transferences to his wife, the belief that it was his role to be all-responsible and self-denying and that anything short of this would bring vile inferences and castigations about his acceptability as a man and as a person.

The traditional model of woman-helping-man would also reinforce in more subtle ways the already guilt-ridden, "earth mother"—fixated orientation of the male. Behind the "helping" posture there may very well lie a one-upmanship, sometimes blatant though usually subtle almost to the point of invisibility. The "helper" is righteous, selfless and deserves gratitude and love from the helpee.

Likewise, the helping attitude within the context of a relationship takes the heat and focus off the "helper" in terms of how he or she partially creates and perpetuates the very problems he or she seeks to "help" and places the blame and focus squarely on the helpee.

Parents of a disturbed child, for example, often see and present themselves as eager and willing to do anything to help the child. At the same time, they tend to unconsciously resist focusing on the family dynamics and the processes within their own relationship that have created the "problem child" and his or her illness. Thus, they would gladly and responsibly feed the child medicines, maintain therapeutic reward and punishment schedules, change the child's school, give the child special attention, alter the diet and so on. Gladly would they act out the behaviors that reinforce their required self-perceptions of being good parents, which keep them in the good light of "helping." But they would at all costs avoid a helping process that requires the really painful and hard work of examining the destructive processes in the family, such as their own double binds on the child, nonacknowledgment of their resistances and resentment toward the child, each other and the role of parenting, plus all of the other fearful and hidden, often unconscious emotions and motivations that would expose the deeper roots of the "problem."

Furthermore, in regard to the notion of "helping," it is my belief that interpersonal problems are created and changed primarily by the "being" rather than the "doing" of the people involved. In fact, those who are the most destructive psychologically, I believe, are the fine interpersonal technicians, those who have the "doing" down to perfection but in combination with an underlying emotional "being" that runs contrary to the "doing."

For example, the parents of a schizophrenic boy had raised him according to sophisticated parent-effectiveness techniques. They always said and did the "correct" and appropriate thing. However, this only obscured and made the communication more destructive, because their body messages and unconscious nonverbal cues constantly telegraphed their underlying resentment and resistance over having to give up time and energy to a son they didn't, on a deeper level, really want. They had him originally for narcissistic reasons, to enhance their image in society and to solidify their relationship, but resented his intrusion on the satisfaction of their own pleasures. Every response of theirs was therefore unconsciously replete with "come here—go away" characteristics. The child would have been emotionally healthier had he received straight-out rejection messages. He might have grown up angry toward the world but he wouldn't have become schizophrenic. He would have known who his enemies were and would have learned to react accordingly and appropriately.

"Helpers" are indirectly saying, "It's really basically your problem, and I'll help *you* with it." In light of the traditional male-female, *actor-reactor* orientation, this only reinforces the end product of the same interaction that results in the man's assuming responsibility and operating with a guilt reflex to the woman in the first place. Consequently, when she sets out to "help" *him* with *his* problem, she only reinforces his "guilty boy" orientation and his fantasy perceptions of the selflessness, altruism, givingness and wonderfulness of the "earth mother."

Another question arises. Will the woman be there to hold the net if he genuinely lets go of the things in him she protests against so vigorously, namely, his power-dominance-success-unemotional-autonomous-performing orientation? In that sense the feminist attitude, while it is freeing women, may also trap them in a paradox at the same time. For while the woman liberates herself, the standard by which she evaluates men may become tighter instead of looser. Rather than appreciating men on a broader, more humanistic basis, the newly assertive, successful, autonomous woman often wants a man who is a success symbol first and a person second. She rationalizes her expectations by saying, "It's not that I have anything against blue-collar workers or men of less education or money. It's just that I don't find them stimulating enough. They're defensive and lack confidence because I'm doing better than they are. I prefer the man who knows who he is and feels good about himself and that seems to be primarily the successful ones." As Gail Sheehy said in a recent interview, "Weak men are not in great demand."[1]

A successful, educated feminist confessed that when her lover, whom she lived with, happened to be sick, she could accept his being in bed for a day or two, but longer than that she found herself becoming increasingly uncomfortable and impatient at his being ill, to the point where she'd be thinking, "Enough's enough. Don't act like a helpless baby."

The paradox produced by raising the woman's expectations rather than broadening them as she becomes "liberated" will increasingly become a problem. Despite oft-heard allegations that things are not "really" improving for women in concrete ways, a recent research study on the changing status of American women in the 1970s indicated that between 1970 and 1974 alone the number of women in college increased by 30 percent while the number of men increased by 12 percent. In 1971 women earned 42 percent of all B.A. degrees and 40 percent of all M.A.s. The proportion of women enrolled in professional schools for law, medicine, architecture and engineering has risen steadily since 1960. For instance, of the total enrollment in law schools, women accounted for 4 percent in 1960, 12 percent in 1972 and 19 percent in 1974. The same trend is seen in enrollments in medical schools, in which women represented 6 percent of the total in 1960, 13 percent in 1972 and 18 percent in 1974.[2]

The question that will arise is simply whether the women who want to "help" men will still find them attractive and be able to love and relate to them when their education, power, money and success symbols are less than hers. If men have been reluctant to let go of the success style of masculine validation, it is as much out of an unconscious fear and awareness that without the success symbols they (the men) would only become progressively more invisible, unlovable and sexually unattractive. They are caught in a double-bind—castigated on the one hand for their power and success orientation and rejected when they don't have them because, as Gail Sheehy pointed out in the same interview, "powerful men are an aphrodisiac for women."[3]

John Dean, in his autobiography *Blind Ambition,* echoed this assessment from a territory and perspective where men observe the impact of power all too clearly. He wrote:

> Maureen went home to California, and I resolved to conquer as many new women as time and power would grant. Henry Kissinger once remarked on power's properties as an aphrodisiac and I found it true.[4]

A major Los Angeles newspaper ran a feature article about a group of men who had fallen on hard occupational times and were experiencing unemployment with little success or hope of getting a new job because of age or a drying up of work in their specialty areas. The common note sounded among them was that with unemployment came shame, invisibility and rejection. Some of the men would even hide the fact that they were at home during the day while their wives were working. They kept their cars locked in the garage, did not answer the phone or the door and kept the window shades drawn. The wife of an engineer whose husband was unemployed for several months reported:

> Normally the phone rings all the time. As soon as word got out, it stopped. One girl left a note on the front porch saying she couldn't reach me. We were here. . . . It's gotten so they don't ask about Gil. Just the kids. It's like I don't have a husband.

The man's son had even asked his mother, "Does this mean Daddy's a bum?" His wife admitted being disturbed by her husband's constant "escape" reading, as she termed it. Also, she told her nine-year-old daughter to keep it quiet that Dad was unemployed.[5] Similarly depressing themes were sounded by the various other men who were unemployed. They were filled with self-loathing and a sense that others looked down on them as if they had committed some heinous act.

The woman who would truly help a man would do so best by working on her own growth. First, by becoming a complete person rather than a gender caricature—assertive, autonomous, sexual and expressive of her aggressive feelings—she would soon find it intolerably painful and boring to become involved or remain with a compulsive, macho-fixated male. She would inevitably find herself drifting away, thereby fomenting a crisis for any man who cared about or had been in a relationship with her. Indeed, in light of the psychologically shut down and rigid state of most men, the only hope for their ever changing, or even just looking at themselves objectively, would be as a result of a powerful crisis that would raise their anxiety to a level where they would be forced to reach out for help or sink and lose the relationship and find themselves completely isolated.

Most women overlook their own unconscious commitment to and benefits from the man's macho style. Particularly if the woman has been raised and conditioned in the traditional feminine mold, her whole tendency will probably be to attach herself to a male who will repeatedly seek to validate himself by the ways in which he can provide for and prove himself to her. Any letting go on his part would demand a balancing assertiveness and strength on her part or else she would feel her own security to be threatened and would have a strong tendency to encourage him back toward regressive masculine-role posturing.

Again, what some women want when they say they want a man to change, to become liberated, is the best of both worlds. They would like him to continue to provide the spinoff benefits of his macho compulsive style while *also* becoming the new, sensual, sensitive, emotional, vulnerable, transparent man. One perceptive, sensitive woman in her early thirties, twice married, examined her own motives in this regard:

> It is one thing to ask a man not to step on people, not to define himself by how viciously and quickly he climbs the success ladder and acquires things. It's another to cancel the charge accounts so that he can play guitar and sing to the children. It would be rather ironic if we one day found ourselves being threatened by men's lib.
>
> Men may have been initially responsible some time in history for the beginnings of this problem, but women have long since learned to be a part of it—have acquiesced and even helped to perpetuate the stereotype. I was just as guilty of "seeing" a man in this way as the man himself was (tough, macho). I wanted a man who was sensitive and in touch, but *in addition to*, not instead of the other.
>
> The question comes to my mind, and I really have to work with it—can I promise that I am mature enough, loving enough, spiritual enough, to let him be as real as he can be even if the neighbors think he's lazy or weird. Maybe his fears aren't so funny—maybe they are more accurate than we women choose to believe.
>
> The woman blows the whole thing if she is somehow implicitly agreeing that, "Yes, men *are* in danger of not being 'male,' of not being respected and loved if they let their emotions go free." If we tell him he can go this far, but no farther, we have done nothing as far as I'm concerned.
>
> I think I could handle such a change and be glad for it. I sure don't underestimate the necessary readjustment though. I'm also very aware that it took three committed relationships, two marriages and once living together, lying in bleeding pieces behind me, for me to get this far.

A woman who wants to "help" a man in his growth and change first needs to recognize how she feeds into, perpetuates and reinforces his tendencies to be driven and dominant and how she disdains and emotionally turns away from the man who is softer, less predictable, more egalitarian and humanistic and generally less concerned about power and success. Then she needs to recognize and alter the consciousness that has taught her to find and attach herself to the man of highest status available to her. Therefore, the best thing she can do to "help" in this regard is to grow to the point where a man is evaluated as a friend-companion-playmate rather than as a provider–protector–success symbol. Without doing that, her liberation becomes an oppressive, destructive treachery that only binds the man who is rigidly caught even further.

QUESTIONS TO ASK

Women who want to be constructive in their relationships with a man in need of, on the verge of, or in the process of change need to ask themselves the following questions:

1) To what extent do I play traditional feminine games and give off messages that indicate my desire to be taken care of, paid for, courted, protected and freed of the need to make decisions?

2) To what extent do I want it both ways—to get the benefits of my liberation when it suits me while retaining the old-time feminine prerogatives when they serve my purposes?

3) To what extent am I drawn to a man because of his status and success symbols, and would I be able to get equally as involved emotionally with a man who made less money, had less education and a lower occupational status than myself?

4) To what extent do I feel that a man owes it to me to take care of me because I have been exploited, have denied myself, was "forced to put up with things" and was held back by men and "society" and gave more than the man did, and am therefore a victim deserving of reparations?

Once clarifying for herself the extent to which she feeds into and perpetuates the destructive gender interactions, a woman would facilitate the growth of a man most if she herself would:

1) Realize that in any relationship with a man she has made a choice to be with him and therefore probably has a stake in his retaining major parts of his style.

2) Refuse to collude with or accommodate to his needs by suppressing her own identity, assertiveness, aggression and sexuality to boost his ego.

3) Acknowledge and own up to the fact that she enjoys some of the fruits of his compulsive, success-driven, power-oriented, dominant behavior and might therefore subconsciously sabotage his attempts to let go of them.

4) Not be afraid to upset the balance of the relationship and therefore precipitate a crisis. For most men, growth will not occur without a crisis that literally forces introspection and self-awareness on them.

5) Acknowledge and own up to the ways she would not want him to change for her own selfish motives because these changes might jeopardize her role in his life. Owning up would at least prevent the communication of double-bind messages that say, "I really want you to change but please don't do it in a way that would threaten my position in this relationship."

6) Tell the truth about her boredom, her sexual responses, even her manipulations so that he can get to know her as she knows herself rather than as he would like to believe she is.

7) Make it clear to him that she is not fragile and easily hurt by his being real, does not want to be taken care of and is quite capable of protecting herself and fighting on her own behalf.

8) Initiate and structure dates, experiences and sex on a level equal to what she expects from him, accepting the fact that he will not always respond with great enthusiasm to her just as she would not to him were she being real.

9) Maintain her own activities, network of friends and schedules that are separate and for herself and assume that he, as a self-caring person, will do likewise. At the same time, she would refuse to play the role of social director by taking responsibility for their social calendar.

10) Never fake anything socially, sexually or by playing "earth mother" roles. Further, she will not fake inter-

est in or accompany him on activities that essentially bore her and where she doesn't want to be present. Likewise, she will tell him she doesn't want him to participate in activities when he is lacking in genuine interest and enthusiasm.

11) Make it clear that his inability or refusal to be transparent and honest out of an alleged motivation to keep the peace or be protective is a turn-off to her.

12) Avoid doing or being anything in the relationship that, if the relationship ended or he in some way rejected her, would cause her to feel martyred, exploited and manipulated.

20. The Emerging Male

All of my life I been like a doubled up fist . . . Poundin' smashin', drivin',—now I'm going to loosen these doubled up hands and touch things *easy* with them . . .[1]

—"Big Daddy,"
Cat on a Hot Tin Roof,
Tennessee Williams

In this age of gender redefinition we are all psychological pioneers. The new directions are uncharted and fraught with the anxieties and pain involved in cutting loose from familiar rituals and predictable responses.

The tendency in times of interpersonal crisis and drastic change is to wish for a return to the known, often in a mood of distorted nostalgic sentimentality. It resembles the phenomenon of the homesick college student who yearns to go back home and remembers it as the warm, safe place it never was.

In fact, we have been witnessing recently the flareup of numerous regressive women's groups advocating that women return to traditional, stereotypical role playing. Undoubtedly, there are many threatened men who would also like to see this happen.

The security of the familiar, even at the price of stagnation, is, in its way, seductive and one major reason why so many people never change their life-style, life pattern or primary relationships, no matter how unsatisfying or painful they are.

One need look no further than the vulnerable, even pathetic stance of most middle-aged and older men to recognize that their human potential has been seriously aborted because their conditioning process has cheated them of so much. The rewards for playing out these assigned roles were interpersonal isolation, emotional repression, rigidity, premature physical deterioration and an increasing sense of futility and cynicism. Only the man's ego defensiveness and the fear of acknowledging the lies he has lived by keep him functioning in so self-destructive a manner.

Aside from its polemical distortions and unfair stereotyping, the women's movement is a profoundly important and freeing one for the male. Books such as this one would probably have found no home and might even have been ridiculed had it not been for the climate of change generated by the women's movement. For men now to stand by without engaging in an equally profound examination and redefinition of their roles would attest to the fact that the masculine defense structure is so rigid and deeply embedded that there is no hope for its alteration and revitalization.

Without a drastic recasting of his role and an equally dramatic change in his consciousness, things can only get worse for him. Specifically, women have already begun filling up the hallowed territories of performance men previously used for defining themselves, and there have been few or no compensations or expansions for him.

His old behaviors with the new woman will not bring him any satisfaction or comfort. The supports of the past, the ones that allowed him to maintain, perpetuate and justify his behavior, are being steadily removed, and he is left exposed as fragile and brittle. He survives by feeding mainly on himself, and precious little nourishment remains within him. He must, for his life's sake, begin to move *past* his age-old orientation of living a life which conforms to external role pressures.

When I am asked about my own motivations for changing, my response is that the alternative of *not* changing seems far worse and more frightening. Mine is not idealistic rebellion or personal sacrifice. From my point of view it is a matter of survival. I do not want to pay the price I see extracted from most of the men around me.

I offer the following basic directions as tone setters and guideposts for men to help them develop a process and rhythm that will break through and beyond their embedded patterns and reflexes. They are, I believe, to be approached in slow motion and with constant questioning and examination. It is not just a matter of the simple development of some cognitive solutions. Intelligent awareness can help define a vision, but the movement toward it will require his total person.

GUIDEPOSTS

1. *Recognize and resist responding to words of sexist masculine intimidation.*

Over the years, the vocabulary of masculinity has become laden with words that menace the male and have the symbolic power to trigger reactions that are self-destructive, because of a deeply rooted tendency in the man to do whatever will allow him to avoid their implications.

These words are often used in wholesale fashion. They are intimidating partially because they cover, in loose and general ways, a wide variety of responses that are actually quite different from each other. Under the spell of masculine intimidation, these labels get reduced to a similar narrow meaning which blocks the man's capacity to see and come to grips with his inner experience: something which would allow him to act on the basis of long-range better sense and the instinct for survival rather than immediate compulsion. To avoid these labels, he settles for the momentary reduction of anxiety. Among these words of sexist intimidation, the following are some of the most powerful motivators.

"Coward": How many men have needlessly placed themselves in jeopardy, been injured or killed because they responded to challenges or threats to their masculinity when little or nothing was at stake except to avoid the label "coward"? In many of these instances, the healthy response would have been to *flee* rather than to *fight*, or simply to refuse to participate.

So too have the words "afraid of" bullied him and made it difficult for him to take the long view. He would assume a responsibility, accept a challenge, put up with an onerous situation, endure an unsatisfactory relationship just to prove that he wasn't *afraid* to do it; that he didn't "chicken out." This made it impossible for him to understand and learn from the important messages his acknowledged fear would have provided.

"Failure": Men are living in an era when they are confronting proliferating and hazardous double-binds. On the one hand, it is suggested to them that success and winning are not the all-important things in life. At the same time, words such as "loser" and "failure" are still applied in derogatory fashion to men who do not effectively compete in the prescribed ways.

Even among the seemingly enlightened segments of the population, subtle evaluations that categorize men in this way are constantly being made. The message is usually indirect—for example, when a successful and powerful man is viewed as charismatic, dynamic, interesting, exciting and so on, while the man who is not is described as "boring," "negative," "drab," "uninteresting," "depressing," and the like.

Even the question "What does he do?" when asked as the source of primary interest in discussing a man has that same undertone. Certain kinds of work imply a positive image and give a man allure. Others immediately fix him with a negative stereotype.

The insidious and pervasive power of such labeling forces men into narrow, repetitive ruts and channels so that they can preserve their image of being a "success" and avoid the alternative negative labels.

"Immature" and *"irresponsible"*: Men in our society often take on overwhelming and debilitating responsibilities at a very early age and burn out prematurely in the cause of proving themselves to be mature and responsible.

A man who marries, fathers, makes a permanent career choice and in general launches for himself a life of "service" and self-denial in his twenties is congratulated by society and defined as a responsible, mature person. In fact, he may actually be a child masquerading as the responsible man. Canny women involved with such men see the immature being that hides behind their socially applauded veneer.

That men in their twenties, who are just beginning to test the waters of their lives, are reinforced for putting themselves firmly in harness at this young age seems particularly destructive. The words "immature" and "irresponsible" are often used indiscriminately to describe any man who moves at a slower pace and chooses to remain uncommitted to a specific life-style for a longer period of time.

Part of the process of freeing the male will be to encourage him to express his playful, emotional and exploratory sides. In the past this would have exposed him to negative reactions. It is within these dimensions, however, that we can see whether we live in an environment whose survival would be threatened if men were to stop fitting themselves into harness and develop a life-style of greater self-care.

"Lazy": The equating of a slower-paced style with nonproductivity and laziness is a psychological trap that results in premature physical deterioration. Part of proving one's manliness is to maintain a high level of activity and reduce to as little as possible one's passive inclinations. A man who naps in the afternoon or sleeps late in the morning is suspect.

The free man will need to come up with a new formula and to recognize that some passivity does not necessarily equal "laziness" or unmanliness. He will need to recognize and respect his fatigue and his resistance to activity and to give them equal play so that he can avoid being a driven, perpetual-motion machine. Learning to turn off the inner accusing voice that labels him "lazy" or something equally negative when he lies back will be a major breakthrough.

"Impotent": This sexist label of intimidation is also loosely and destructively applied to define myriad responses and motivations. The first time they fail to get an erection, many men think of themselves in the negative context of "I was impotent with her," or "I couldn't get it up." The underlying implication is of sexual failure or of a shadow on their masculinity.

In general, the word "impotent" serves no useful purpose and is clearly sexist because it implies a standard of acceptable masculine sexual performance that makes a man abnormal if he can't live up to it.

The diagnostic quality of this word is also devastating. Men who are labeled "impotent" are also inevitably subjected to self-hate and to pity from others. The word "impotent" clearly needs to be rejected, and those who apply it should be confronted with its sexist bias.

Even if a man has a serious, chronic "problem" with his erections, to apply the word "impotence" to him is still destructive, because its effect is to pressure him to "overcome" "his problem" as soon as possible—at whatever cost to his personality. The process of becoming aware of the meaning of his responses is put under great pressure. He wants his erection back and in top functioning condition as soon as possible so he will no longer be labeled "impotent."

Likewise, other labels for male sexual problems, such as "premature ejaculation" and even "sexual dysfunction," are often sexist and I believe destructive in their connotations. Self-caring men would not apply such labels to themselves, nor would they tolerate their being applied by others.

"*Latent homosexual*": These words have had a particularly devastating impact on men in terms of blocking the development of affectionate, warm, caring experiences between them. A man who finds himself responding to another man with loving and sensual feelings, unless he has a strongly rooted sexual identity and equally strong self-esteem, tends to be flooded with anxiety and self-doubt. "Maybe I'm a latent homosexual," he tells himself.

Most men, to ensure that they will not be suspect, therefore keep a deliberate and self-protective distance from other men and do so with a defensive, isolating rigidity that loudly signals the message "Don't touch me."

If the words "latent homosexual" imply the potential for an affectionate and sensual response toward a man, practically all men could be considered "latent homosexuals." It is only that most men have rigid and powerful defenses against this tendency that allows them to masquerade as being "totally masculine."

Very simply, all males who have been raised in our culture and who have had women as their primary nurturing and identification figures are "latent homosexuals," in that they have a strong feminine imprint and potential. Their powerful reaction against closeness with men is psychologically defensive; a phobia protecting them against this very threatening interest and desire.

Except in limited instances, the label "latent homosexual," as it is so loosely applied, is a term of sexist intimidation. Warmth, affection, physical touching in a gentle, caring way and attention paid to the needs and feelings of a man all fall under the hostile, intimidating rubic of this label. This is particularly unfortunate and destructive because it sets up such powerful barriers to supportive, loving friendships among men, which are absolutely imperative if he is ever to free himself from his dangerous emotional isolation and his inordinate and debilitating dependency on "his" woman.

"Woman hater": The nature of the traditional male-female relationship is such that women's passive-submissive posture results in the development of unconscious anger and rage toward the man she inevitably comes to resent being controlled and used by. All traditionally conditioned women are therefore potential or latent "man haters."

Likewise the pressure on the traditionally conditioned man to:

1) Constantly prove himself;

2) Repress his needs and emotions;

3) Take responsibility which results in feeling guilty;

4) Be granted sex on a limited and controlled basis subject to his "good behavior";

5) Thwart his own impulses to be playful, spontaneous and expressive in order to live up to the image of the mature husband and father;

6) Experience and yet have to deny intense dependency and therefore vulnerability in relation to the woman in his life;

7) Be unable to express and deal directly with his

resistance, boredom, conflict, resentment and so on in the relationship;

8) Put himself second,

all build up underlying currents of anger and resentment. All traditionally conditioned men are therefore potential or latent "woman haters."

It has, however, been fashionable and tolerable for women to express this anger directly toward men without becoming suspect, because women are perceived as the "victims" and the exploited and "used" ones. The male, who has been considered "top dog," has been given no such justification for anger and therefore his feelings toward women must be hidden and denied. If it is openly expressed, he becomes sexually and psychologically suspect and open to derogatory labeling.

In a repressed, polite, ritualized society where male-female resistance, resentment, anger and so on are not readily surfaced and dealt with unless they can be well justified and tied to an obvious external cause ("You were late"; "You looked at another woman [man]"), significant amounts of hostility build up. The traditionally conditioned woman avoids both anger and conflict, while the male sees his role as being protector of the female and feels himself to be the "heavy" if he initiates an argument or fight.

Consequently, anger in these relationships is always lurking underneath and searching for an outlet or acceptable channel. In the meantime, it surfaces in numerous indirect ways, such as detachment, indifference, boredom, insensitivity, lack of sexual responsiveness, forgetfulness, guilt-making, manipulation and sundry psychological and emotional symptoms. The extremely romantic, never-fighting couple usually have the most fragile, potentially explosive relationship because conflict is never surfaced, dealt with and resolved directly.

Today, women's consciousness raising has provided acceptable channels for the expression of female anger and rage, while men's anger still tends to remain dormant. Potentially, male anger toward women is just as great as women's toward men. However, the controls against its expression are still extremely rigid and powerful. The chivalrous protectiveness many men exhibit toward women, even when the women don't desire it, and the common male perception of women as very fragile are, I believe, part of the defense structure by which the man denies and defends against these angry feelings.

It is both interesting and significant that, while most men would deny having anger and hostility toward women, many women perceive men as having tremendous anger, to the point where some of them fear most men and see them as potential rapists. The important point is simply that anger in men toward women exists just as powerfully as in the opposite case, and the label "woman hater" as a form of accusation is one other term of sexist intimidation that tends to incite his guilt and block him from experiencing and dealing with a real part of his internal experience.

If men are to grow beyond their present rigid positions, they must experience, openly acknowledge and come to terms with their anger toward women, just as women have toward men. The man with no experienced and acknowledged anger toward women is a repressed individual just as the woman who denies any anger toward men would be. This kind of repression often produces unexpectedly cruel and cold behavior in an intimate relationship, so that the person who persistently denies anger may suddenly abandon the relationship, get involved in a secret affair, become detached, all the while denying any negative motivation.

In the long run, women will find men who *do* experience and express their anger toward women openly and directly easier and more satisfying and comfortable to relate to and be with than "Mr. Nice Guy," and potentially capable of significantly more intimacy and love.

"Chauvinist pig": It has been acceptable and fashionable in the last decade to keep men psychologically on the defensive through the intimidation of accusing labels such as "oppressor" and "chauvinist pig." This has played directly into the large potential for guilt in men toward women. Consequently, the sexist ways women behave toward men and the ways women reinforce male sexist behavior have not been focused on and dealt with. In the meantime, many men are finding themselves self-conscious, unsure

and somewhat paralyzed in their responses toward women lest they be accused of saying or doing something sexist.

Male acceptance of such derogatory labels clouds his understanding of what it is that he is reacting to and why. Such accusations can also be self-serving on the part of women, who may use them to keep a man off balance, accommodating and bending over backwards to prove that he is *not* sexist.

The vocabulary is rife with many other words of masculine intimidation that need to be rooted out and exposed for their toxic impact.

2. *Cultivate buddyships.*

It is my belief that well-founded and self-caring, meaningful change and growth for men can only happen if they develop same-sex support systems that would lighten their dependency on women and would also allow them to go through whatever changes they need to go through without fear of alienating their sole source of intimacy.

The one factor more than any other that has facilitated the changes in women's consciousness in fairly rapid and smooth fashion is their ability to take and give support and comfort to each other and to get enough satisfaction from these relationships to compensate for the periods when their relationships with men were in crisis or entirely absent. Because of a sense of mutual support, women did not feel the need to ask for men's permission to change, nor did they fear alienating the man or incurring his disapproval if they risked change.

Likewise, unless men can go through their changes without the terror of losing their woman's love, any change will be contingent on and limited by her approval. In addition, a caring, loving buddyship relationship in a time of unpredictable and volatile heterosexual relationships can provide roots and sources of pleasure, warmth and comfort. The most exciting and dramatic potential in the cultivation of a buddyship orientation is the reduction and softening of the defensive, guarded, detached and competitive posture most men have toward each other.

3. *Avoid the "earth mother" and embrace the woman-person.*

The surgeon general should caution that regardless of how inviting and seemingly satisfying the "earth mother" seems to be in her submissive, adoring, Madonna-like giving posture, she is ultimately extremely dangerous to the man's psychological health. The "earth mother" reinforces his self-destructive, regressive tendencies to dominate, control, prove himself, perform and take major responsibility while also feeling himself in competition with other men for "his" sexual property. The rewards he gets for playing this role are illusory because the "earth mother" will reinforce his tendencies to feel guilty for everything while she herself develops strong latent anger which may emerge as sudden rebellion, raging explosions, unexpected abandonment of the relationship or an endless catalogue of psychosomatic and psychological symptoms.

Above and beyond everything else, intimacy with an "earth mother" is boring, stagnant and devoid of surprise or spontaneity. It is true that a relationship with a woman-person who relates as an equal, responds according to her needs and rhythms, surfaces and negotiates conflict, expresses her anger directly, shares in decision making and the expenses, initiates activities and is a friend and partner as well as a lover and nurturer might prove temporarily threatening because she will not go along passively and submissively with things and will therefore upset the man's long-time orientation of controlling these relationships. However, the growth and freeing aspects of being with a woman-person, relieving the man of the need to put himself second, to feel chronically guilty and responsible when problems arise—as well as providing the freedom for him to concentrate on loosening and expanding the boundaries of his consciousness—more than compensate.

"Earth mother" is destructive to a man's growth. An aware, self-caring man will avoid such a relationship just as an aware woman-person will not involve herself in the destructiveness of a relationship with a sexist-macho male who chronically needs to dominate, control and deny emotions and needs.

4. *Reintegrate your feminine side and revel in the pleasure of experiencing and giving expression to these denied parts of your personality.*

A counterpart to assertion training for women ought to be passivity training for men. As women have been integrating their masculine side, men need to integrate their feminine side in order to move beyond the present liberation crunch. In other words, men must take the benefits of women's growth and not just stretch their capacities thin to handle more stress and responsibility.

Specifically, as women integrate their previously repressed assertiveness, autonomy, sexuality, anger and aggression, men need to reclaim emotions, dependency needs, passivity, fluidity, playfulness, sensuality, vulnerability and resistance to always assuming responsibility. Men too need to become balanced people.

If all that the growth and change in women's consciousness will mean for men is an adaptation to her expanded identity, he will be locking himself into an unbearable position. Women's liberation must not be allowed to mean for men accommodation to her new image. Rather, it must herald the opportunity for men to become fully human themselves, and in the process, like her, reconstruct or even abandon relationships where their changes and growth are not accepted, nurtured and cherished.

5. *Postpone binding commitments.*

The powerful external pressures on the man as a young, growing person, I believe, make it necessary for him to take a number of adult years to establish and develop an autonomous, inner-directed focus on who he is and what he wants.

The traditional male harness has meant the early and often premature establishment of career, marriage and family, which gave the man the appearance of maturity but actually made genuine self-development very difficult, because he was constantly struggling to deal with external pressures. Just as women are realizing and rebelling against their traditional role harnesses, men need now to recognize and alter their self-damaging orientation of assuming and striving to live up to the inordinate demands and pressures laid on them early in life.

6. *Recognize and acknowledge emotions as critical guides to reality.*

The masculine orientation to emotions has characteristically been to perceive them as an interference, threat or challenge which he needed to learn to control and transcend. Consequently, men have given up one of the truest indices for self-understanding and the accurate perception of their relationships. It is perhaps the most harmful aspect of male conditioning that emotions have been made synonymous with femininity and that men have thus been deprived of access to their humanness. Identification and acceptance of fear, affection, resentment, boredom, resistance, longing, sadness, hurt, frustration and so on are crucial to men's development as full people.

7. *Be your own child.*

It is axiomatic that fathers attempt to compensate for personal frustrations and unrealized fantasies through their sons. Fathering a son can be seen as a symbolic passing of the baton, a way of saying, "Here, you fulfill the dreams that I couldn't."

It is perhaps time for men to father themselves, to become their own children and to give themselves what they never got; in effect to undo some of the destructiveness of their own parental conditioning. It will make him that much better a father to his own children later on, as he will father for the *pleasure* of the process and not as a way of acting out his own unfulfilled desires. The effective father therefore will not be the man who works at the role but comes to it fully conscious and fulfilled himself.

8. *Change yourself first!*

It is very much a part of the masculine orientation to want to change the world at the same time or before he works at changing himself. Fortunately, the important changes required for male growth and emergence are intimate and can be effected with great benefit to himself *even if nobody else* changes The development of a buddyship relationship; experiencing and acknowledging emotions; accepting and recognizing his sexual response as an honest expression of himself without making negative judgments; enhancing his capacity for sensuality; developing relationships with women who take equal responsibility and relate as friends and partners; altering self-destructive body habits; giving play to passivity, dependency, vulnerability and fear; postponing intimate commitments; and disengaging from the stranglehold of the obsession with success or fear of failure, can all be worked at and reached without having to change the world in the process. While it produces changes in his life-style, new energies will also be released that make him more productive and his life more fulfilling than it ever was when he was driven by the compulsions of a rigid masculine orientation.

9. *Remember that "masculine" and "feminine" are conditioned phenomena and therefore always in the process of redefinition and change.*

Gender definitions are always transitional. The model of what a man or woman "should be" changes from year to year. Being a "hero" at a heavy personal cost, proving oneself just for the sake of proving when it is detrimental to oneself, is to trade foolishly for temporary approval or adulation. The important thing is to separate the necessary and meaningful challenges from the mindless, compulsive activities one engages in from day to day to allay the anxiety and concern over how it will fit one's gender image and look in other people's eyes.

10. *Support and insist on the continued emergence and growth of women.*

The addictive power of traditional femininity in its ability to stimulate fantasy is so great that few men can withstand its pull. Regressive women's movements that encourage women to resume traditional feminine role playing are highly destructive to the man. The genuine woman-hero is the one who risks relating as a fully and honestly participating, equal and responsible person. It is time for men to see through the webs woven by the femme fatale and old-time female manipulators, who play on men's emotions, learn to push the correct buttons and therefore draw the major attention and interest from most men.

11. *Ask for help.*

It is in the masculine orientation not to ask for help, to go it alone, to seek quick, unambiguous answers and to reject any approach that is not clear-cut and obvious in its logic.

In matters of the emotions and psychological processes, only charlatans hold out the promise of rapid, dramatic change. Defenses cause a person to see himself and reality as he wishes. Change is difficult because it requires bringing back into awareness and integration disowned and threatening parts of oneself.

The ability to ask for help is important in allowing oneself to accept support. It is equally important as a symbol of one's capacity to recognize that the problems and issues are often too complex and overwhelming to negotiate by oneself.

Help can come from many sources, not necessarily professional. The important part is being able to acknowledge one's confusion enough to say, "I need help."

12. *Custom-make your life.*

Look around and ask yourself if on a personal and interpersonal level it still makes sense to live up to old models. Technologically we are living in a highly sophisticated space age, while on the level of human interaction most of our expectations and value systems are ages old and anachronistic.

We are all pioneers in this era of loosening and changing gender definitions to fit human needs rather than to reinforce masculine and feminine stereotypes. It is both an exciting and a threatening time. There will be periods when the changes seem to be too painful, even impossible. The solace I choose in those moments is to ask myself,

"Do I want to repeat the cycles, fit the patterns and play the games that seem to have been played by others from time immemorial? Do they feel good, and do they yield what they're supposed to?" That, I believe, is enough of a spur to maintain momentum in those threatening moments when wresting oneself free from very powerful, very established and very debilitating sexual role models seems like an impossible challenge.

References

CHAPTER 1

1. Mark Strand, "About a Man," *New Yorker*, October 10, 1977, p. 44.
2. Bureau of the Census, *1970 Census of Population. Vol. 1: Characteristics of the Population: United States Summary*, pp. 1–259. Bureau of the Census, *Current Population Reports: Population Estimates and Projections*, February 1975, tables 2, 3, 4.
3. Aaron Latham, "My Lost Generation," *New York*, November 19, 1973, pp. 53–56.
4. Barry Farrell, "The Power Politician behind the Badge," *New West*, December 19, 1977, p. 30.
5. Sandra Lipsitz Bem, "Androgeny vs. the Right Little Lives of Fluffy Women and Chesty Men," *Psychology Today*, September 1975, pp. 58–62.
6. *The Way of Life according to Lao-tzu*, Witter Bynner, trans. (New York: Capricorn Books, 1962), p. 73.

CHAPTER 2

1. *Time*, April 25, 1977, p. 67.
2. *Los Angeles Times*, April 27, 1976.
3. *Newsweek*, July 4, 1976, pp. 30–31.
4. Michael J. Kaufman and Joseph Popper, "Pee Wee Pill Poppers," *Sport*, December 1976, pp. 16–25.
5. George Simpson, "College Football's B.M.O.C. Crisis," *Sport*, November 1976, pp. 19–30.
6. Eileen Brennan "Epitaph for a Dead Mercenary," *People*, August 23, 1976, pp. 18–20.
7. "Abe Maslow—1908–1970," *Psychology Today*, August 1970, p. 16.
8. *Time*, November 22, 1976, p. 61.
9. *Los Angeles Times*, January 15, 1976.

CHAPTER 3

1. *Newsweek,* December 27, 1976, p. 59.
2. George E. Vaillant, M.D., and Charles C. McArthur, "Natural History of Male Psychologic Health. I. The Adult Life Cycle from 18 to 50," *Seminars in Psychiatry,* vol. 4, no. 4 (November 1972), pp. 415–27.

CHAPTER 4

1. Richard M. Coffman and Larry J. Pinter (U.S. Air Force Academy), "The Sex Ratio of Post-industrial America," p. 5. (This paper was presented at the Western Social Science Association Annual Meeting at Tempe, Arizona, April 28–May 1, 1976).
2. "Life Expectancy Statistics in U. S. Take Sudden Jump," *Los Angeles Times,* July 25, 1977, Part I, p. 2.
3. David C. Glass, "Stress, Competition and Heart Attacks," *Psychology Today,* December 1976, p. 57.
4. William Shakespeare, *Macbeth* (Cambridge, Massachusetts: Houghton Mifflin Company, 1931), Joseph Quincy Adams, ed., Act II, Scene II, p. 36.
5. Simpson, George, "College Football's B.M.O.C. Crisis: Battered & Maimed on Campus," *Sport,* November 1976, p. 30.
6. Christing McKee, M.D., Billie F. Corder, Thomas Harzlip, M.D., "Psychiatrist's Responses to Sexual Bias in Pharmaceutical Advertising," *American Journal of Psychiatry,* vol. 131, no. 11 (November 1974), pp. 1273–1275.
7. Rose Dosti, "Shedding Light on Diet and Athletics," *Los Angeles Times,* July 7, 1977, Part VI, p. 1.
8. "Latest in Health and Medicine," *U.S. News & World Report,* Vol. 82, No. 2, January 17, 1977, p. 69.
9. *Los Angeles Times,* April 30, 1978, Part I, p. 18.
10. Erik Eckholm and Frank Record, "Worldwatch Paper 9: The Two Faces of Malnutrition," December 1976, p. 46.
11. Quote taken from the film *Men's Lives* filmed by Will Roberts and Josh Hanig, *New Day Films,* Franklin Lakes, New Jersey, 1975.

CHAPTER 5

1. John Le Carré, *The Honourable Schoolboy* (New York: Alfred A. Knopf, Inc., 1977), p. 533.
2. Gail Sheehy, "The Life of the Most Powerful Woman in New York," *New York,* December 10, 1973, p. 51.

3. Ibid., p. 57.

4. David C. McClelland and David H. Burnham, "Power-Driven Managers: Good Guys Make Bum Bosses," *Psychology Today*, vol. 9, no. 7, December 1975, p. 69.

5. Jack Horn, "Good Guys Make Unchallenging Bosses," *Psychology Today*, vol. 9, no. 3, August 1975, p. 55.

6. David C. McClelland, *Power: The Inner Experience* (New York: Halsted Press, 1976), p. 276.

7. *The Collected Works of Henrik Ibsen, Volume III, An Enemy of the People, The Wild Duck* (New York: Charles Scribner's Sons, 1913), pp. 187–188.

CHAPTER 6

1. Louis I. Dublin, *Suicide—A Sociological and Statistical Study* (New York: Ronald Press, 1963), p. 41.

2. Kate Frankenthal, "Suicidal Differences of the Sexes," *Proceedings of the Sixth International Conference for Suicide Prevention* (Ann Arbor, Mich.: Edwards, 1972), p. 182.

3. Robert E. Litman, M.D., "The Prevention of Suicide," *Current Psychiatric Therapies*, vol. 6 (1966), p. 271.

4. Harry Levinson, "On Executive Suicide," *Harvard Business Review*, vol. 53, no. 4 (July-August 1975), p. 118.

5. David Lester, Ph.D., "Suicide Behavior in Men and Women," *Mental Hygiene*, vol. 53, no. 3 (July 1969), p. 340.

6. Warren Breed, "Occupational Mobility and Suicide among White Males," *American Sociological Review*, vol. 28, no. 2 (April 1963), pp. 179–88.

7. *Los Angeles Times*, September 4, 1977.

8. Don D. Jackson, "Suicide," *Scientific American*, November 1954, pp. 88–92, 94, 96.

9. H. Goldberg and R. T. Lewis, *Money Madness: The Psychology of Saving, Spending, Loving, and Hating Money* (New York: Morrow, 1978), pp. 126–58.

CHAPTER 7

1. Jules Feiffer, *Village Voice*, December 12, 1977.

CHAPTER 8

1. Ashley Montagu, *The Natural Superiority of Women*, rev. ed. (New York: Collier, 1974), pp. 181, 182, 183.

2. Lester Gelb, "Masculinity—Femininity: A Study in Imposed Inequality," *Psychoanalysis and Women: Contributions*

to New Theory and Therapy, Jean Baker Miller, M.D., ed. (New York: Brunner/Mazel, 1973), pp. 369–77.

3. Joseph Epstein, *Divorced in America* (New York: Dutton, 1974), p. 206.

4. David G. Winter, Abigail J. Stewart and David C. McClelland, "Husband's Motives and Wife's Career Level," *Journal of Personality and Social Psychology*, vol. 35, no. 3 (March 1977), pp. 159–66.

CHAPTER 9

1. Robert Frost, "The Hill Wife," from *Complete Poems of Robert Frost* (New York: Holt, Rinehart & Winston, 1949), p. 162.

2. Evelyn P. Stevens, "Marianismo: The Other Face of Machismo in Latin America," in *Female and Male in Latin America: Essays*, Ann Pescatello, ed. (Pittsburgh: University of Pittsburgh Press, 1973), p. 91.

3. Rogelio Diaz-Guerrero, "Neurosis and the Mexican Family Structure," *American Journal of Psychiatry*, vol. 112, no. 6 (December 1955), pp. 411–17; "Adolescence in Mexico: Some Cultural, Psychological and Psychiatric Aspects," *International Mental Health Research Newsletter*, vol. 12, no. 4 (Winter 1970), pp. 1, 10–13.

4. Stevens, loc. cit., p. 95.

5. J. Mayone Stycos, *Family and Fertility in Puerto Rico* (New York: Columbia University Press, 1955), pp. 136–42, 158; Theodore B. Brameld, *The Remaking of a Culture* (New York: Harper, 1959), pp. 107–8.

6. José B. Adolph, "La emancipacion masculina en Lima," *Mundo Nuevo*, April 1970, pp. 39–41.

7. Salvador Reyes Nevares, "El machismo en Mexico," *Mundo Nuevo*, April 1970, pp. 14–19.

8. *Los Angeles Times*, June 10, 1977.

9. Carroll, Smith and Rosenberg, "The Hysterical Woman: Sex Roles and Role Conflict in 19th-Century America," *Social Research*, vol. 39, no. 4 (Winter 1972), pp. 652–78.

10. David H. Stoker, Louis A. Zurcher, and Wayne Fox, "Women in Psychotherapy: A Cross-Cultural Comparison," *International Journal of Social Psychiatry*, vol. 15 (1969), pp. 5–22.

11. *Los Angeles Times*, September 9, 1976.

12. Robert S. Weiss, "The Emotional Impact of Marital Separation," *Journal of Social Issues*, vol. 32, no. 1 (Winter 1976), p. 135.

13. Ibid., p. 143.
14. Carol A. Brown, Roslyn Feldberg, Elizabeth M. Fox and Janet Kohen, "Divorce: Chance of a New Lifetime," *Journal of Social Issues,* vol. 32, no. 1 (Winter 1976), p. 129.
15. Ibid., p. 126.
16. Ibid., p. 129.
17. Ibid.
18. Ibid.
19. Ibid,
20. Weiss, loc. cit., p. 137.
21. *Los Angeles Times,* September 9, 1976.

CHAPTER 10

1. Helen Singer Kaplan, "Friction and Fantasy: No-Nonsense Therapy for Six Sexual Malfunctions," *Psychology Today,* October 1974, p. 80.
2. Leonard R. Derogatis, John K. Meyer and Bridget W. Gallant, "Distinctions between Male and Female Invested Partners in Sexual Disorders," *American Journal of Psychiatry,* vol. 134, no. 4 (April 1977), pp. 385–90.
3. Reproductive Biology Research Foundation, Seminar on Human Sexuality, December 5–6, 1977, Los Angeles, Calif.
4. Gloria Steinem, "Is Child Pornography . . . ABOUT SEX?", *Ms.,* August 1977, pp. 43–44.
5. Susan Brownmiller, *Against Our Will: Men, Women and Rape* (New York: Simon & Schuster, 1975), p. 290.
6. Ibid.
7. Ibid., p. 294.
8. Dick Hobson, "Survivor's Notes from the Sexual Revolution," *Los Angeles Magazine,* April 1977, p. 107.
9. Terri Schultz, "Getting It On," *Penthouse,* April 1974, p. 46.
10. Warren Mintz, "The Male Sexual Cycle," *Humanist,* vol. 36, no. 6 (November–December 1976), p. 11.
11. Mary Harrington Hall, "A Conversation with Masters & Johnson and Mary Harrington Hall," *Psychology Today,* July 1969, p. 55.
12. Schultz, loc. cit.
13. Herb Goldberg, *The Hazards of Being Male* (New York: Signet, 1977), p. 22.

CHAPTER 11

1. Karen Durbin, "How to Spot a Liberated Man," *Mademoiselle,* April 1973, pp. 172–73.

CHAPTER 12

1. *Time,* May 9, 1977, p. 85.
2. *Time,* August 31, 1970, p. 16.
3. Ibid.
4. Phyllis Chesler, "Men Drive Women Crazy," *Psychology Today,* July 1971, pp. 18–98.
5. *Time,* August 31, 1970, p. 16.
6. Marilyn French, *The Women's Room* (New York: Summit Books, 1977), p. 161.
7. *People,* February 20, 1978, p. 33.
8. Jackie MacMillan, "Rape and Prostitution," *Victomology,* Vol. 1, No. 3. Fall 1976, pp. 414–420.
9. Eric Kroll, "Testimony," *Sex Objects* (New Hampshire, Addison House, 1977). New York. Printed in U.S.A. by Foremost Lithographers, Providence, R.I.
10. Herb Goro, "Portrait of a Marriage That Couldn't Be Saved," *New York,* September 18, 1972, pp. 31–42.
11. Meredith P. Smith, M.D., "Decline in Duodenal Ulcer Surgery," *Journal of the American Medical Association,* Vol. 237, No. 10, March 7, 1977, pp. 987–988.
12. Nancy Allen, "Suicide in California 1960–1970," State of California Department of Public Health, 1973, pp. 6 and 10.
13. Robert C. Steppacher and Judith S. Mausner, "Suicide in Professionals: A Study of Male and Female Psychologists," *American Journal of Epidemiology,* Vol. 98, No. 6, December 1973, pp. 436–445. (Published by Johns Hopkins University.)
14. "Cigarette Smoking Among Teen-agers and Young Women," published by the National Cancer Institute in cooperation with the American Cancer Society, p. 5 ([NIH] 77–1203). U.S. Dept. of Health, Education and Welfare, National Institutes of Health. Note: The findings reported in this pamphlet are part of an extensive research project on smoking among teen-agers and young women conducted in 1975 for the American Cancer Society by Yankelovich, Skelly and White, Inc.
11. " 'Gentler Sex' Turns to Guns, Knives, Bombs," *Los Angeles Times,* September 2, 1974, Part I-B, p. 6.
16. Frieda L. Gehlen, "Legislative Role Performance of Female Legislators," *Sex Roles,* February 1977, Vol. 3, No. 1, p. 1018.
17. *Los Angeles Times,* September 8, 1977.

CHAPTER 13

1. Diane and Dick O'Connor, *How to Make Your Man More Sensitive* (New York: E. P. Dutton & Co., Inc., 1975), p. 175.
2. David Bond, "Letters," *Village Voice*, April 12, 1976, p. 3.

CHAPTER 15

1. Julia R. Heiman, "The Physiology of Erotica: Women's Sexual Arousal," *Psychology Today*, April 1975, p. 91.
2. Ibid., p. 93.
3. "Ratio of Male to Female Admissions to State and County Mental Hospitals by Age for Behavior Disorders and Adjustive Reactions, U.S., 1973," *National Institute of Mental Health Statistical Note* 115, Table 3, pp. 10–13.
4. Ibid.
5. "Ratio of Male to Female Residency in State and County Mental Hospitals by Age for Behavior Disorders and Adjustive Reactions, U.S., 1973," *National Institute of Mental Health Statistical Note* 115, Table 3, pp. 10–13.
6. Janet S. Hyde and B. G. Rosenberg, "Tomboyism: Implications for Theories of Female Development"; paper presented at the Western Psychological Association Convention, San Francisco, Calif., April 1974.
7. Carol Tavris, "Woman & Man," *Psychology Today*, March 1972, p. 58.

CHAPTER 17

1. *U.S. News & World Report*, April 15, 1974, pp. 59–60.
2. Helena Lopata, "Widows and Widowers," *Humanist*, vol. 37, no. 5 (September-October 1977), pp. 25–28.
3. Samuel Wallace, *After Suicide* (New York: Wiley, 1973), p. 78.
4. *Los Angeles Times*, August 29, 1976.

CHAPTER 18

1. Bernie Zilbergeld, *Male Sexuality: A Guide to Sexual Fulfillment* (Boston: Little, Brown, 1978), p. 56.

CHAPTER 19

1. Martin L. Gross, "Conversation with an Author: Gail Sheehy, author of *Passages,* on 'Crises of Adult Life,'" *Book Digest,* August 1977, p. 32.

2. Roxann A. and Sheldon Van Dusen and Eleanor Bernert, "The Changing Status of American Women: A Life Cycle Perspective," *American Psychologist,* vol. 31, no. 2 (February 1976), pp. 106–16.

3. Gross, loc. cit.

4. John Dean, *Blind Ambition* (New York: Simon & Schuster, 1976), p. 127.

5. *Los Angeles Times,* February 26, 1978.

CHAPTER 20

1. Tennessee Williams, "Cat on a Hot Tin Roof," *Best American Plays,* Fourth Series 1951-1957, Gassner, John ed. (New York: Crown Publishers, 1958), Act 2, p. 60.

Index

ABOUT THE AUTHOR

Herb Goldberg received his Ph.D. in clinical
psychology from Adelphi University. He has
been on the faculty of California State University
since 1965, where he is presently Professor of
Psychology. In addition, he has had a private
practice with individuals, couples and families
for over ten years and conducts workshops
across the country. He is a contributor to numerous professional publications and the author
of several books, including the best-selling THE
HAZARDS OF BEING MALE, available in a
Signet edition.

SIGNET and MENTOR Books of Related Interest